Dream big &
Dance loud!
Deb

DANCING

to my

HEARTBEAT

A Mother and Daughter's Journey from Victim to Victorious

DEBORAH LYSHOLM

Contributing author Kristin Freya

2013

BEAVER'S POND
PRESS

ISBN 13: 978-1-59298-991-1

Library of Congress Catalog Number: 2013907595
Printed in the United States of America
First Printing: 2013
17   16   15   14   13   5   4   3   2   1

Cover and interior design by Alan Pranke
Cover photo: Rick Norling, and courtesy of Freya/Wonsavage
Editors: Connie Anderson, Anita Coolidge, Betty Leidtke, Mary Miller

BEAVER'S POND
PRESS

Beaver's Pond Press, Inc.
7108 Ohms Lane
Edina, MN 55439-2129
(952) 829-8818
www.BeaversPondPress.com

To order, visit www.BeaversPondBooks.com or call 1-800-901-3480.
Reseller discounts available.

Inquiries and permissions can be sent in writing to:
New Beat Productions LLC, 7661 West 145th Street, Apple Valley, MN 55124,
or visit: Deborah Lysholm, Author Facebook page.

DANCING TO MY HEARTBEAT

Table of Contents

NOTES FROM THE AUTHOR

This book is dedicated to my lovely daughter, Kristin—my shining star and delicate angel. Keep dancing, sweetie! I love you beyond words. You have blessed my life with meaning.

To my precious family—embrace the "explorer spirit" inherited from our ancestors. Place one foot in front of the other, feeling warmth and love. Our bond is a gift.

To readers who find themselves in a quest to start over—know that you have it in you to hear sweeter music, see brighter colors, and flash a smile that is genuine.

To my dear friends and dance family…

We dance!
Our celebration is life.
We dance!
Our souls are revealed.
We dance!
Our burden is broken.
We dance!
Our hearts are healed.
We dance!

…Love, Deb

The events described in this book are based on real events recalled from our memory, legal documents, print and television media, and personal journals. We understand that there may be people in our lives who experienced or remember some of the events differently than our perspective, so we apologize for the differences. Some names and other identifying factors have been changed to protect the innocent.

NOTES FROM FRIENDS

From desperation, betrayal, and heartache emerges the triumphal victory of the human spirit in this journey about a woman who refused defeat to follow her dreams and passion for dance. Deborah Lysholm's strength, tenacity, and unfailing love for people and her art is an inspiration to everyone that knows her. See why Deborah is my personal hero in this compelling autobiography detailing her journey from abuse to freedom, fear to faith, and hopelessness to achievement.

Patty Taulbee, Owner, Plantlife Body Products, San Clemente, CA

Whether or not you have suffered at the hands of an abuser, this is a story of survival and triumph that should be read.

Deborah Lysholm has captured the trials of a wife and mother dealing with physical and emotional abuse from her husband. She details her life story from the beginning, as a child from a loving and traditional household, to the day when her husband pointed a gun at her and she knew she had to leave her desperate and dangerous situation to begin her life again. This decision came at a time when these horrifying experiences were not talked about, let alone made public. And the more insidious danger that lurked was that a woman and her child would feel forced into staying in a relationship which could result in generations being imprinted with violence, or worse, victims losing their lives.

It could have happened this way for Deborah and her daughter. There could have been a small, vague article in the newspaper one morning that only mentioned names — and didn't accurately reflect the vicious attack that ended their lives — but only that two people were found dead. But thank God! This is not what happened with Deborah. Not only did she and her daughter leave the horrible existence they'd known for years, but even more miraculously, they prevailed over years of discriminatory court battles, financial crises, emotional fallout, and resistance at every turn to found a performing arts studio that is unparalleled in its reputation, community exposure, and curriculum. They built their new lives from the ashes and have become happy, fulfilled, and successful entrepreneurs, as well as strong and determined women who overcame.

The reason I can speak with certainty of these things is that I was there when it was happening. I was a student and friend of Deborah's, and I was there when all the secrets Deb tried so hard to withhold for years came rushing out as a torrent of battery, betrayal, violence, and threats. I watched as Deb's life came crashing down, but I was there also to watch her summon strength to tackle all the battles to come. I want the readers to know this book is not just a collection of horrible memories, but more importantly, of the glorious victories that were achieved. For anyone who has felt there is no path out, there is no redemption, there is no hope of a sane life filled with happiness and productivity, Deb's story shows there is, indeed, life and happiness and fulfillment if you make the decision to believe it and take that first step. Deborah Lysholm shares how she took that first step, and her hope and prayer is that those who read the accounts will do the same.

To my friend, Deb, who is a beautiful, dancing Phoenix from the ashes.

Laurie Holien, Executive Assistant, Orly Company, Los Angeles, CA

FOREWORD

When Deb first walked into my office, she had been laid low by a marriage that had left her with deep emotional scars. As I listened to her tell her story, I realized I had heard it many times before. The divorce laws simply required proving of irretrievable breakdown of the marriage and if that were agreed upon, there was no place for a person like Deb to be heard as to the events that lead to that breakdown.

Until now, victims who told me their stories had simply divorced their spouses and tried to recover as best they could. Deb was determined to speak up and use her voice against her former spouse in a court of law. She had experienced physical and emotional harm from her former spouse, but because the lingering threat was primarily emotional, the criminal justice system was, at the time, able to afford no help. I was in the process of transitioning out of the practice of law en route to becoming a mental health professional. Additionally, I had no experience with this kind of case so I was at first reluctant to represent her. However, there was a resolve about Deb that was compelling. It was clear from the start, she was not just waging a war for justice for herself and her daughter, but for all women scarred by what they experienced in an abusive relationship. Confronting her spouse in court was what we did, and shortly after a jury heard the evidence that would be introduced, the case settled.

The remarkable part of Deb's journey is what followed and what you will read about here. It is a story of hope from a woman who refused to give up. A woman who refused to let her past define her future. A woman who would not be tamed by forces seeking to disregard her and silence her truth. A woman who recovered by refusing to give in. It is a story about the power of resolve and truth when it is told.

Don Horton, J.D.
Attorney at Law (Retired)

INTRODUCTION BY KRISTIN

Deborah's Daughter

This memoir is my mother's recollection of how we managed to navigate my father's never-ending abuse and how the hours we spent in dance classes gave us healing, freedom, and strength for our souls. With each dance, we poured out our stifled frustration and rescued our self-confidence from drowning in my father's personal darkness.

My memories of home are shrouded in fear and revolve around a looming, dark figure that required mine and my mother's ultimate obedience and attention. As a young child, I told Santa that what I wanted for Christmas was for my father to go away and never come back. I clearly recall Santa's shocked face looking down at me sitting on his lap. He then looked out at my parents who stood waiting for me to take my holiday picture. My mother was smiling and my father simply looked bored. Unfortunately, Santa, like many other adults in my life, neither did nor said anything to change the situation. But on that day, I realized I had found my wish. Every shooting star I saw, each time I dropped a coin in a wishing well, each bedtime prayer I said and every time I blew out my birthday candles, I made the same wish: for my father to go away and never come back.

As early as age seven, I realized that my family dynamic was different from my friends' family dynamics. Up until then, I thought that everyone's father was like mine. I learned to look for what I called "Dad's dark cloud." I saw him as a shape shifter, with two personalities living inside him. When enraged, his transformation began like this: his blue eyes would dilate and become nearly black, then his focus on his victim would sharpen and finally his aura would become what I can best describe as a swirl of dark gray smoke. This cloud made it difficult to see him clearly. This dark cloud became my warning, a "tell" for where he was going emotionally. I became grateful for it in many ways. I learned to take it as a sign to run out of the house and find a place to hide for a few hours. My favorite spot was my neighbor's house across the street. He usually never followed me. I think public displays for the neighbors were somehow unacceptable to him.

If my mother was at home, his dark cloud warning gave me a moment to prepare for what would inevitably become a very long night. I would hide in closets or under beds, anywhere close by. Once the yelling stopped, I would crawl out and find my mother to help her and hug her. She would often be silent, shaking and moving very slowly as if she were under water. Sometimes she would say things like, "He didn't mean it" or "It's okay, honey, I'm okay." Deep down, we both knew differently. Once the dark cloud appeared, there was no way to talk him down. When he became enraged, it did not matter to him that we were all expected to be somewhere. It would not matter if we were expected at a family Easter gathering, dinner with neighbors, or if I were on my way to school. Once it took over, nothing could deter the sad, angry, and violent man who lived in the dark cloud.

When I reached age eleven I no longer viewed him as a father; he was simply an angry, violent intruder who would not leave. I began to interfere when he beat my mother. This, of course, backfired and he often refocused his attack on me. Over time, I was actually relieved and strangely proud that I could derail his focus from my mother to me, especially if he had already beat her so badly that she had passed out. I was always afraid that he would not know when to stop and that one day, he would kill one or both of us.

By the age of fifteen it was clear to me that no one was going to save my mother and me from this person. We were on our own. On my sixteenth birthday, I took the first step to self-preservation and ownership of my life. I told my father that we needed to have a brief talk. I was admittedly shaky and nervous as he sat down calmly, a bit shocked and confused himself, as this was something that usually did not happen. In fact, I normally went out of my way to not engage with him. During this conversation I announced what I believed was wrong with him. I told him I had always thought that he was very bitter and frustrated with many things about his life: his job, his choice to get married, and feeling trapped for having had me. I told him that throughout my life, I had loved him as well as feared him. I further told him that I had futilely prayed to a god who never answered my prayer that one day he would stop hurting us. Instead, he became more bold and violent over the years.

Then, I bravely announced that I did not either love or fear him any longer. All of the emotions I had for him, good or bad, had run dry. I felt nothing for him anymore. He was visibly shaken. His shoulders hunched forward and he would not make eye contact. I told him that this conversation would be the last time I would speak directly to him. Lastly, I told him that I would fight back because he did not know when to stop. The last words I spoke directly to my father were, "From now on, know that I will fight back and not stop until you do."

I walked away shaking, but I felt for the first time that this was my house and that I was capable and strong.

The two years of living at home while I finished high school were a roller coaster. He began to make apologies to me, similar to the ones I had heard him give to my mother. I knew it meant nothing. He only wanted to control me again. Sometimes he displayed good behavior and other times he would become angered by my silence. He would then burst into my room to yell at me for being disrespectful to him, often calling me an "ungrateful bitch" and demand that I speak to him. When I said nothing, he would either leave, slamming the door behind him, or he would physically attack me. I would now fight back to protect myself or my mother from him, however, I would not utter a word from my lips. It is interesting now to look back and realize that no one in my family noticed that we never spoke to each other during family gatherings.

During those years, I spent as much time away from home as possible. I immersed myself in dance and theater like it was a lifeboat. And it was! I felt free in a dance class. I was in control of myself and I began to dream of my own future as a choreographer. In college, I majored in dance and began shaping my long and deeply fulfilling career as a choreographer, director, and teacher. Through the inner strength dance gave me and the final realization that I had the power within me to triumph over my oppressor, I learned to manage my environment and reach for a brighter future.

In 1996, my ultimate wish finally came true. My father went away and never came back. It took the two of us, my mother and me, to make that wish come true. As you read my mother's memoir, I am positive that you will also share in the tremendous respect and pride that I have for my mother. Her strength and courage is awe-inspiring. She not only took a stand against my father, but saw her own experience as a way to help other women find their way out of similar abusive situations. She, in a profound way, discovered her own strength and built her dream. She is incredibly strong, brave, and generous. She taught me about resiliency, inner strength, and conviction. She exemplifies the virtues of digging deep, trusting yourself, and not being afraid to dream big.

"I love you, Mom!"

Kristin

Looking in the **Rearview Mirror**

"How are you doing, Deb?" exclaimed the energetic and happy surgeon as he threw back the curtain.

"I'm scared out of my mind."

"Why? I'm not!" he responded, causing me to laugh, and defuse my anxiety. My heart was beating very fast as Dr. Andrew read my chart one final

time before escorting me to the operating room. Today, finally, my noticeably damaged left eyelid would be repaired. Nervousness can make a few minutes seem like an eternity, and thankfully, my daughter, Kristin, and her husband, Paul, were with me, lending their support. All three of us were nervous, and I really don't know who was most frightened.

"Follow me," Dr. Andrew said, heading down the corridor through double doors. Blinding surgical lights made me squint as I felt the pinch of the needle. "To put you in la-la land," Dr. Andrew assured me. "Count back from ten."

"Ten, nine, eight, seven..." I feebly attempted to articulate; and as my vision blurred, I knew that the next time I looked into a mirror, I would no longer be reminded of the terror and horror of the past...

My Roots

My roots are in the sweet soil of the small town of Madison, Minnesota, near the South Dakota border. This lush green farming community of rolling hills was dotted with white houses, red barns, steepled churches, and many happy and contented full-blooded Norwegians, including my parents, Robert and Jalma.

My dad was in the midst of his military service when I was born on March 1, 1950. While he was away, Mom and I lived in a small, humble, wooden box of a home, covered top to bottom with green roofing shingles, and nestled in a row of dwellings meant for summer migrant workers. We had electricity but no running water or indoor plumbing. During the winter months, Mom carried in buckets of snow to melt on the stove so we could bathe in a galvanized steel scrub tub. She hauled our drinking water home in a gallon jug from the town pump.

My earliest childhood memory was the day Dad returned home from military service. His dad proudly welcomed him home at the Minneapolis airport and then drove him back to Madison in Dad's trusty old Ford pickup.

"We will see your dad soon. Just keep listening for his truck," Mom assured me as she gently pushed me, now a toddler, back and forth on the rope-and-tire swing suspended from the mighty oak tree in our backyard. "He will be so surprised to see how big you have grown. Keep your pretty dress clean until he gets home."

Mom and I wore gingham-checked dresses with puffed sleeves that she made for this special occasion. My white patent leather shoes touched the blue summer sky every time she pushed the swing. "I think I hear the truck!" Mom screamed in delight. In the distance, beyond the white picket fence that encircled our yard, over the green cornfields, we could see plumes of dust spewed by my dad's pickup truck speeding down the gravel road. Dad shifted gears to a lower rumble as he turned his truck around the corner and coasted to a stop.

"You're home, you're home!" Mom cried as she ran from the swing and into my dad's arms. The love of her life was back.

Meanwhile, back at the swing, the offspring of their love clung tightly to the tire to avoid falling off and getting her dress dirty.

"There's my girl," Dad said as he ran and lifted me from the swing, holding me high over his head, smiling. Now I was flying high against the blue summer sky.

Within a year, my first sibling, Shirlee, was born.

"Let's move to Minneapolis. Jobs are better there," Dad encouraged. "I need to get away from this small town. Minneapolis is a good place to raise a family, I hear." Mom agreed. They sold everything they owned, sandwiched their daughters between them on a motorcycle, pointed it east, and rode off to a new life in Minneapolis. Dad was able to find a job within a week, and we became official residents of the "Cities."

In short order, my parents' blonde-haired, blue-eyed brood grew to four when brother Butch and sister Nancie joined the family. Our weekdays were spent at our Minneapolis home, and weekends spent piling into our 1957 Chevy station wagon heading back to the Minnesota/South Dakota border to visit my paternal grandparents, Alice and Fred, on their farm. This was the most incredible playground that any child could imagine. Riding horses bareback, making forts out of bales of hay, flying through the air like "Tarzan" on gunnysack swings, or bouncing on bed-pillow "toboggans" at rapid-fire speed down the wooden staircase while our vibrating voices squealed in delight, gave our creative minds rigorous exercise. Grandpa Fred showed us how to milk cows, and the precise aim needed to squirt milk into a kitten's mouth. We witnessed the birth of many farm animals, and saw crops return year after year to the rich fertile fields. The focus of farm life was essentially the rebirth of many things. To cap off our weekend, we stopped to visit my maternal grandparents, Josie and Jalmer, at their small home in Madison, where they made sure their grandchildren had plenty of reading and math workbooks to keep them busy and quiet.

We grew up with one foot in the city and the other foot on the farm.

"Come on kids, time for church," Grandma Alice said, as we reluctantly emerged from under many layers of warm flannel blankets in her cozy farmhouse. One by one we climbed into our grandparents' 1948 split-windshield Chevy, and drove the well-worn gravel road to the country church where some of the hymns were still sung in Norwegian.

"Being the oldest child in the family, you must sit quietly and listen, setting a good example for your brother and sisters," Grandma Alice whispered to me before the sermon began. I fondly remember the scent of the old wood pews, and the wild rose fragrance of her perfume. Grandma glowed in her favorite form-fitting black dress dotted with red flowers, and her red wide-brim straw hat adorned with ribbons and netting. The *piece de resistance*, I must say, were her red high heels. Grandpa Fred was a man of few words—an occasional "*Uff da!*" would be the extent of many conversations, followed by a huge smile, both eyes twinkling.

My roots, as far back as the stories go, were people from Norway, including the indigenous Sami people who were adventurous, nomadic reindeer herders, and farmers who emphasized the importance of families and perseverance, and of doing the right thing for their children. One such ancestor was my great, great, great-grandmother, Ingeborg O. Sjolie, born March 12, 1828 (a Pisces like me), who married for love, not social status, which angered her aristocratic family. On May 15, 1861, she and her farmer-husband sailed to America, in part to flee her family's shunning and disapproval. In a letter found several generations later, Ingeborg had written one last letter to her family—a plea for them to come see her off at the pier in Oslo before she left forever.

She ended her letter with: *"We write to tell you that we intend to leave Norway to get independence for our children, and this is a parent's first duty after the duty to God. We are convinced that everything will be good if we trust God, as we know that he is everywhere, and also in America. America is a good country, as many of the people there trust God. And now we end this letter with a greeting to all of you. We want you to pray for us that God will bless what we are going to do and keep his strong hand over us, both body and soul. We shall never forget you. But now, good health!"*

Her family never met her at the pier before she sailed away to America. Ingeborg died in Erskine, Minnesota, in 1920 at the age of ninety-two.

Forgiving love was the glue that kept my extended families' marriages together. The only family breakup I knew of was when Grandma Alice divorced her first husband. No one talked much about the divorce because divorce, by nature, had an intensely negative stigma in a small town. Even when I was too young to understand, I heard the discomfort in Grandma Alice's voice when it was brought up, and that made me sad. I loved my grandma, and did not like hearing that people took pity on her or talked negatively about her situation.

What I did understand at that young age was that I never wanted to be in the same situation as Grandma Alice.

My Third Parent

I looked up to my parents and wanted to be like them in many ways. Dad (an Aries), had a James Dean look about him, and was our caring leader. He became quite an entrepreneur, owning three businesses in the auto and heavy-duty equipment industry. Dad often took his daughters shopping for pretty dresses, and his sons to check out the latest in the auto showrooms. He was a talented artist and regularly surprised us with murals he painted on the basement's cinder block walls.

"Do you see the fawn and the baby bear I painted in the forest?" he quizzed, as his panoramas always hid little visual treasures. He taught us that it was the journey that counted when trying to reach a goal and to always take time to play. Dad gave me a little dime-store aquamarine birthstone pendant necklace—which I still wear today—on the day that I learned to walk. When I was ten years old, he taught me how to waltz.

"Come here, Deb, and stand on my feet. You will eventually figure it out," he said as he reached out his hand to hold mine.

Mom (a Libra), had a fashion model's high cheekbones, full lips, and silky hair, a Lauren Bacall-type look. Out of financial necessity and love, she sewed most of our clothing, and was the one who made sure we did our homework and learned to be self-sufficient. Mom was a social butterfly with a beautiful voice and took pride singing in the local women's choir. Being of the June Cleaver era, she instilled in her daughters a woman's responsibility to be the glue that keeps a family together.

"You must always be willing to forgive and forget. Always take the high road and don't look back. People are always sorry after they hurt your feelings. And, Deb, you are the oldest, and sometimes that means you get the short end of the stick when things go wrong. You must set an example and forgive."

My siblings were precious to me. They were full of compassion, and had lovable personalities that masked mischievous streaks. Adept at writing, drawing, dancing, and singing—creativity was in their DNA—it was abundantly manifested in many directions. Shirlee was sweet and big-hearted, and her compassion limitless. We hung out together and shared many of the same friends—in fact, they often got us mixed up. Nancie was gifted at poetry and fascinated with animals. Even though six years younger, she joined us in our drive-in and shopping adventures. Neighbors would proclaim, "There go the Lysholm girls," as we sped down the street on our bicycles.

Butch had to navigate through childhood with three sisters—quite an accomplishment. A combination of Dennis the Menace and Cato, a character in the original Pink Panther movies, Butch skillfully choreographed surprise pounces out of nowhere, scaring the daylights out of us.

When I was in high school, two more brothers arrived. Kurt was admirably full of kindness for the underdog. Equipped with the familial mischievous streak, his laugh made others laugh. Mark was special. His big blue eyes, long eyelashes, little rosy lips, and white-blonde hair that stuck up in an unmanageable Mohawk, made him resemble the cartoon character, Tweety Bird. Mark was also my hero. Born with neurofibromatosis, he courageously beat the odds after lengthy surgeries and rehabilitation.

My responsibility was to set an example for my five siblings, and when things didn't go my way, I had been groomed to know how to forgive. In future years, this "forgiveness programming" worked against me and became an albatross.

Dance!

At age four, I received my first pair of tap shoes from my parents, who were themselves jitterbug champs. Daily, my little pointer finger gently rubbed Vaseline on the patent leather to make them shine. Nightly, before going to bed, I danced in my tap shoes to make sure they still worked.

"Mom! Dad! Listen what I can do!" I squealed, dressed in red flannel pajamas and shiny, black tap shoes with big bows. Because of the discipline required, the art form I was learning in those special shoes became my "third parent." Little did I know, at the time, that dance would also become a coping mechanism and my future salvation.

In grade school I became a "studio rat," practically living in the dance studio. Being very shy, dancing gave me a creative voice, a new and safe way to communicate. Dancing taught me to see the big picture, and all of the little pieces that made up the big picture. It also taught me diligence and persistence because, if I didn't get a step or movement right, I kept at it until it was perfect. The fortitude required to learn to dance complemented my now-instinctive responsibility to set an example. These are admirable skills, to be sure, but in a perverted twist unbeknownst to me, these skills would render me a pawn in a wicked game where the stakes were high, including my survival.

My sisters and I made many friends at our dance classes, including the three Anderson girls. The "six sister" group was practically inseparable, becoming our own support network. While in high school in the late '60s, dance created opportunities to forge friendship bonds with my classmates, both guys and girls. During our summers, the six sisters, along with an assortment of other entertainers, performed at numerous festivals around the state. We were bused from one location to another to perform, and during these trips, musicians and singers became our new boyfriends. Slumber parties were frequent with young girls in those days, as our innocent minds attempted to predict what life had in store for us—certainly boyfriends and marriage. Our voices erupted into song when we played hopeful tunes like, "When a Man Loves a Woman", "My Guy", and "I Got You Babe". For the evening's grand finale, a Ouija board helped us see what our futures held. If only I could have gotten a clue.

My Dating Years

In high school I wasn't into long-term dating, partly because I was so busy with dance lessons and teaching dance. I was never with a boyfriend very long, and most were friends rather than romantic interests. My girlfriends, who were in long-term relationships, were wrapping too much of their identities into their boyfriends. I never felt comfortable with that because I didn't want to disappear.

In my mom's generation, it was more or less expected that after high school, a girl should just get married. A romantic at heart, Mom truly believed that her daughters wouldn't be happy unless they were whisked away by a knight in shining armor, so—she placed high importance on me having a man in my life, even as a teen.

During my junior year, I didn't have a date for the homecoming dance, and Mom let me know she was not happy.

"It's embarrassing for me at card club when all of the other women are bragging about the boys taking their daughters to homecoming." I had disappointed Mom, and the entire episode eroded my self-confidence. Thoughts of "I'm worthless and ugly" found a home in my brain.

On the other side of the spectrum, Dad was intimidating and judgmental toward any boy I dated.

"Young man, what is your phone number in case I need to talk to your parents?" he demanded. After my date nervously recited the number, Dad also warned him not to take me into neighborhoods he considered dangerous, even if it was simply to wait for a bus.

Expectations and Responsibility

During my mid-teens, in addition to schoolwork, household chores, and dance lessons, I helped Mom take care of Kurt and Mark. Feeding Mark his bottle while cutting Kurt's food into chewable bites, or rocking one to sleep while reading a book to the other, introduced me to multitasking.

Besides being taught to forgive, I was also expected to take on a lot of responsibility. For a while that was okay, until the situation became more complicated when Mom began to drink a lot. I wanted to help her recover, and at the same time protect my siblings from the horrors that alcoholism can bring to a family, and to try to make our household seem normal. Mom eventually, and admirably, stopped drinking, but during our adolescence, the stress of having a family member who drinks too much made my siblings and me feel like we were the problem—and that we had done something very wrong. We learned coping skills to cover up the chaos at home—which was yet another rehearsal for later in my life.

My grades were excellent, as were my college entrance exams, and I yearned to go to college.

"Please, can I go to college?" I begged, even though I knew that with six children, it was a struggle for my parents to make ends meet.

"We will try our best to help you pay for your tuition, but if you have to take a bus through a bad neighborhood, I'm going to drop you off and pick you up each day," Dad said. I agreed, and so a plan was set in motion for me to go to the University of Minnesota after I graduated the next year.

During the spring of my high school junior year, I became aware of social dances hosted by the university for potential new students. I decided to attend one of these dances to groom myself for the transition out of high school. It was here that I met Richard, my future husband, a soon-to-be sophomore at the university. We danced and talked, and I definitely felt an instant connection. Apparently he did, too, though at the time we did not exchange telephone numbers.

Fast-forward a few months to the summer, and Richard and I happened to meet again at another university dance.

"Very glad to run into you again. There is a new movie I would like to see. Care to join me?" he asked. This time, we exchanged numbers and went on a few dates. Richard (a Gemini), was a gentleman, a good conversationalist, and good looking—my mom's dream for me come true. I felt comfortable and natural with him. As my high school senior year progressed, so did the frequency of our dating. While Mom adored Richard, Dad was cordial, but did confront me one day.

"Why would a guy in college want to date a girl still in high school?" he asked.

During our courtship, I entered the university, majoring in art education because the university did not have a dance major program at the time. Richard and I were taking the same art history class, and one day he said, "Since both of us are finding it difficult to study at home, we should start meeting at the library to study." This is when we entered into an even more exclusive relationship.

My time at the university was pre-personal computer, so students often rented a library typing booth to work on their assignments, which Richard and I did together to save money. One afternoon while I was rapidly typing a paper due the next morning, he said out of the blue, "What do you think... should we get married?"

"Okay," I said after catching my breath. Richard fashioned a ring out of a foil gum wrapper, and we walked out of the booth engaged to be married. At the time, it seemed like the next natural step. Mom would be ecstatic to hear the news, but I didn't tell my parents for a couple of weeks. While I thought I was ready — maybe I wasn't.

"Deb, you're the one. We are meant to be. You're the one that I want. I love you," Richard kept reassuring me, but at times it felt like pressuring. No one had ever said these things to me before. He was a master at smooth talk, something that should have put me on guard rather than make me giddy.

After letting the dust settle on our whirlwind engagement, and when I felt confident to yell to the world that I was in love, I revealed the news to my parents.

"Mom, before Dad gets home I need to share something with you. Guess what? I'm getting married!" Surprisingly, both Mom and Dad were thrilled. I was entering into my new life, seemingly a most natural passage. I was ready, and I was happy.

And the Award for "Best Actress" Goes to...

"Deb, stand on the stool so I can mark the hem. I found the veil material you wanted. You are going to be a beautiful bride," Mom beamed as she pulled out her pincushion. She insisted on making my wedding gown, just as she had always taken care of my other special occasion dresses.

"I'll wear the necklace Dad gave me when I learned to walk. I think that is appropriate, since he will be walking me down the aisle," I added, smiling.

Richard and I wasted no time planning our wedding so that the blessed day would take place during our next break in university classes. The setting for our special day was a picturesque white-stucco church with beautiful stained-glass windows, nestled in a clump of willow, evergreen, and white birch trees located next to a sparkling lake.

Dad looked very handsome as we walked side-by-side down the aisle, and his voice quivered, "Her mother and I," while answering, "Who gives this woman to be married to this man?" Richard and I chose silver wedding bands due to our limited budget, but they were priceless gold in my mind. Our ceremony went smoothly until one little soul objected to our getting married. Halfway through the service, I heard a familiar voice crying, "Debbie! Debbie! Debbie!" I looked back and saw my little brother, Mark, frantically running down the aisle toward me. He had escaped from my wildly interesting and lovable Aunt Elsie who was sitting in the back of the church with him, just in case he fussed. Mark reached his desired destination: me—one of his other "moms"—and stood for a moment before my parents, seated in the front pew, were able to snatch him.

Maybe this toddler had a premonition about my future.

Our wedding was beautifully simple, and our honeymoon even simpler. We spent a weekend at a small resort in western Wisconsin, and upon returning, moved into an old brownstone apartment overlooking the freeway that was not in the best neighborhood of Minneapolis. It was all that we could afford, and gave us our first sense of freedom as young adults. Fortunately, the landlady was my Aunt Elsie. We had our place to call "Home," and looked forward to a good life together.

Our furniture consisted of an eclectic array of hand-me-downs from extended family members. Thick, dark, wood moldings framed the doors and windows, and accented a ceiling covered with old metal tiles embossed in floral design. My kitchen was tiny, but had a roomy pantry. Our bathroom boasted floor-to-ceiling pink ceramic tiles and a white claw-foot tub. A fusion of incense and mustiness permeated the entire building.

We dreamed of the day when we would own a home, or have the luxury of actually flying to an exotic vacation spot, rather than camping in a tent on road trips. Nevertheless, we possessed adventurous spirits, and while hiking, biking, or canoeing, never ran out of things to discuss.

A few weeks after our wedding, Richard and I purchased our first used car—an original "hippie" Volkswagen Beetle, complete with tie-dyed upholstery and a brush-painted lime green exterior. The car had seen better days, and often, to get it started, one of us sat in the driver's seat while the other gave the car a push to engage the motor. Some of our most adventurous hikes happened when we had to walk back home after the car broke down.

During our courtship, Richard was very charming, and I believed that we were head-over-heels in love. I found him to be very loquacious and polite— that is, until we crossed paths at the grocery store with one of my male friends from the dance studio.

"Who was that guy? Did you date him? Why were you so happy to see him?" Richard became jealous and enraged as he fired off questions.

"No, we never dated. He's just a dance friend that I haven't seen for years. Dancers share a supportive bond because we've all been through the challenges of learning how to dance. No different than the camaraderie of a sports team," I said, hoping he would understand.

In a similar instance while dating, Richard reacted negatively when a stranger at one of the university dances tried to talk to me. He flat out kicked at the guy, who was simply trying to be cordial. Since it was so crowded at the dance, we left immediately, and nothing came of it. My first thought was: "He cares about me," but I also wondered if perhaps I was doing something wrong. When I questioned him about his behavior, Richard insisted that his possessiveness was because he loved me.

The saying, *Love is blind*, comes to mind when the "jealousy" red flag is not heeded.

Richard was happier when my life became structured to have no time for anything but him. I was becoming increasingly isolated, though it was not really obvious to me at the time, nor did I realize what was happening. During the early years of our marriage, we moved to apartments farther away from my family, and closer to his. Unbeknownst to me, Richard's maneuvering to isolate me from those who cared about me was another sign of danger ahead.

My Early Years as a Newlywed

As college kids, we scrimped by on very little, and concluded that having both of us in college was too much for our budget.

"It's important for me to finish college first because I have only one year remaining. You put your college career on hold, and work to support us, and you can go back to college when I graduate." Richard's demand left no room for negotiating.

To support us, I worked full-time as an office manager for my dad's business, and taught dance at various studios in Minneapolis. Each day after his classes were done, Richard headed to the library for several hours to study, after which he worked a few hours at a manufacturing company in the evening. Because of our staggered schedules, we hid love notes around the house to surprise each other. I giggled in delight when I found the notes he left in places like my dresser drawer or makeup bag. He found my notes in his book bag or dangling from the shower faucet. One morning, instead of finding a love note from me, he found a tiny surprise gift box by his pillow. Inside was a pair of white satin baby shoes with a note that said, "Can hardly wait to meet you, Daddy!" We had wasted no time in getting pregnant, either.

Richard drove the car; I got around by bus.

"Since I don't know how to drive a manual-shift car, perhaps we should trade ours in for an automatic transmission because it would make life easier for me. That way I won't have to bother you to drive me places, or have to wait at a bus stop in the winter, especially in my condition," I suggested.

"Only a wimp drives a car with an automatic transmission. I don't have the patience to teach you how to drive a manual-shift car."

I became resigned to the fact that my method of transportation was by bus—or by him, and did not recognize this as one of his control mechanisms.

The pending "little arrival" was a glorious and joyful surprise to me, and it seemed that he felt the same, at least until it became obvious that I needed to don my first maternity clothing. That is when Richard began to ridicule my figure with comments like, "Man, you look like a walrus. Do you think you'll ever see your feet again?" Thanks to all of my dance training, and the physical conditioning that goes along with it, official maternity clothing was not part of my wardrobe until six months into my pregnancy. Richard's unrealistic expectation that I maintain an hourglass figure while pregnant was just the beginning of his determination that I be perfect, and meet all of his needs, no matter how impossible. His criticisms put me on a psychological treadmill. I tried and tried again, putting forth incredible energy over many years to be what he wanted.

Deep into my quest to meet his needs, I neglected to see the "crazy maker" red flag.

Somehow, the months of my pregnancy simply flew by while I continued my involvement in dance until our baby was born. I proved that a dancer with a big tummy could still manage to do a pirouette. Even with Richard's occasional negativity, I still felt very fortunate. As far as I was concerned, I was in love, and life was good, and getting even better.

To my astonishment and delight, gourmet cooking intrigued me. I had excelled in my high school chemistry class, and being in the kitchen felt like I had my own chemistry lab—a place where I created tasty entrees pleasing to the eye and stomach. An ever-growing collection of cookbooks lined the bookshelf, with each recipe becoming another fascinating science experiment. One particular evening, nearly eight months into my pregnancy, I was so overwhelmed with joy about our baby that I stayed up late to surprise my husband with a romantic dinner, complete with candles, flowers, and gourmet cuisine. I was in love, and knew that in a short time, we would be a family with the miracle of a new baby. It was very evident that we would have another dancer in the family, based upon the kicks our baby was frequently executing in the womb. I was glowing and euphoric.

Very late that evening I heard the hippie-mobile pull up in the driveway. I had just enough time to light the candles for our romantic dinner and adjust the flowers so they were perfect. When the apartment door opened, I saw my loving husband standing in the doorway with his arms spread wide, signaling that I should rush up and give him a passionate kiss. I ran toward Richard with a big smile, and my arms reaching out. Just when I thought I would feel safe and secure in his arms, my body was whirled around and violently slammed against the kitchen counter. Instead of the warmth of a hug, I was brutally shocked—by my first full-on beating.

No, I did not see it coming. I lost my breath for a moment and tried desperately to wake up from this sudden nightmare.

"You bitch, because of you, I have to work late. You've ruined my life!" Like the flick of a switch, Richard went from light to darkness, and I couldn't tell what hurt worse, his words or the shock of the physical pain. Protective instincts took over, and I wrapped my body around my baby to create a shield from Richard's violent outburst.

Most of the night I cowered in a corner of the kitchen. My cozy chemistry lab now became the scene of a crime. Instantly, my self-image went from glowing and joyful to being shocked, and feeling completely worthless. In a flash, I was reduced to believing that I must certainly be the most horrible, disgusting person in the world. Why would a man do this to his wife, especially a pregnant wife? There must be something wrong with me. My mind was paralyzed, preventing me from understanding that there was, instead, something very wrong with him. These feelings dug deep into my soul and my mind, and firmly planted their roots. Over the years, they raised their ugly heads frequently, and without warning.

During Richard's attack, my left arm hit the edge of the kitchen counter so hard that an egg-sized lump and bruise developed on my wrist. The next day, when people at work asked me about the bruise, in my embarrassment, I lied, "Oh, I'm just so clumsy with this big tummy. I slipped on the kitchen floor after I had just mopped it." Unable to concentrate, I wished I had called in sick.

I was absolutely unprepared for this first shocking assault of extreme physical abuse, not only to me, but also to our baby who was due in just over a month. The most frightening thing that evening was the vacant look in Richard's eyes, as if he was devoid of any soul.

The person I loved, I now feared tremendously. There was a cavernous disconnect. Fear, love, fear, love—these emotions played a fierce ping-pong game in my heart. When would this confusing traumatic nightmare end? I was too frightened to tell anyone about the assault because letting the words leave my lips would make it real. I tried to will it away in my mind, but after a moment, the bruise on my wrist brought back the horrific reality.

My pre-programming to "set an example" and "to forgive" was entrenched. I did not want to be a failure, especially at marriage.

How could I possibly tell my parents, and risk having them be disappointed in me?

How could I let my siblings down?

How could I break up my new family before it even had a chance to start?

I loved Richard, and I loved our baby, but who was this alien who suddenly possessed my loving husband's mind and body?

I thought I had the answer. Tomorrow I would call Richard's parents and brother to ask for help, because they obviously knew him better and could probably suggest the best ways to approach him. My mind went into justification mode again, and I began to think up all kinds of excuses for his behavior. My upbringing dictated that "I must fix the problem" and keep our family together. I just needed to explain the situation to my in-laws, and thereby get the emotional tools to help him. I actually started to feel bad for him because I thought that he must certainly feel terrible and guilt-ridden. I knew he loved our baby and me, and this was just an isolated blip in our young marriage.

After work the next day, I immediately called my mother-in-law and brother-in-law to explain what happened the night before.

Their reaction was that Richard meant nothing by his outburst, and that it most likely would not happen again. Neither of them asked if I was okay. I was now more confused. Was this behavior typical in marriages? Was this now my lot in life?

The raging war between fear and love became more extreme. This was the man I married, and shortly, we would be parents. On this emotional and psychological overload, I took my first steps to becoming an "actress," one who excelled in making something seem what it was not. I was programmed to forgive—*even though I believed this was something that should not be forgiven.*

My ability to forgive now started to morph into a masterful cover-up skill. Outside of our home, the world saw us as a perfect couple. Inside the home, I was a prisoner of Richard's inner war, and became his convenient target whenever he felt the world was mistreating him. I had never experienced this emotional and physical pain before, and simply did not have the skills to know how to respond correctly. However, I did have the skills to keep at it until I got it right. As an emotional diversion from my newfound feelings of worthlessness, I began to obsess about my impending motherhood. I knew my baby would certainly love me.

On a damp and chilly November night a couple weeks later, Mother Nature was giving me many signals that delivery day was coming. Richard came home from work, and things seemed more or less normal.

"I've got more studying to do, so make some coffee to help keep me awake," he lamented. While the aroma of brewing coffee filled our apartment, his expletives began flying as he complained, "My boss asked me to come into work early this afternoon, so I missed my study time at the library. I've got an important final exam tomorrow, which means I have to stay up all night to study." I placed a cup of hot coffee on his desk, gave him a kiss, and whispered, "I'm heading to bed now. Good luck on your exam tomorrow." Alongside the coffee, I slipped him a piece of warm homemade gingerbread topped with fresh whipped cream.

At this late point in my pregnancy, my gait was more like a waddle. In the bedroom, I looked at the empty crib set up with loving care for a precious new baby who'd now occupy that space. A smile crossed my face, and I placed my hand on my tummy to enjoy another encore performance of our dancer-baby. A violent shove from Richard suddenly interrupted my happiness. My yellow nightgown whirled around my body as I fell to the floor.

"If it wasn't for you, I wouldn't have to be studying right now!" he yelled. Trying to get up, I felt another fierce pain in my lower back as he kicked me like a football, knocking me down again. I was afraid to move because a sharp and incapacitating pain was pulsating down my left leg. The impact of his kick caused our baby's position to shift inside my body, putting pressure on a nerve. Even through my paralyzing pain, I kept my cry to a whimper because I thought he would kick me again. When I asked him to take me to the hospital, Richard threw the car keys at me and screamed, "Drive there yourself!" He knew I couldn't drive a manual-shift car. I didn't have enough money for a taxi, and was terrified that if I called a taxi, or called someone for help, Richard would become enraged and hurt me or the baby again before anyone got to our apartment. So there I stayed.

In the morning, Richard tearfully apologized, saying he was under a lot of stress at work and at school.

"Please believe me—I will never do that again. I love you and our baby. If you leave me, I'll kill myself. I can't live without you. You stay in bed and rest today, and I'll bring home dinner. I don't want you to exert yourself, and if it weren't for this exam, I would stay home and care for you. I'm sure your leg pain is just part of the pregnancy because of your close due date." However, he added, "You cause me to do these things that I really don't want to do, so maybe while you rest today, just think about how you can be a better wife. Things will be better after the baby is born, and you get back into shape."

A classic red flag: placing guilt and responsibility on the victim. Being blamed for the abuser's anger and his suicide threat, and causing the victim consuming guilt and worry.

This was the beginning of twenty-three years of being trapped in an abuse cycle: violent outbursts, followed by Richard's tearful promises that it would never happen again.

"After all," he would say, "you made me do it." He was effective at manipulating my emotions to the point that I believed the things he told me. My self-image sank very low, and it was even hard to look in the mirror. Who was this person who was so horrible and ugly that a man would beat her up even when she was pregnant?

For a short period, our relationship would seem to be fixed, but it would break again, and then be fixed again before breaking again. It was a vicious cycle. I later understood that this cycle was the trademark of domestic violence.

FACT: This cycle keeps its victims trapped inside a forceful centrifuge that is impossible to flee, and if you try, the act of fleeing is often fatal.

My New Motherhood

On a sunny but cold late-November morning three weeks later, I woke up feeling extremely nauseated. My back pain was excruciating, and I went into the bathroom and vomited. I had incredible cramps in my stomach and legs. For a moment, I thought this was from being kicked in the back a few weeks earlier. Mother Nature sharply clapped her hands and said, "Wake up, honey, you're in labor!" Today was the day of our baby's debut! I waddled back to bed and lay there breathing slowly to ease the labor pains. Richard seemed excited, but he said our first big snowstorm was in the forecast and that, "We'd better hurry and get snow tires on the car on our way to the hospital!" My contractions were still far apart, so I thought a trip to the tire store would be okay. Besides, my doctor had said contractions can go on for a very long time. I grabbed my hospital suitcase, to be prepared just in case our baby's entrance into this world was sooner rather than later, and we headed out the door.

First we had to stop by the university so Richard could drop off an assignment that was due. He parked our hippie-mobile and suggested, "Walk with me to the professor's office just in case your contractions became more frequent." Up to this point, we had had only a little snow and freezing rain. Richard walked several paces ahead of me as I waddled carefully along the snowy sidewalk that edged the top of a small hill. Whoops, I slipped on the snow and proceeded to slide down the hill with my arms wrapped protectively around my baby. Instead of helping me, Richard paused briefly, seeming embarrassed by my mishap. Uttering words of disgust, he continued walking to drop off his assignment. I caught my breath and lay still for a moment to make sure my body was in one piece. Placing one hand in front of the other, I carefully crawled up the hill and back into the car.

Unbelievably, people who witnessed my fall, and saw Richard's reaction, didn't offer to help me. "Is Richard right? I must be a horrible person". Name-calling was another way for him to make me feel that I caused his outburst, and this destroyed my self-esteem even further.

Richard returned shortly, and we headed to the tire store. After about a ten-minute drive, my contractions suddenly went from thirty minutes apart to just a few minutes apart. Something happened when I fell and slid down the hill.

"Our baby is coming now!" I cried. Richard didn't believe me at first, and kept driving toward the tire store until I cried out in agony. He abruptly turned the car around and headed to St. Mary's Hospital near the university campus. My hospital check-in was speedy, followed by a dash to the labor room. A friendly and comforting nurse assured, "Your doctor has been notified and is on his way." Richard sat next to the bed, studying for more exams. Billions of beads of sweat rolled down my forehead as I tried as hard as I could to not vocalize my agony, knowing that if I did, he would ridicule or hurt me. Our baby was about to make a grand entrance.

The nurse came to check me again and blurted, "Oh my, your baby isn't going to wait for the doctor." Panic set in as she grabbed the bed and rolled me toward the delivery room. "Just breathe slowly," she kept saying. The nurse sprinted down the hallway that had now become a speedway to the delivery room. I looked up and watched the ceiling lights flicker by like strobe lights. Just as we reached our destination, a caring hand touched my shoulder. It was my doctor, still dressed in his winter boots and coat. He had been running neck-and-neck with my "race car" to the delivery room. We made it with just a few seconds to spare. My doctor laughed and said, "You pulled me from a card game, and I was winning. Just give one more push, Deb."

Then it happened! I heard a cry that I will never forget. It was beautiful music coming from a beautiful little girl. My doctor held her up—a perfect angelic face with a dimple in each cheek. Her arms flailed like wings trying to fly, and I cried, "She is dancing already." When the doctor laid her on my stomach, I felt her warm little body wiggle and squirm. "So this is the dance you have been working on, my little Kristin. One moment you were dancing *in* my stomach, and now you are dancing *on* my stomach."

Love and completeness filled my entire being.

"I am a mother," I exclaimed. "I will love and care for my baby forever. I will teach her the dance of life. I will make sure she feels loved every day of her life." I will never forget the gifts Kristin gave me at that moment—the music of her cry, the warmth of her body, and the promise of her love.

The next morning my doctor announced that Kristin was a perfect baby.

"From your comments during delivery, I take it that you are a dancer. Don't go back into that activity until I give you the okay sign," he cautioned. A nurse brought Kristin into the room, and my doctor offered up his opinion, "Yup. She'll be a dancer, too." He winked and patted my foot as he walked out of the room.

I held Kristin with gentle care and love. Nothing is as soft or smells as good as a new baby. Kristin's eyes had not opened yet, and while resting, I gently stroked her silky blonde "peach fuzz" hair. Richard was also full-blooded Norwegian, and on a canvas in my mind, a portrait was emerging of the Nordic goddess she would become.

Contented, I turned to feel the warmth of the sun's rays on my face as it streamed through the big window. We never did get the predicted snowstorm. I whispered, "What a glorious day to welcome a new life!" Tears of pure joy welled up in my eyes until I was distracted by someone staring at me. Slowly looking down, I saw one little bright blue eye open for the first time. Kristin was intently studying me as if to say, "So, you're my mom." The split second that we first looked at each other was miraculous and blessed.

Richard had been at the university taking his final exams, so later that evening he quietly entered the room, holding a stuffed koala bear. He placed the bear next to me and said that he would have come earlier—but that he had to come to terms with the fact that he had a daughter instead of a son.

"The main thing is that she is healthy and perfect," he sighed. I sat there in utter disbelief at his self-pity. Gathering my courage, coupled with a powerfully direct voice that he had never heard before, I said, "The main thing is that she is a human being who will always be loved!"

The next two days were full of visits from family and friends who eagerly cooed at Kristin through the nursery window. It felt so good to be around smiling and happy people. Dad was extremely proud, and monopolized holding his first grandchild. Thinking ahead, as he usually did, he brought a brand new pink tricycle adorned with pink bows, balloons, and a ringer bell on the handle bar. He said he wanted to be the one to give Kristin "her first set of wheels." Whenever my family gathered, it was quite an event, full of conversation and laughter. Our joyfulness was probably not appreciated by some folks in the hospital, especially when Dad had fun ringing the bell on Kristin's tricycle. Richard received many compliments from our families about his new daughter, and he openly began to radiate pride. I thought, "At last, we will be a happy family."

On the third day, Richard picked us up in the VW. We drove home in a car full of flowers, baby toys, stuffed animals, numerous newborn outfits, and a pink tricycle, to begin our journey in life. Because I had helped Mom care for my younger siblings, I was very equipped for my new responsibility. Even in my new life, my pre-programming to set an example kicked into high gear, right along with my newly-developed acting skills needed to make things seem what they were not. I was hopeful that things would be different. After all, we had a daughter now, someone to protect, love, and nurture into the finest human being she could be.

When we arrived home, Richard carried in the gifts, and I carried in life's most precious gift, our daughter. Richard and I put our arms around each other and stared at our lovely child in her crib. I truly believed that the dreams we had when we were first married would bloom again, and life would be good. I gave him a passionate kiss and whispered, "I love our new family."

Later that evening, I warmly expressed to Richard, "Even though our budget is tight right now, our beautiful baby makes us richer than anyone in the world." I gave him another kiss and headed to take a shower before resting. Richard lifted Kristin from her crib, and I wished I had had a camera to capture the loving image of him smiling at his new daughter. After my shower, I went into the kitchen for a drink of water, and as I walked into the living room, Richard grabbed me from behind and threw me on the floor. He yelled, "If it wasn't for you, I could have a new car or motorcycle! You bitch, you've ruined my life." To make his point more clear, he kicked me in the back. I quickly got Kristin from her crib and curled up on the sofa with my beautiful and perfect newborn. Holding her gently throughout the night, I tearfully and quietly cried out to my own mom for help because I was so afraid of my husband. Even though she lived ten miles away, I hoped Mom would hear my cry from a distance. I knew, however, that I was caught in an emotional catch-22. Whether I stayed with Richard or went home to a family still trying to cope with an alcoholic parent, I would be in a situation where I would be made to feel horrible about myself. That night, before Richard went to sleep in our bedroom, he repeated that he was angry we had a girl instead of a boy.

The next morning I awoke to the sound of the old wood floor creaking as Richard walked toward the living-room sofa where Kristin and I rested. He lamented, "It will never happen again. I just feel like you can't give me all of your attention now."

I recalled a magazine article that I had recently read, explaining that the arrival of a new baby can be difficult for some men. Instead of recognizing this as another red flag, I used the article to rationalize his most recent outbursts of violence. During the next few weeks, Richard actually seemed to take joy in helping out with our new baby. When family and friends came to visit, he was the first to boast about Kristin, and our life together actually seemed blissful and perfect. We made it through the turbulence, and now it would be smooth sailing ahead. I was very happy.

Soon it was Christmas. This was my family's favorite holiday, and the time we followed family tradition—a trip to Grandma Alice's farm to join more than thirty aunts, uncles, and cousins for Christmas Eve festivities that included feasting on the world's best home-cooked food, taking turns reading from the Bible, singing hymns, and wildly opening gifts. Oh yes, and an occasional "Uff da" from Grandpa Fred punctuated the celebrating. Laughter and youthful glee filled the huge farmhouse until, one by one, we drifted into a deep sleep from pure exhaustion and full stomachs. Outside, moonlit glistening snow quietly blanketed that remote part of the world.

This Christmas was decidedly more special to my extended family because joining us would be Kristin, the first grandchild for my parents and the first great-grandchild on both Mom's and Dad's sides of the family. We rode with my parents on the three-hour car ride from Minneapolis to the farm, and when we arrived, Dad proudly said, "Please let me carry her in," as he lifted Kristin from my arms.

Carefully cradling his first grandchild, Dad crunched his way through the deep snow into the Currier and Ives picturesque farmhouse.

"The rebirth of many things," I thought. When the front door opened, I could hear my relatives' excited chatter to see the new baby. Dad set Kristin, nestled in her infant seat, on the kitchen table, and my extended family quickly gathered around to see the beautiful new baby girl. Kristin was wearing a red-and-white Santa's elf pajama-and-stocking cap set that Mom had lovingly made.

Kristin was greeted with smiles and gentle touches, and with my grandparents' kitchen enveloped in love, Richard grabbed my left hand and squeezed it in what I thought was a secret gesture of pride. Instead, in his frightening Dr. Jekyll and Mr. Hyde transition, he kept squeezing my hand so hard that I expected my fingers would break from the pressure around my wedding ring. He leaned over and sternly whispered in my ear, "Get your things because we are going back home. I can't stand the smell of a farm, and your family is a bunch of hicks."

I fought back tears. I would not ruin my family's joyful moment. We, of course, could not drive away as we had traveled to the farm in my parents' car. Richard sulked until it was time to drive back to Minneapolis.

My new life was not what I had expected.

Silent Screams

Because we needed the money, I returned to work when Kristin was less than a month old. In a perverse way, Richard used this as an excuse to make me feel like a horrible parent. On one hand, he would ridicule me for working outside of the home, and say that I was neglecting Kristin, even though Mom and Aunt Elsie provided excellent daycare. On the other hand, he'd say, "No wife of mine is going to stay home and sit on her ass. You need to bring more money into this household, so find a second job if you need to."

One more in the myriad of red flags: keep changing the rules, and control through chaos.

The beatings continued throughout Kristin's first six months, while we were living in our apartment in south Minneapolis. A couple of the attacks occurred because, as he said, "I want to remind you what will happen if you ever make me angry." I had learned to let my body go limp because the beatings hurt less.

Always his false promise followed: "It will never happen again." Just as he made me believe that I was the cause of his violence, I also believed his promise that it would stop. I desperately wanted the love we felt for each other on our wedding day to survive. I did not want Kristin to be from a broken home. I was consumed with trying to mend what was becoming hopelessly shattered. I knew how to be diligent and not give up. I knew how to stay, not leave. And if I did leave, I would die if he took Kristin from me.

By the time Kristin was two years old, Richard had graduated from the university, and had found a good corporate management job. To be in a safer neighborhood, we moved to an apartment located in a northern suburb of Minneapolis, far from my work and my family that lived on the south end. When I reminded him of our agreement that I would work to support our family and pay his college tuition until he graduated, and next it would be my turn to go back to school, he offered up numerous excuses of why I should still wait.

My greatest nightmare emerged at this time by his frequent proclamation, "If I wanted to, I could leave you now and get full custody of Kristin because you earn less than I do." This threatened me to the core. He was a master at feeding his insatiable need to control by keeping my emotional and psychological state in chaos. He knew the threat to take Kristin away from me was the main button to push to keep me in line. Sadly, I could not see a way out of this trap.

During the two years after Kristin's birth, through dancing and just doing the everyday things, I had lost my pregnancy weight, but had not shopped for any new clothes. I was down to one pair of badly worn denim jeans that were now too big. On a shopping trip with Richard, who often bought two or three expensive suits at once, I stopped to look at a pair of jeans on a clothing rack. In front of several shoppers, he grabbed me by the hair and pulled me out of the store, yelling, "You dumb shit, you're wasting all of our money!" Again, no one intervened, further deepening my feeling that I must be a very worthless person.

In spite of the physical and emotional abuse during the next few years, our lives did seem to settle down as he began to rapidly advance through the ranks at his job. We even had a new car, but it was still a manual shift. One day he actually agreed to teach me how to drive it, but the lesson abruptly ended when, as a manual-shift beginner, I made the engine chug and lurch while trying to shift gears.

"Get out of my car, you stupid bitch!" he yelled. I got out of the car, thinking that we were going to trade places and go home. Instead, he left me standing there as he drove away. I ended up walking the five miles home. What else could I do?

The next day, while bagging up garbage to bring to the dumpster, I noticed that Richard had given Kristin his new car keys, and she was playing with them. When I heard the jingling of the keys stop, I looked up and saw Kristin trying to stick one of the keys into an electrical outlet. In sheer alarm, I bolted toward her, grabbing the keys in time. But in my dash, I tipped over the pail, sending garbage flying all over the kitchen. Richard immediately slapped my face, grabbed me by the hair, and dragged me into the bedroom. Holding my shoulders, he shook me so hard that I got a stiff neck. I was again helpless and speechless.

The Essence of Kristin as a Child

In spite of these outbursts, Kristin for the most part seemed to have a decent and playful relationship with her dad during her early years. She was a strikingly beautiful child with an incredibly cute personality. As a toddler, she often sat by the window in her little white rocking chair, waiting patiently for her dad to come home to play with her. She was always seeking her dad's approval and attention in her preschool days. Occasionally, when he was engrossed in reading the newspaper, Kristin playfully ran full speed across the room to bounce off a sofa cushion, fly into the air and execute a smash landing on his lap. Her performance ended with the flash of an irresistible smile and a big hug for her dad.

Growing up, Kristin (a Sagittarius), made friends easily, and always looked after the underdog. She loved transcending limits and relished exchange of ideas. I saw many of my siblings' personality traits and talents in her. A big heart, love of animals, a sweet streak as well as a mischievous streak, a laugh that made you laugh, a gift for writing and drawing, admirable independence, and a natural talent as a dancer. She adored all of her grandparents, and her ever-increasing crew of cousins were more like siblings. Kristin and my wildly interesting and lovable Aunt Elsie developed a deep and special closeness—as if Kristin had a third grandma.

Kristin also had an innate sense of right and wrong, and of being fair. She never lied, and always took responsibility for her actions. For example, when she was only nine years old, she overheard me on the telephone angrily scolding a furniture salesman about the huge dent that I had just noticed in the wall of our newly remodeled basement. I accused their delivery staff of causing the damage when they delivered a large bookshelf while I was at work. After I hung up, I remembered that Kristin had offered to vacuum the new basement carpet the day before, and being a little suspicious, I pushed the edge of the vacuum up to the hole in the wall. It was a perfect match. My detective work solved the mystery, and Kristin boldly took responsibility as she said, "I'll take care of this, Mom. Don't worry." She looked up the furniture company's number in the telephone book, asked to speak to the manager, and confessed to what had happened. She apologetically said, "I don't want the delivery people to get into trouble, because the damage is my fault. I'm sorry." Two days later Kristin received a letter in the mail from the furniture store manager, who expressed his admiration for her strong character, stating that her parents should be very proud.

Our First Home

In the spring of 1975, while our first home was under construction, we moved in with my parents for a few months. Mom had sought help for her drinking problem, and seemed healthier than she had been for a long time. I thought that living with my parents during those months would be a respite for me from the abuse, but I was wrong. Richard still found moments—and took advantage of them. Times during our stay I certainly thought about talking to my parents about what my married life was like, but it seemed overwhelming to reveal the unspeakable and continuing abuse, even while staying in their home. I was never sure what he would do. Without provocation, he had already wreaked such havoc. What would he do if he were found out, or challenged? I did not want to appear as a failure to my parents—because my husband already viewed me that way. I did not want to be a cause for my mom to drink again. Also, my youngest sibling, Mark, had been diagnosed with neurofibromatosis, and my parents had their own relationship issues to deal with. I did not want to further burden anyone else's life. My self-esteem and self-worth were severely compromised.

I was no longer even capable of making the decision to talk with my parents, because being in an abusive situation for so long, it had obliterated my decision-making skills.

In the fall of 1975, when Kristin started kindergarten, we moved into our first house, a small split-level in Apple Valley, Minnesota. One of the first projects she and her dad worked on was building a house for her new puppy, Goldie. Kristin loved to sit by her dad and watch hockey or hand him tools as he worked on one of his cars. They often played catch in our huge backyard. Kristin was also proudly involved in dance lessons, just like her mom. Later in our lives, Kristin revealed to me that in her childhood, working with her dad was sometimes scary because some of the tools were sharp, and by that time she was keenly aware of his temper. She also shared that he used to tell her that he still wished she had been a boy. During these early years, she somehow felt that it would be better to try to appease "the monster in him," rather than aggravate him, which she was afraid would put her and me at risk. Her wisdom far exceeded her age.

In the early years of our marriage, my life was in chaos, even as the world was in chaos from the Vietnam War. I was in a war zone at home, and I never knew when the enemy would strike next. The long, dark night had begun, and now two of us were living the nightmare at the hands of one who should have been caring for us. Not only had the responsibilities of setting an example, and of forgiving, been deeply rooted into my being, but so had the societal bombardment of keeping a family together at all costs for the sake of the children. I read numerous articles about the adverse effects divorces have on children, and watched countless experts on television talk about the virtue of the intact family as it related to healthy child development. I cherished the concept of "family." This became Richard's ultimate element of control by threatening that if the marriage were dissolved, he would take Kristin away from me. I had to keep it together. And to survive the daily mayhem—we had to act like there was none. Battered women are truly the best actresses—no amount of acting training can teach you what my daughter and I learned as a result of our experiences.

Obsession to Control

So now, with this foundation, I'll return to the day-to-day of my marriage. Sleeping in the same room with Richard, let alone in the same bed, was not easy. It became especially clear one night when, while I was sleeping, he again jabbed his right elbow into my left thigh. I woke up from the pain, unable to move my leg. After this incident, I learned to sleep almost motionless, and to breathe in a shallow manner during the night. My worry was that if I tossed or turned and accidentally woke him up, he would hurt me. Fear became all-consuming. Although this had happened before, and he didn't actually say it at the time, I felt that his attempt to hurt my leg had to do with his jealousy regarding my dancing. I kept dancing nevertheless, because dancing was my sanctuary, and even though she was still young, I observed Kristin also choosing dance to define herself.

Throughout our marriage, I continued to take dance lessons regularly in Minneapolis, and master classes with professionals from Chicago, New York, and Los Angeles. When Kristin was older, we began to take dance classes together—even the master classes. We felt safe in a studio; we felt whole in a studio. For us, a dance studio was the most natural environment. It was where we were alive, where we smiled and reclaimed who we were.

In addition to continuing with my own dance education, I directed a dance program in the local public school district, and taught around the Twin Cities area with increasing frequency. I performed with a professional jazz dance company based in St. Paul, and for several years, my summers included choreographing community theater productions.

Kristin's natural talent as a dancer blossomed early. When she was only twelve years old, she was already performing with me in the jazz dance company, and at fifteen, was doing her own choreography for summer community theater. Having the opportunity to perform with one's own child is something not many parents experience. Every time we were about to dance together, I became emotionally choked up, and the thrill of it all gave a double meaning to my feeling of genuine happiness and comfort on stage. As I had done, Kristin spent a lot of time after school in the dance studio, and it became a haven. The creativity and physical demands of dance would prove to be one of the major saving graces for my daughter, as it had been and continued to be, for me.

Student enrollment in my classes grew substantially each year. At every opportunity, through beatings and sabotage, Richard tried to put an end to my involvement in dance, and to jeopardize my teaching career—but he could not stop me. One of his shining moments was in June 1985. Prior to my leaving for my students' most important annual dance concert, he went so far as to take my costumes out of my car trunk. After a frantic search, I found my costumes in the garage dumpster, and I danced in them that night with the added accoutrement of potato salad and pickle juice.

Control was the issue. Control fed his larger-than-life ego, larger-than-life narcissistic personality, and larger-than-life insecurities. Years later, after we had separated, I found out for the first time that he would threaten Kristin over simple things, like not unloading the dishwasher or not walking the dog when he thought she should. He often made clear threats to use his hands or a gun to cause harm to me, and to our daughter when I was away at work.

Kristin also revealed that in her early grades, when I was away, she knew to walk on eggshells around her dad, and to have an escape plan until I returned home. One day she hopped on her bicycle and pedaled as fast as she could to run away from him. Upon realizing that she did not know where to go, she began to sob, and headed back home, only to experience her dad laughing at her unsuccessful flight for freedom. Compassion was not one of his virtues.

The one thing in our lives that he did not understand enough to control was our passion for dance. From his viewpoint, why should he let us dance? And by the same token, how could we stop?

Father/Daughter Relationship Changes

As we hope all healthy little girls do, they grow into bigger girls and into their adolescence. As Kristin got older and became an independent, bigger girl, her relationship with her dad changed dramatically. His playful demeanor toward her was fading, and he took as personal insult, rather than pride, any attempt on her part to be independent. Kristin also started to try to intervene whenever he became abusive toward me.

After I separated from Richard, Kristin and I felt safe enough to finally reveal things to each other that the other didn't know. Even though each assault was horrible, one in particular has haunted me ever since Kristin explained what happened. When she was about nine years old, on an afternoon before I returned home from shopping, she recalls Richard hitting her with a rolling pin, giving her several bruises on her back. During school the next day, Kristin panicked as she stood in line for the students' annual scoliosis check, afraid that her teacher and other students would see her bruises, causing her dad to get into trouble. Kristin bolted from the line and ran home, hiding in our front bushes until the school bus passed at its normal afternoon time. She knew that her dad would be angry if he was found out. Once the bus pulled away, Kristin went to the neighbor's house, as she usually did for daycare, until I got home from work. By keeping silent and not revealing what her dad had done, this precious young child believed she was protecting her mom and herself from further abuse.

As Kristin told me the story, I sobbed. Why hadn't I pursued this mystery further at the time? I remembered coming home, carrying the grocery bags into the house, and seeing a broken rolling pin on the counter. Richard claimed that I should quit buying cheap utensils and get a better one next time. I never thought to ask him why he suddenly decided to take up baking.

Hindsight is 20/20, and can cause immense heartache and incapacitating regret. It can invoke cries for forgiveness. In my attempt to keep our family together for the sake of Kristin's well-being, I had unwittingly taught her how to be a good actress, to make something seem what it was not. I pray each night for her forgiveness, and that she will always understand that I tried to be the best mom I could.

The year following the rolling-pin incident was relatively calm, and we were finally financially able to go on a luxury family vacation, one that we could only dream about years earlier as newlyweds. Our destination was an eight-day Caribbean cruise, and we were filled with anticipation. At last our departure day arrived. We eagerly boarded the airplane, and a few hours later boarded a mammoth cruise ship.

As a cruise ship tradition, the second night is the captain's welcome dinner, where everyone struts around the ship in fine formalwear. An endless assortment of delicacies was paraded around the dinner table, and after we were more than full, we brought Kristin back to our cabin to help her settle in for the night.

"Dad and I are going to take a walk around the ship, and go to the lounge to listen to music and dance a bit," I explained to Kristin. She climbed into her bunk, and I knew that with a full tummy, sunburned cheeks, and the gentle rocking of the ship, it would be only a matter of minutes before she fell asleep.

Richard and I strolled around the entire circumference of the ship, detouring toward the sound of loud music and laughter. We came upon the liveliest lounge on the ship, and quickly joined in the celebration. Great music, coupled with an incredible dance floor, meant that *I was in heaven!* After we danced for several minutes, we sat down to order a glass of wine. Before our waiter returned, a man walked up to Richard and said, "Sir, I watched you and your wife on the dance floor, and I respectfully ask permission to dance one dance with your wife." Before Richard could answer, I interrupted and said, "I am complimented by your request, but this is our special vacation, and I am happy to just dance with my husband." After the gentleman walked away, Richard angrily accused me of doing something to cause the man to request a dance. With a vacant look in his eyes that I knew all too well, he proceeded to grab my arm and force me back to our cabin.

Once inside, where our eleven-year-old daughter was sleeping, Richard grabbed me tightly by the throat. I began to feel faint, and called to Kristin for help. I couldn't catch my breath, and thought I was dying. I yelled again for Kristin to get help, and when she tried to go out the door, her dad grabbed her by the neck and threw her back, yelling threats at her. She hit her head against the wall and started to cry. The cold look in his eyes was terrifying, and I thought that night would be my last. I couldn't console my baby because I was in the midst of being strangled.

When I woke up the next morning, Richard had already left the cabin. I had a lot of bruises on my face, neck, and chest, which I covered up with tons of makeup. Kristin innocently and carefully studied me as I applied the makeup. We said no words to each other, except that we were both okay, and held hands as we walked through the cabin door to face the day.

This horrendous attack simply drove Kristin and me into more fear and avoidance, and there was, to be sure, an unbreakable bond between us. We continued our long, lonely walk down the ship's corridor, knowing that when we stepped into the sunlight, we would transform into actresses executing another command performance.

While eating dinner the evening we returned home from the cruise, Richard's anger about my involvement in dance roared once more. He unexpectedly grabbed my left arm and began to pummel my left shoulder repeatedly with his right fist. Within minutes my entire left shoulder and upper back area swelled, turning a sickening dark purple and black color, sharply contrasting the red of multiple broken blood vessels.

In her reflection of those years, Kristin revealed that her perception of her dad was that he didn't have what it would take to be gentle or considerate. She basically got to the point where she ignored him. She says that even as a younger child, she could actually see the energy around him "go dark, and his eyes start looking like a dead fish." She remembers feeling the energy that seemed to take him over, and early on, she knew she needed to "appease the monster." She also recognized that he seemed to try to change, but failed every time.

Scared Silent

It may seem impossible to believe that:
- anyone could have been so abusive to another human being; especially a wife and daughter;
- we somehow survived;
- we didn't say anything about it; or
- no one noticed or, if they did, they didn't try to do something about it.

I often prayed that someone would see the hurt in our eyes and ask what was wrong. Because we had been conditioned to be silent, I tried to talk with my eyes, and hoped that someone would see into my soul, where dreadful secrets were kept. If anyone had asked, "Deb, what is wrong?" I would have been given permission to talk. That simple question would have opened a door that I would have dared to go through.

But I was also terrified to say something, knowing that the abuse would get worse. When people made mention of the bruises on my arms and legs, I explained them away as a result of an over-exuberant dance class, or that I fell. Oftentimes, during the beatings, I would mentally drift away to another place to avoid having to deal with this reality that took too much out of me. I simply didn't have enough energy to ask for help. Kristin later told me that she would mentally drift off to Africa.

Dance had become my only way to communicate and to feel alive. An inner strength came through every time I set my body in motion. In my case, Richard kept knocking down the building blocks of self-confidence, self-esteem, and self-image—things that make us who we are. Whenever I tried to reassemble the building blocks of "Deb," he would crash them into a heap. Before long, the building blocks became too heavy for me to lift and carry. Domestic violence is a systematic whittling down of a human being's makeup. It renders them unable to make any decisions, including the decision to leave. Perhaps, partly because of her youth and spirit, Kristin had moments of being proactive about our situation. Among other things, I later found out that she and a childhood friend had built a little fort in the woods behind her friend's house, and planned an escape route for us in case Richard hit us again.

Being the rolling stone that gathers no moss, Richard decided that we should move again, into a bigger house with a garage large enough for his cars. In 1986 we signed a purchase agreement to build a new home a mile from our current home in Apple Valley, and as part of the agreement, Richard opted for us to do most of the paint, stain, and ceramic tile work ourselves. Even though we could have afforded to let the professionals do that work, he claimed, "They'll just rip us off." Richard also opted to use violence towards me to ease his frustration when the do-it-yourself projects became overwhelming. As building blocks were assembled for our new home, the building blocks of me continued to crumble.

Chaos—the Ultimate in Control

In 1988, Kristin's senior year in high school, she yearned to major in dance at the University of Minnesota, and it was a blessed day when she received the letter of acceptance into their dance major program. She lived on campus her freshman year, and later in various lofts and apartments with friends up through her senior year. During summers, Kristin spent periods of time living back home to save money.

Before she moved out, Kristin told me that she was very worried about my safety now that I would be alone with her dad. She made frequent calls of, "Are you okay?" and periodic visits home to do her laundry in order to survey the situation. It was at this time that Richard embarked on another method to send me on an emotional roller coaster of a different kind. The physical abuse would intensify, followed by disappearing acts when he would not return home until very late.

Artfully, Richard tried to isolate me even more when he announced that even though we had lived in our new home only two years, he wanted us to move again, either to a condo in Minneapolis or out of state.

"I'm sick of mowing the grass," he lamented. The thought of moving to a location where I didn't know anyone but him terrified me. He knew that the only way he could control my involvement in dance was to pull me away, geographically, from the strong student base and reputation I had built in the local dance community. He insisted that we spend our Sundays looking at condos and townhouses.

His actions were insane for us financially, and packed boxes still sat in our basement from this move. One afternoon I decided to tackle a few of the boxes, and began the unpleasant task of sorting through old financial files. A few hours later, Richard came into our office to see the status of my project. My heart beat wildly as I saw the all-too-familiar steely rage in his eyes. His first blow hit the top of my head. The second blow hit my left cheek and eyelid. The impact of his fist against my skull rang through my ears, and the resulting head trauma rendered me motionless. Demeaning remarks flew effortlessly from his mouth.

"When are you going to get a real job? Teaching dance isn't work, you're just out having fun. I should have married someone from a decent family—with money. If I left you, you'd just end up living in a ghetto. That's all you deserve. You're just a hick like the rest of your family."

With another angry sweep of his arm, stacks of papers and file folders that I had been sorting flew into the air and sashayed back to earth like confetti. My eyelid immediately swelled up from his blow, and my head felt like it was going to explode. I gazed down at the file folder still clutched in my hand—a folder now marked forever with blood droplets.

The beatings, intimidation and control tactics, were constant, and too many to mention. It was only after I had decided to separate from him that Kristin and I felt safe enough to talk to each other about them. She said she had not told me about things that happened when I wasn't home. In addition to being afraid that he would be more abusive, she sensed that, over the years, I was getting more and more depressed about the abuse, and she didn't want to burden me more.

The more I tried to protect myself, the more violent he became, so I was trained to just take it—and pray that it would end quickly. Whatever he felt was wrong in his life, he blamed on me. If it weren't for his daughter and me, he would have a better lifestyle.

What kind of lifestyle did he think he had provided his family?

The Road to Freedom

This analogy describes the situation Kristin and I were in: *"If you throw a frog into a pot of boiling water, it will jump out. If you throw a frog into a pot of cold water and slowly turn up the heat, it will acclimate itself to the rising temperature, until it dies."*

A late April 1992 event finally triggered my decision to escape from this nightmare. At day's end, I was already in my nightgown. Richard started yelling at me because I was upset that he was out until four in the morning. Although he had threatened to shoot us before, he never actually picked up a gun. This time he did. During his angry outburst, he marched into his closet. I thought he was reaching for his slippers on the lower shelf, but to my horror, he spun around, aiming his rifle at me. His vacant look was as cold as the metal of his gun. I bolted for the front door, literally dashing for my life out into the blustery, rainy night.

"Oh, God! Please help me outrun a bullet," I prayed. My heart pounded like thunder as I splashed through the puddles in my bare feet. Pure terror consumed me, and in seconds, the rhythms of my beating heart and running feet were in sync. To this day I remember that rhythm. It will still occasionally resurface when I tap dance—I call it my survival rhythm.

Never before had I experienced this horror, and as I fled, I could not make my legs run fast enough. With each running step, I was either one step closer to surviving—or one step closer to being killed. I managed to reach the end of the block and hid behind a cluster of bushes. Richard followed me in his car, and when he found me, he shoved me into the front passenger door, bruising my left shoulder. He quickly opened the car door and pushed me inside. For half-hour, he drove around, yelling at me and pounding his fists on the dashboard. I remembered seeing three neighborhood teenage girls watching from across the street when I fled the house just thirty minutes earlier. I prayed that they had called the police, and felt sure that officers would be at our house. But I learned later that although the girls had, indeed, frantically run home to report what they had seen, their parents did not want to get involved. So no one called the police.

As horribly abusive as Richard had been for twenty-three years, this was no doubt his most terrifying action. The memory of that night still haunts me.

Aside from being killed, one of my fears in those days was that if I went to someone for help—and was refused—it would validate Richard's claim that no one cared about me. Now basic survival was the issue. Around three that morning, while Richard was asleep, I quietly gathered some clothing, put it in a laundry basket, and tiptoed to the garage. I opened my car door in slow motion, and held my breath as I turned the key to start the car. I said a prayer that nothing would wake him. So far, so good! He had not come into the garage. For the first time I was going to flee to safety. One more hurdle: I pushed the remote control button and held my breath as the overhead garage door loudly creaked and moaned. I let out a deep sigh of relief— and inhaled hope. Putting the car into reverse, a sudden horrific "bang" came from the rear of the car. In the rearview mirror was, like a scene in a horror movie, Richard's enraged face as he pounded on the trunk.

"Get back into the house," he screamed.

I almost made it—until he blocked my exit to freedom!

Back in the house, I lay still, dressed in my escape clothes, afraid to breathe. When morning came, I pretended to be asleep while Richard got ready for work. When he drove away, I called in sick to work. For several minutes I sat quietly at the kitchen desk before I became somewhat aware of my surroundings. Warm sunlight flooded my face, and the faint laughter of school children at the bus stop fluttered through the air. The house became magically quiet as I saw a hand dialing the phone to call the police. I saw my hand reach for the phone, but it did not seem like it was my hand. Was this an out-of-body experience or divine intervention? Perhaps it was my guardian angel. For the first time, I was actually going to ask for help. A spirit was telling me that I could not take this anymore.

"Deb, you are going to die if you do not leave."

When the police dispatcher answered the phone, I cried, "I need help because my angry husband pointed a gun at me." I was transferred to another officer who informed me that the current law stated that if someone was threatened with a gun, the incident had to be reported *within four hours*. Ten hours had elapsed since Richard aimed the gun at me; therefore, there was nothing they could do. I gasped and said, "Sir, I am afraid for my life. Is there nothing that can be done? What do I do?"

"You and your husband just need to learn to get along," he advised.

I was speechless, and begged for a multitude of guardian angels to help me. This can't be! Deep, dark sadness enveloped me—that is, until a small flame flickering inside me grew to a roaring fire. In an instant, I knew what was in the angels' plan for me. They would step aside to make way for me to learn, on my own, the skills needed to regain the strength to lift, carry, and reassemble the building blocks of me. The first block for me to lift was courage, for I needed profound courage to fuel my quest for help.

That night after work, Richard had another of his outbursts, complete with pounding his fists on the wall. In response to the gun incident the night before, he said, "What do I have to do to get you out of my life? Now I know why there are murder-suicides. I have friends in probate court, and I can have you committed."

In what seemed like a stroke of instant insanity, his comments abruptly changed direction when he announced that he wanted our marriage to become more of a "business arrangement," because being married had better tax deductions—and divorces were too expensive. Now that Kristin was in college, he felt that he should be able to date other women and carry on how he wanted to. He further stated that, "You are not allowed to do any of this because it would make me look bad if you were seeing someone else. I also want you to get a second job so our household has more money."

Richard had been coming home late more frequently, and that evening he admitted to having an affair with a co-worker. I had always been faithful during our marriage, and the emotional blow of this revelation, heaped on top of years of abuse, left me almost lifeless. My heart had just been ripped from my body. With my entire being, I knew at that moment that he truly believed it would be easier and less expensive for him to get rid of me than to go through a divorce. Terror set in, and I could hardly move. I was living with a monster, and I prayed that I would make it through the night. Immediately, survival instinct kicked in like it never had before, and through the remainder of the night I was on full alert.

After Richard left for work the next morning, I drove straight to the police department, walked directly to the dispatcher window, and said, "I fear for my life. My daughter and I have suffered many years of abuse." The dispatcher called for an officer and asked me to wait in the lobby. The first police officer to enter the lobby spoke two sentences to me: "We see this all the time," and, "You and your husband should work this out." He then turned around and walked back into the department. At that moment another police officer emerged to inform me that he couldn't do much about my situation other than to refer me to the Robert Lewis House Women's Shelter.

I had no idea what a women's shelter was or how they would help me. I drove home and called the Robert Lewis House. That phone call saved my life. The warm woman who answered asked me to come in immediately to talk to an advocate. Someone actually wanted to hear what I had lived through. I had a voice for the first time! Someone finally asked the question that I needed to hear: "Deb, what is wrong?" I had been given permission to talk. Thus began the filing for a restraining order—and a divorce.

Advocate Angels

In early May, 1992 with the help and guidance of the Robert Lewis House advocate, I obtained a temporary order for protection, which was effective for one week. I was immediately put in touch with an attorney, Rita, who prepared an order for protection request that would extend it for one year, as well as a petition for divorce. By the end of the week, the year-long order for protection was granted by the judge on duty—even though Richard said in court it wasn't necessary, and he completely denied everything—and Rita filed the divorce papers. During the hearing, Kristin and I sat next to each other, and behind us was Richard who, to show us in his not-so-subtle way that he was still in charge, repeatedly and irritatingly kicked the back of our bench. At first, Kristin felt sad about the hearing, but by the end of the proceeding it was apparent that this was our only option.

A week after the gun incident, Richard was allowed to return to the house, escorted by a police officer, to collect his belongings. Thanks to the intervention by the Robert Lewis House, the police were now responding to my cries for help. The officer was very kind to me, and I noticed that he kept his hand close to his gun while he was overseeing Richard's final visit to the house. After Richard left, the officer stayed for a while to make sure he didn't come back, and made the comment, "I have never seen someone wound so tight. He's like a spring ready to pop." Even though he had now moved out, I was still filled with apprehension that Richard might return. As he left, his last words were, "The problem with you, Deb, is that you don't obey."

Still in Fear

The locks on the front and back doors of the house were changed, but one day, upon returning home, I was more than a little upset to see that the broomsticks, which I had threaded into the garage door framework to prevent it from opening, were on the garage floor instead. Rita said that Richard admitted he had been at the house to retrieve some tools while I was away, and had to shake the garage door hard and rapidly to make the brooms fall out. Even though he couldn't get into the house, dread overwhelmed me. I started sleeping with a phone on the other pillow. For several months, I was often sick to my stomach, and it seemed to be a different kind of stress that I was feeling now. According to statistics, the initial time of separation is the most dangerous time for victims, the time when the abuser generally retaliates. The women's shelter advocate had warned me of this, and on a mental and emotional level, I was registering every horrible possibility, often giving me nightmares of his breaking in. The daily call from the advocate to make sure I was okay was most comforting, as was immersing myself in the beauty of dance, as it gave me a respite from my feelings of fear.

To help me get through this difficult time, Kristin and a few of her college friends spent a week at my house camping out on the sofa and in sleeping bags. They created a very busy social calendar for me, including tickets to an outdoor Lollapalooza rock concert. While Kristin and her friends went upstairs to get dressed for the big concert, I scanned my closet downstairs to pick out an appropriate outfit.

"Hurry up, Mom, so we aren't late!" As I proudly walked out of the bedroom in my rock concert splendor, Kristin and her crew gave me a horrified look and gasped, "You can't wear that! You look like you are going to church!" Kristin ran up to her closet and came back with some of her clothes and told me to change. She fixed my hair and makeup until I looked more "hip," and not like a mom tagging along. I was ready for a good time. Yahoo! We spent the day at the outdoor concert and continued our partying into the night, dancing at a popular music club in Minneapolis. How blessed I was to have such a fun daughter.

Kristin and her friends graciously included me in many of their eventful evenings. We were still relying on some tried-and-true methods of coping, of living well, of finding joy that would overpower the fear.

Sideways Moves

My newfound freedom felt good. However, even though the order for protection was supposed to prevent Richard from abusing or harassing me for one year, he still found ways to torture me. In October 1992, I received a letter responding to an ad in a dating publication called *Di's Meet People*. I immediately drove to the publication's office and learned that they had run an ad which said, "*Sexy disease-free DWF, attractive blonde, sincere and passionate. Searching for a S/DM who likes to dance and romance. Let's hear from you!*" Other letters followed that were lewd and suggestive. I was mortified.

The ad upset me, but I became much more upset when the receptionist in the publication office gave me the original application for the ad, and I saw that it was in Richard's handwriting. Rita contacted Richard's attorney and asked her to advise him that such harassment was a violation of the order for protection, and sent her a copy as evidence. Rita told me that Richard completely denied having made the application for the ad. I had a forensic document examiner look over the application along with several examples of Richard's handwriting, and her conclusion was that, indeed, it was his handwriting.

The county attorney's office subsequently brought criminal charges associated with this incident against Richard, and subpoenaed me as a witness. Richard did not hire an attorney to represent him but, instead, opted to proceed *pro se*, meaning that during the trial when I was on the witness stand, I would be forced to be questioned by my soon-to-be-ex-husband, whom I still greatly feared.

Richard used this as an opportunity to badger me, and to try to provoke me during his questioning because he knew that I could not run away. A few times the judge did intervene to stop Richard's behavior toward me, but it happened nevertheless. Prior to the trial, I told Sherry, the prosecuting attorney, that I was panic-stricken at the thought of even being in the same room with the man who had threatened me with a gun and abused me for so long. Sherry said, "You have no choice, but after you are off the witness stand you can go home. You do not have to stay for the verdict."

Leaving the witness stand after Richard's badgering was difficult because my legs felt unsteady. Sherry took my arm and helped me to the door, interrupting an emotional breakdown. She said she would call me when the verdict was in. I drove home, and after two hours had passed, Sherry called to say, "Richard was found guilty and, based on his reaction, I worry for your safety. I advise you to leave your house immediately and stay in a safe spot for the night." I packed a bag, grabbed my new Bichon puppy, Misha, and drove to my parents' apartment because they had a security system.

Richard was fined a few hundred dollars. Even though the judge reprimanded him from the bench for his abusive questioning of me, and even with Sherry's take on his behavior in the courtroom and her subsequent concern for me, he was found guilty of only a misdemeanor.

More Help

By the fall of 1992, Kristin and I were seeing a psychologist, Dr. Lund, and in that process we began to truly face the horrors of living with Richard. Now that we were away from him, it was finally safe enough for me to talk to Kristin about it, and for her to tell me what had happened to her.

We had so many suppressed emotions concerning the abuse that we both had endured. Kristin did not know all of the details of my abuse, nor I the details of what she had experienced. I needed to hear her details, as she began to feel comfortable talking about them. When she started actually telling me what had happened when I wasn't at home, I simply broke down sobbing and cried every time we talked about it.

One episode in particular tore at my heart, as Kristin revealed what had happened. When she was about twenty and had moved back home for the summer, I was out walking the dog while she was in her bedroom getting ready to meet some of her friends. Her dad came up the stairs, and from the hallway said, "So, what are you doing tonight?"

Kristin cautioned, "Don't come in here. I'm getting dressed." She pushed the door shut, but it slammed accidentally because of a gust of wind blowing through her window.

Her dad became enraged and burst through the door yelling, "Don't ever slam doors on me! Why didn't you answer me? You are going to have to start talking to me. You can't just ignore me anymore."

She responded with, "I did answer you. I'm getting dressed, obviously." When she asked him to get out so she could finish getting ready, he had his back to the door and proceeded to grab her by her ears and ram her head into the wall. He pulled her by her hair, but she escaped and ran out of her room, stopping at the top of the staircase because she didn't think the terror would go on anymore. His rage continued as he ran out of her bedroom and pushed her down the stairs, causing her to hit her head repeatedly along the way. When she landed, he pulled her up again by her hair and kicked her in the lower back and out the front door. She ended up on the front steps on all fours.

I recalled returning an hour later from walking the dog, and noticed that Kristin's face was flushed as she walked out the door to meet her friends. When I went inside and demanded to know what was wrong, Richard calmly said to me, "Oh, we just had a little argument."

As Kristin detailed her dad's assault that night, I rocked back and forth, unable to breathe.

After Richard moved out, people would often ask me, "Why didn't you just leave?" That question immediately assigned blame to me—and threw me back into a psychological place that I was trying so hard to leave. That question would infuriate me and is as insensitive as asking prisoners of war, "You outnumbered the guards. Why didn't you just walk out?" Would these same people ask of Richard, "Why did you do that to your wife and daughter?" Victims of abuse are erroneously viewed as weak. The reality is that incredible stamina and courage are required to gain the strength to leave an abusive situation.

Our meetings with Dr. Lund helped me conclude that all of us on this earth get only one chance in life, and no one has the right to take away the opportunity another person has to become who they were meant to be. If someone knocks down the building blocks of who you are, move immediately to another construction site. Once an abuser crosses that line, he or she will most likely do it again.

I was unable to recognize this glaring red flag during my married years because Richard had slowly and completely undermined my self-esteem.

The Meltdown

About 10 p.m. the night of November 25, 1992, I experienced a complete meltdown. I had been shopping for the Thanksgiving holiday at a supermarket when suddenly I recalled how Richard had humiliated me at that same store. After I paid for my groceries, all I remember about the drive back home was that my car suddenly veered off the freeway's cloverleaf ramp and stopped just inches in front of a huge tree, and that a lot of car horns were honking.

As I drove, my mind had been running a virtual slideshow of abuse against my daughter and me that repeated over and over from years of madness, culminating in the final run for my life the night Richard chased me with a gun. That image had taken over my mind when I lost control of the car.

No one was hurt in the near-accident, and somehow I managed to drive home. I called Kristin, who was by this time living with a roommate in an apartment in Minneapolis. I could hardly talk, so overwhelmed with what was going through my mind that it was difficult to form sentences. She finally understood that, indeed, I was okay physically, but I really needed her or someone to come over and be with me. There was alarm in Kristin's voice, and she said she was going to call my sister, Shirlee, who called me back right away. Shirlee kept me on the phone until she knew that Kristin had arrived at my house. While waiting, I had no strength to even hold up my head. Every ounce of energy in my body had disappeared. The world was going in extremely slow motion.

Kristin tried to call Dr. Lund, but she was out of town. When Kristin and her roommate arrived at my house, I was still talking to my sister, but I can't even remember what I was saying. Kristin tells me that my eyes were glazed over, and I couldn't communicate with her. The horror slideshow was still going, and I kept seeing myself running down the block, believing every step might be my last because I thought Richard would shoot me. Kristin decided to take me to my parents' place, and she literally had to help me walk out to the car because I had no strength or stability in my legs.

Kristin said that on that drive, all I could do was stare straight ahead, trancelike, and that every few minutes I would become very upset and yell, "Don't hurt my baby!" In the scene I kept reliving, Kristin was a toddler, and we were in the car with Richard. Kristin was eating ice cream and dripped some on the seat. Her dad's temper exploded, and he proceeded to dump his iced drink on her head in retaliation for her ice cream accident. I simply couldn't stand it—still. "Don't hurt my baby! Don't hurt my baby!" I sobbed. My sadness was suffocating.

As Kristin continued driving, she held my hand and said, "Mom, I'm okay. This is Kristin, and I am taking you to Grandma's house." In my mind, I was really back in time reliving the abuse. When we arrived at my parents' apartment, I fell to my hands and knees in the hallway leading to their door. I was inconsolable. Mom's fright and concern were audible as she ran toward me.

"Oh, my darling, Deb! What is going on?!"

I was tearful the entire time I stayed with my parents. They didn't really know what to do for me. Frankly, it was the safety of their place that let me reach into my deepest caves of sadness. Just being there was healing; they didn't really have to do anything. It wasn't something I was trying consciously to do, to release my pent-up emotions; I just couldn't help it. I also know it was part of my healing that I could finally express what had been buried for so long. When I was again able to see Dr. Lund, she was not surprised that I had had this flashback episode. She explained that it was part of my healing as I tried to purge painful memories from my mind.

I still hadn't told my parents what actually happened in my married life. I thought: "They didn't need to hear my problems." Dad had recently been diagnosed with Parkinson's disease, and had to shut down his business, which meant that they had to move from a lovely home by a lake to an apartment by a busy freeway—a major life change. Mom, as I mentioned earlier, admirably recovered from a drinking problem, and I did not want to upset or reverse her victory.

No Patch Big Enough

Filing for divorce forced me to look at our marriage relationship from the outside, like a snapshot in my mind. The most vivid image was the violence and abuse he heaped upon me. It ripped the fabric of our marriage, and made it impossible to reconnect the threads.

Throughout our marriage I catered to every one of Richard's wishes—and put mine last. He had a talent for undermining my self-esteem by his "crazy makers."

I kept the house spotless, but he would yell, "This place is a pigpen!"

I was a gourmet cook, but he would complain, "What kind of crap is this?"

I was a good mom, but he would say, "You're not fit to care for Kristin."

He was angry that I worked outside of the home, yet demanded, "Get a second job. No wife of mine is going to sit around on her ass."

He ordered that if I ever saw him in public talking to a co-worker, "Act like you don't know me. I don't want to be embarrassed."

He became more and more controlling to the point that, toward the end of our marriage, I would face his angry outbursts if I dared to go into a different room than where he was. His narcissism dictated that he be the center of attention, and when he wasn't, he became cruel. For instance, when my family and friends had gone to great lengths to plan a surprise fortieth birthday party for me, Richard secretly called everyone and told them to cancel the party because he thought it would be a waste of time and money.

The Divorce

My parents came to support me at the divorce hearing in May 1993. While we were waiting in the courthouse lobby for the hearing to begin, I took a moment to go to the restroom to splash some water on my face to help calm me. In my absence, my parents looked at the folder of my notes that contained the trial affidavits Kristin and I prepared. These notes described in detail some of the instances of abuse we had experienced. I returned to see my parents crying in great distress while they read the affidavits.

Across the lobby, we could see Richard go to the men's restroom. Dad became enraged, and even though he moved with great difficulty due to Parkinson's disease, he shouted, "I'm going to get him!" Very slowly he shuffled his way toward the restroom. Each step was unsteady, like a toddler taking first steps, and the shaking of his body from the disease was made worse by his tremendous emotional stress. Dad wanted to confront Richard on his own, and would not let anyone help him walk. I know in my heart that he wanted to show Kristin and me that he would be our protector. It took Dad several minutes to reach the men's room, only to have Richard walk briskly past him out the door. Several minutes later Dad made his way back to my group of family and friends and proudly said, "I got there too late to punch him, but I gave him a dirty look when he walked past me." I will never forget Dad's act of love that day.

While we were waiting for our divorce hearing to begin, Richard suddenly walked over to Kristin to give her a necklace, which she would not accept. He had no contact for over a year, and it felt like a way to try to make himself feel better. It did not come with an apology. Kristin bravely walked away.

The divorce court hearing lasted two hours. My attorney, Rita, tried to bring up the abuse Kristin and I had suffered for over two decades, but in the hearing, Judge Redford wouldn't hear it, not even to help determine a fair spousal maintenance award.

"That's for another court on another day at another time," he sternly ordered.

DANCING TO MY HEARTBEAT

Awarded the house, I lived there for another couple of years. Richard was ordered to keep me on his employment health insurance plan for a few more years. The spousal maintenance was not even enough to cover my expenses, which is exactly what Richard had hoped. He knew I would be forced to move out of the house, and took delight that his often-stated prediction would come true: "You're going to end up living in a ghetto. That's all you deserve."

I was devastated. The most disappointing and unbelievable thing was that Judge Redford forbade allowing the abuse to be discussed. Kristin and I needed to be able to say what had happened. We had been forced into silence for so long. I could feel my body start to shake uncontrollably, and I felt faint. At the end, Judge Redford asked each of us to stand and state if we understood the proceedings that day. Richard said, "Yes." When it was my turn to answer, no words came out. Judge Redford looked at me, first in a puzzled manner, and then with concern as I collapsed into my chair. I was having another severe meltdown because I was being silenced once again—but this time by the judge. My emotions weighed so heavily on me that I literally could not move. Another slideshow of the abuse came back in my mind, and I sobbed. Likely Richard's vanity made him think that I was just distraught at the thought of losing him. In truth, I was consumed with the reality of the unfairness of not being able to tell Judge Redford what a monster Richard had been.

Mom had her arms around me until I could sit up again. Looking at Judge Redford, I finally said, "I understand the proceedings today. I also understand that you will not let me tell you what happened to my daughter and me for twenty-three years."

I signed on the dotted line, thus ending my nightmare marriage. Richard was out of the house. My daughter and I were at last on the road to safety and freedom.

The Persistence of a Dream

Following the divorce, my life expanded in good ways—and in challenging ways. At the time, I was working several part-time jobs, teaching dance and choreographing community theater productions whenever I had the opportunity. Kristin was teaching with me now, as well. My dance student base was increasing, and Kristin and I considered our students our new "family."

Only puppy Misha and I lived in my home, and occasionally, Kristin, depending on her college schedule. Eventually I got a full-time job managing the shared office of a marketing research company and law firm. And, I continued teaching dance.

Because I did not want the divorce to jeopardize Kristin's future, I worked as much as I possibly could to pay for her college tuition. Her first two years of college were paid by an insurance settlement from a car accident we were injured in when she was seven years old. A semi-truck traveling at a high rate of speed rear-ended us, causing both of us to be whisked away in an ambulance, and Kristin needing plastic surgery above her left eye. The settlement was put into a savings account until she graduated from high school. Often miracles and blessings happen in difficult situations, even if we can't see them in the moment.

Kristin's last two years of college were paid by us being extremely frugal. She and I scrimped and saved and dined many evenings on breakfast cereal in order to cover her tuition. Her dad did not offer to pay one penny. He also ridiculed her constantly because she was majoring in dance instead of business. He could not understand the precious gift of dance that she was blessed with and would pass on to others. He would never see her extraordinary contributions to this beautiful art form and the many honors and awards she received. He would not see her selected Choreographer of the Year by the University of Minnesota, or see her receive the Woman of Substance Award from the College of St. Catherine. He would not see her start her own dance company, Vox Medusa, and its rise as one of the most prominent modern dance companies in Minnesota.

A Flock of Angels

In spite of our financial strain, I still held in my heart my childhood dream of having my own dance studio. Frequently, I thought about the studio, even when confronted with the never-ending struggle to make ends meet. I started talking with various realtors to psychologically ease myself into accepting the idea of selling the house, necessary in order to pursue my vision. I learned very quickly how to maintain the yard and house. I took delight in staining the deck, seal-coating the driveway, pruning bushes, and mowing the lawn. My garden was gorgeous. I wanted to have a beautiful home, and to make it especially attractive to the next family who might purchase it.

At the urging of two dear California friends, Patty and Laurie, I met new male friends, but had learned to guard my heart with a lock and key. Many of them are still my "best buddies." I found it difficult to accept a compliment or receive an admirer's attention because I had been made to feel worthless for so long. One evening I met Kristin for dinner, and when she saw me walking into the restaurant, she said, "Mom! You look beautiful! You are glowing!" During our dinner, Kristin kept saying, "Mom, a table full of men next to you can't keep their eyes off you. Don't you see them?"

Because my feelings of being ugly were so entrenched, I didn't have the radar to pick up on glances of that type.

Following the divorce, Kristin and I were still dealing with the emotional and psychological fallout from the years of abuse. Both of us were having trouble healing, largely because we were not given the opportunity to say in divorce court what had happened. Even after the divorce, Richard threatened to cut off my health insurance, and expressed anger about the spousal maintenance payments. Still trying to control me from a distance, he demanded, "Get a second job, or sell the house."

Also, from a distance, Patty and Laurie encouraged me to sell my house, but for different reasons.

"Why work ten jobs to support your house when you can sell the house, and it can support you?" They knew of my dream to build a dance studio. Besides helping me map out my future, they made sure life was not boring. Our friendships developed while I was still married. Before they moved to California, Patty and I worked for the City of Minneapolis for a period of time, and Laurie was my long-time dance student. At the end of our get-togethers, our cheeks hurt from hearty and loud laughter. We never stop talking, and simply love life. Our strong faith in God keeps us close, and we will always be a dynamic trio.

With the nudging of angels, I somehow managed to begin major research work to write a business plan for the dance studio. I attended several dance festivals in order to network with professional master teachers and choreographers. At one of these festivals, I met Dianne Walker (another Pisces like me), a world-renowned tap dancer, and told her of my dream to build a studio. Dianne and I talked for many hours about the abusive marriage that I had just left, and she admired my spirit to pursue a career in the arts. We found a common bond in our passionate interest in tap dancing, and it wasn't long before we became close friends. She also became my mentor and teacher, and counseled me on many decisions. Our friendship was destined since we were both tap dancers, governed by the astrological sign that rules the human foot. Dianne became like a sister, and offered to be an honorary board member of my studio when it was built.

Around this time I ran into a childhood friend, Barry, at a high school class reunion. We had lived across the alley from each other during elementary school, and I was often the target of his relentless teasing. Barry was now an architect, and I told him about the circumstances of my recent divorce, and of my dream to build my own performing arts school. Without a moment's hesitation, Barry said, "That's great, Deb. Let's sit over there and talk." He pointed to a quiet corner in the ballroom filled with former classmates. Barry grabbed a pile of napkins as we made our way through the crowd. Surrounded by the din of the reunion, Barry asked me to describe in detail my vision of the studio. While I talked, he carefully sketched out building plans on a napkin. I thought he was just trying to show me an example of how the floor plan might look.

A few weeks later, this generous and kind-hearted soul presented me with blueprints he had prepared for my dream studio. He felt the design would fall within my budget, except for the added cost for architectural fees. Without telling me, Barry had also submitted the plan for my studio to be considered as the one free project that his architectural firm did every year, to give back to the community. After their committee meeting, Barry called: my studio was selected as their special project. I am eternally grateful to them.

The following few months were filled with focus-group meetings, attended by families of my student base, and many meetings with my CPA. I spent countless hours in the library, preparing demographic studies of the area to pinpoint a good location.

I had ample time over the years to observe what worked, and what didn't, in many dance studios. My mind was clear about what I wanted to offer my students because I took the time to listen to their desires and dreams. Most of all, I wanted to provide a safe haven for dancers to reclaim who they were, if they needed to, and to release their creative spirit. My inner drive was to make sure that dancers in my studio felt good about themselves while receiving high-quality dance education. An important part of my dream was to share the art of dance with dancers overseas because I truly believed this art form to be a universal language.

The Business Plan

The activity that now filled my life—that is, developing a business plan—also served as a diversion to help keep me from being emotionally and psychologically swallowed by past horrors. I wanted to show the world, my parents, and my siblings that Kristin and I were survivors. Like a swinging pendulum, however, at times moments of healing were overwhelmed by an uncontrollable flood of bad memories.

Seven months after my divorce, and while busy writing the business plan for my dream, I received a call from a local high school inviting me to teach a master jazz dance class to students in their dance program. It was a sunny day in December 1993 when I walked into the classroom full of dancers with equally sunny smiles. The dancers were sitting on the floor, some stretching and some sipping from a can of soda or a bottle of water. After introducing myself, I began the class with a rigorous warm-up to get us through the winter chill in the room. We were having a wonderful time, and in minutes the heat from our hard-working bodies began to frost the cold windows and fog the mirrors. Being Minnesotans, we knew these were signs of a good class.

My class continued with accelerated energy and pauses for the dancers to drink water. Now we were ready for the really fun part of the class—the grand jetés. These lofty leaps make dancers feel they can defy gravity and fly. I felt very happy as I prepared to demonstrate the leap pattern. I soared through the air with an incredible sense of freedom, and loved feeling the power of the human body, and the air rushing against my face. Obviously, every leap that goes up must also come down. My perfectly executed grand jeté ended with my left foot landing on a puddle of water accidentally spilled by students. Instead of sliding into a split position with my left leg forward, my leg bent sideways at the knee and I heard a loud POP! I crumbled to the floor, crying in agony. Instantly, my knee swelled to the size of a grapefruit, and my body went into the trauma of knowing that something terrible had just happened. My ears were buzzing, and I felt nauseated and faint. The pain was unbearable.

Survival instinct kicked in, and instead of waiting for an ambulance, I hopped out of the classroom to my car in the parking lot. Along the way I stopped to fill my scarf with snow, wrapping it around my knee before driving to the nearby hospital. While in the emergency room, I reassured myself that my injury was simply a whopper of a sprain, and with a little TLC, I would be back dancing in no time. Wrong!

The emergency room physician put my leg in an ankle-to-mid-thigh brace, gave me medication for pain and swelling, and made an appointment for me to see Dr. Robert, a highly regarded orthopedic surgeon, the next day.

"Why would I need to see a surgeon?" I asked.

"I think you may have done some significant damage, and Dr. Robert can order an MRI. Keep your leg elevated and ice your knee ten minutes every hour," he ordered. I hopped out of the hospital and tried to ease myself into my little Chevrolet Cavalier. This is definitely not a graceful maneuver to make when your leg is in a brace.

When I arrived home, I hopped through the front door, and the first thing I saw was my dance studio business plan laying on the desk, and next to it, the file cabinets full of volumes of research work for my dream. I was sad and depressed because I had been through enough already. I needed more than family and friends now; I needed a flock of angels. I couldn't sleep because I cried and prayed all night while Misha gently lay by my injured knee. Ah, the unconditional love of a dog. Maybe he was my angel for now.

Another Obstacle

While heading out to my morning medical appointment, I awkwardly got into my car. After Dr. Robert examined my injury, he ordered an MRI.

"You may have torn your anterior cruciate ligament. Keep icing and elevating the leg until we get the results back."

A few days later my heart pounded like it was going to break loose from my body as I waited for the verdict in Dr. Robert's office.

"Just as I thought, you didn't just tear part of your ligament; it has completely separated from the bone."

"How long does it take to grow back?"

Dr. Robert explained, through words and drawings, the extent of the repair work needed, and that the ligament does not grow back.

"You will need major reconstructive surgery of the ligament. That means total removal of the damaged ligament, which will be replaced by a harvested section of your own patella ligament or a ligament from a cadaver, which we screw into place to reinforce where we drill into your tibia and femur to place the bone plugs at each end of the harvested ligament."

Whoa! Wait just a minute here! Harvested ligament? Cadaver? Screws and drills? These words sent shockwaves through my body and brain.

"I am a dancer with a dream. I need to dance again or I will die. It's as simple as that. So, when do we begin? And by the way, let's keep it in the family—no cadaver parts, please," I pleaded.

Aware of my career as a dancer, Dr. Robert said that I would need to regain the same strength and stability in my knee as that of a gymnast. He specialized in sports injuries and was actually quite well versed in dance terminology, so I felt very confident.

"It will take work from both of us to get you back on the dance floor. Are you ready to begin the hardest dance of all?"

"Let's boogie," I laughed.

February arrived, and it was time to go under the knife. My parents met me at the hospital just as I was being wheeled into surgery. One of the nurses handed me a marker and said, "Please make an 'X' on the leg that is injured so we make doubly sure the correct leg is operated on." Instead of an 'X,' I wrote on my left thigh, "Precious tool of a dancer."

As an incentive to get through the surgery and recovery, I brought my tap shoes to the hospital, and had the nurse tie the shoestrings together and hang them at the foot of my bed. I knew that if I ever wanted to wear them again, I had to be diligent. For the next four days, many family members and dancing friends visited me in the hospital, and my room was filled with flowers and stuffed ballerina bears.

Kristin took over teaching my dance classes, serving as my "legs" until I could get back to normal. I didn't want the momentum of my increasing student base to suffer due to my injury, so as fast as I could, I returned to the dance classes, even if just to observe.

Living alone after surgery was hard at times because basic day-to-day things were impossible to do in a leg brace and on crutches. Before my surgery, Kristin helped me get the house ready by rigging up a chair and hand-held nozzle in the shower. We rearranged furniture and made sure things I needed were within reach. Living alone also posed another problem in that during the three weeks I was not allowed to drive, I had no one to take me to daily physical therapy sessions. Kristin and everyone else had jobs or school, but thankfully, a pastor from my church called every morning to find out my schedule, and took me to my appointments and to places like the grocery store. He even tied my shoes because I was unable to reach them. He was one of my angels.

When I was finally able to retire my crutches, my physical therapist put me on a walking regimen that lasted for three months. I wore the brace for stability as I alternated walking and mildly jogging for three miles each day—rain or shine. I followed the same route every day at the same time, and passersby in cars on their way to work would honk and wave or shout, "Keep it up. You're doing great!"

Unbeknownst to me at the time, it would be an entire year before my knee felt somewhat normal and I could dance at my pre-injury pace. It felt good to be teaching again and to put energy behind my movements. I still had a little "grand jeté phobia" to deal with, but that soon passed. A new rule was added to any class that I taught: All liquids must be consumed *outside* of the studio.

I still struggled endlessly with what felt like the universe being unfair. I wanted to be genuinely happy and joyful again, and smile without feeling like I was hiding behind it to mask sadness. But it seemed like the minute I felt good about something, something bad followed, so I avoided feeling good because I did not want to face what always seemed to follow. At the time, I was not cognizant of it, but both the good and bad experiences in my life were really moves that the universe was making to send me on a purposeful journey. I was a pellet in a cosmic slingshot, about to be propelled toward light instead of darkness. Oh, it took so long for me to finally learn how to let go—and put complete trust in God.

It was definitely my love of dance, my students, and their families that kept me going. I also loved to watch Kristin gain their respect and confidence as a teacher, dancer, and exceptionally talented choreographer. Kristin had an aura about her when she danced, and audiences could not take their eyes off her. Once her body moved, they were spellbound. She had a sweet, but direct and effective, method of teaching, and she now was in demand. As I used every spare moment to plan for our studio, Kristin was organizing and promoting her dance company.

The Lawsuit

While our new lives unfolded post-divorce, Kristin and I faced our next major mutual challenge of bringing up the issue of domestic violence before a judge on "another day at another time." Yes, the dream of the dance studio was still very much alive, but we knew our complete freedom would not manifest until we were finally allowed to tell the truth in court about what we had lived through for two decades.

A few months prior to my divorce, in addition to Rita, I had been in touch with another attorney, Don, who was very interested in domestic violence issues. After my divorce, I met with Don to explain in more detail the violence Kristin and I had experienced, and how we could not heal because our voices had not been heard during the divorce proceedings. Kristin and I would never get those years back, but we could start a new life if we, for the first time, stood up for ourselves. Don was a very kind and compassionate person, and I was very appreciative of his time. He recommended that Kristin and I continue meeting with Dr. Lund, who was counseling us through our healing process. We had a long way to go, and our journey would be nothing short of an odyssey.

A First-Ever Civil Court Suit is Filed

A little less than a year after my divorce, with the continuing concerned guidance of the Robert Lewis House, Don, Dr. Lund, family, and friends, we proceeded to file against Richard. This was the first-ever domestic violence lawsuit in the United States in civil court. Kristin filed the lawsuit with me, in spirit, because enough time had passed since she had moved out of the house that the statute of limitation laws now prohibited her from being named as an additional litigant. Nevertheless, we were in this together, and our voices would be heard, whether on legal documents or not. Kristin was a witness for the trial, and she *would* have a voice. I *would* have a voice.

We decided to be proactive, not only for ourselves, but to attempt to awaken the justice system to the prevalent and pervasive—and ignored— dangers of domestic violence and abuse in this country. Don said his law firm had never handled a case like this before, and all of their research work indicated that this was the first of its type in the country. We were all pioneers. Suddenly, I was in the company of my ancestors who, through passion and yearning, dared to begin an uncharted life. So, as my leg was healing, as our finances began to stabilize, and as the business plans for the dance studio were finalizing, we were also about to head into the intense and emotionally wrenching depths of a lawsuit.

During the two years that legal filings and motions were prepared for a court date, relentless nightmares plagued my slumber. Visions of the past woke me from a deep sleep, and I gasped for breath.

Even with all the tremendous support—I had never felt so alone.

Blessings and Miracles

In late January 1996, a good friend called to see how I was doing. Bob was a film archivist who specialized in the preservation of old movies, and was especially fond of those featuring tap dance luminaries like Fred Astaire, Sammy Davis, Jr., and the Nicholas Brothers, and jazz musicians like Duke Ellington, Fats Waller, and Cab Calloway, to name a few. Our conversation included that not only did I want to someday have my own dance studio, but that I also longed to be able to take a master tap dance class from my idol, Gregory Hines. I had often wondered if Gregory even had the time to teach

master classes since his movie and television career seemed so full. Bob said
that his cousin in New York thought she lived in the same apartment building
as Gregory, although she was not absolutely sure.

"Here is the building address, and perhaps if you send a letter to Gregory
at that address, it might get to him."

Before writing the letter, I called Dianne to ask if she thought sending a
letter to Gregory was a good idea.

"Send it, Deb!" she said without hesitation. Saying a little hopeful prayer, I
dropped it into the mailbox. This is my letter:

February 7, 1996

Dear Gregory,

*My name is Deborah, and I first of all want to thank you for all you have
contributed to the art of tap. As a tap dancer, I am very grateful that you have
brought so much attention to this American original art form.*

*I am in the process of selling everything I own, including my house, to help
finance the construction of my own dance studio. My plans were delayed a bit
in pursuing my dream because I had to first recover from an injury to my left
knee. I have a passion for teaching and a passion for tap, and I am sure you
understand the drive that it takes to do those things. I have admired your talent
and style for many years and have also always dreamed of being able to take
a master tap dance class from you, but I do not know if you still teach master
classes and, if so, how would I find out more information about them?*

*My daughter, Kristin, is a dancer, too, and together we want to build our
studio, in part to prove to ourselves that we are survivors. In 1993, I finally
divorced my abusive husband of twenty-three years. Dance helped us survive all
those years, and dance will give us a new life. I firmly believe that dance must
come from the heart, and I know that dance has been my lifeblood. As I write
this letter to you, I finally know what I will call my dance studio—"Heartbeat."*

*Thank you for your time to read my letter. I would love to hear from you,
and my work and home telephone numbers are noted below. Again, thank you
for your amazing talent and grace.*

Deborah

On a beautiful sunny afternoon about six weeks later, my telephone rang while I was juggling heavy grocery bags and carrying them into the house from the car. Grabbing it before the last ring, I was a bit out of breath.

"Hello," I gasped.

"Is this Deborah?"

"Yes, this is Deb."

Then I heard, "Well, how are you, Deb? This is Gregory Hines."

(NOTE: Let me explain something before you read on. At that time, Kristin was dating Dereck, who was a talented magician, actor, voice impersonator, and a bit of a jokester. Dereck knew about the letter I sent to Gregory, and how much I hoped to hear from him. By this time I thought perhaps Gregory never received the letter because of a wrong address, or if it did reach him, it was stuck in a pile of fan mail. Now you can read on.)

In total disbelief, I blurted, "Oh, hello Dereck. What is this, another one of your magic tricks?"

After a very long pause and change in tone of voice, he said, "No...this is the REAL Gregory Hines."

"Oh, I am so glad we are on the phone right now because it means you cannot see my very red, embarrassed face."

Gregory discussed his admiration for my desire to build a studio, and I discussed my admiration for his genuine kindness and talent. We also talked "tap dance" for a long time. He instantly made me feel comfortable, as if we had known each other for years. He was sincere in his interest about me and the studio, and my love of tap dancing.

At the end of our forty-five-minute conversation, Gregory said, "I haven't taught master classes for a long time, so I think it is about time that I do that again. When we hang up, I will call my manager and tell her to contact you the next time I am scheduled to be in the Midwest. If there is a day that I can spare from my Midwest location, I will fly to Minneapolis, and you can arrange to have you and your advanced students take my master class. I want to see where Heartbeat will be built and support your effort. In talking to you, Deb, I feel like you do not fully realize the incredible sacrifice you are making for the arts. I admire you."

After we hung up, I sat motionless for several minutes, trying to integrate what had just happened. Another angel had visited me. Even if I never heard from Gregory again, a dream had just come true, and I knew that through my letter, my voice on at least one subject had been heard.

Right after Richard and I separated, my sister, Shirlee, gave me a chubby little angel figurine to protect me, and it did its job from my nightstand. I reached over to hold the angel, but was startled when the telephone rang again. This time it was Gregory's manager calling me to get my contact information. She informed me that Gregory's schedule changed frequently, making it hard to pinpoint when he might be free.

"It may be in a few weeks or not until next year. We simply do not know, and it may be that you only get a day's notice," she said.

Many weeks passed after Gregory's call, so I gave up hope for the master class, but was very thankful for his generosity to take time out of his busy schedule to call me. In spite of all the physical and financial challenges I was continually facing, my dream of a dance studio was still very much alive. The euphoria of Gregory's phone call stayed with me for a few months until I received another phone call that swung my emotional pendulum in the other direction.

"Deb, I just received a court date of August 12 for the domestic violence trial. I will need to meet with you more frequently now, as it is only two months away. The date you have been waiting for is finally here," Don said.

My studio planning effort had to be put on hold now. I was worthless at work because my mind was on overload with fear and anticipation—a deleterious combination. Prayers were now sent hourly, not just nightly. In the days leading up to the trial, my daily routine was kept very simple and very strict to avoid becoming overwhelmed. Each day I got one step closer to having to be in the presence of a man who still deeply frightened me. Knowing the psychological turmoil I was struggling with, and expecting that I might become a basket case if I did not keep it together, I decided that writing a journal would help keep me grounded. My fears and anxieties left my brain and found a home on paper. Now my journal's notations could memorialize and relay the events of this first-ever trial that lasted three days.

Driving Without a Map

TRIAL DAY ONE - AUGUST 12, 1996

The alarm went off at six. I lay motionless for a long time, staring at the ceiling. Today was another milestone along the way to a new life for Kristin and me. I have worked very hard to get to this point, and yearn for both of us to heal. My love for Kristin is strong, and she is my angel and my life. More than anything, I want the trial to release our creative spirits and open doors that have been closed for so long. I pray that I am setting an important example for Kristin to become whatever she wants to be, and to spread her wings, and not be held back by anyone. Nothing means more to me than to know that she feels her mother's love always, because nothing is stronger or more comforting.

It seemed my life was on cruise control. I fed and walked Misha, and made breakfast but had no appetite. Stepping into a steamy hot shower, a feeling came over me that finally, today, the horrid hurt from the past would also be washed away. The warmth of the water permeated my body through to my bones, as I stood there and breathed deeply. I had done all that I could to stand up for my daughter and myself, and the final step would happen today to free us from the past. We would have a new life.

After the shower, I started to have alternating moments of nervousness and euphoria. The trial day was here. Dread stormed through me like a tsunami because it also meant that I would have to be in the courtroom with Richard, a man who threatened me with a gun the very last time we were in this house as a family. Being conditioned to fear him during our marriage, the process of realizing that I would see him today made me terrified. It was an automatic reaction. My movement around the house seemed like a movie going fast forward. I kept thinking, "I've got to get Kristin. I've got to get Kristin."

Was my panic a desire to protect Kristin—or for her to protect me?

The weight of every battered woman and child was on my shoulders, a weight I gladly carried. I want to make a difference—and I want us to heal. Confidence and strength fill me, but at the same time, solitude. Glorious hopes ricochet through my mind that when I return home tonight, I will be a new person—a survivor. I gave Misha one more pat on the head, and as I turned the key to lock the front door, I imagined what it would be like to arrive home and unlock the door to a new life.

A renewed calmness came over me as I drove away.

Kristin was waiting curbside when I pulled up to her house, and gave me one of her gorgeous smiles as she fastened her seatbelt. She has a beauty that is rare and breathtaking—blonde hair, blue eyes, and great Norwegian genes. The atmosphere in the car seemed as if more than the two of us were passengers.

"Aha!" I said, "The angels are already with us." Pulling away from the curb, I reached over to hold Kristin's hand as we smiled at each other.

We did not say much. Sometimes more is said in silence. During the years we were abused, Kristin and I had learned to communicate and support each other on a different level—one without words. We had developed many psychological and spiritual mechanisms of survival because Richard had threatened us into silence, and we knew what the violent outcome would be if we ever said anything about the abuse.

Today, we would be silent no more.

We arrived at Don's office at 7:45 a.m., and sat quietly in his conference room until his assistant, Suzanne, entered with some coffee and donuts. Our anxiety would not allow us to eat or drink. My friends, Patty and Laurie, arrived a few minutes later and joined in the silence. I had flown them in from California to be witnesses in the trial. The silence was deafening. Suzanne opened the conference room door to say that Don would need to talk to each of us separately before we headed to the courthouse.

First Patty met with Don, followed by Laurie, and Kristin. Next, Suzanne asked me to follow her. Don gave me a hug and comforted me by saying, "You are strong, Deb. Don't worry. All you have to do is tell the truth. Richard needs to be held accountable, and after the trial, your life will be new. It will be yours." Don grabbed his suit jacket and said, "Come on. You have worked hard for this day."

The few-block walk to the courthouse seemed like miles and miles. Don filed this lawsuit in the county where Richard now resided, and where we had lived while married, rather than with the county that handled our divorce, where I now live. Walking arm-in-arm, Kristin and I were surrounded by the love of good friends and a caring attorney. My emotions were on high as we entered the courtroom. For a moment, the room felt like a hospital delivery room, sterile and quiet in anticipation of the cries of a new life born. Suddenly, commotion erupted as Richard, his new wife (or girlfriend), his new baby, and James, his attorney, entered the courtroom.

Kristin and I were shocked. We had no idea that these new people were now in her dad's life. Kristin looked at me and said, "I feel like I should tell her to run for the hills. Get away from him as fast as you can." Then she made simple sense of the situation, "Mom, you and I are going to be free to do with our lives what we want. Dad is just going to be changing diapers." History repeats itself! Again Richard had, within two years, met someone, married (perhaps), and had a baby.

At that moment, Richard picked up his crying baby and paced rapidly. He exaggerated his parade in front of Kristin and me to the point of being obnoxious. He was going out of his way to act like the perfect dad, but it didn't work. His antics were to hurt Kristin and me, as if to say, "Look, I've replaced both of you because you weren't good enough for me." The baby's crying got worse, so Richard and the woman departed with their baby into the hallway.

"Did you know about this?" I asked Don. He said he had just found out the day before. However, he didn't think Richard would be stupid enough to bring his new family to a trial where he was being accused of assault and battery, among other things.

"What a way to impress your girlfriend," Don said sarcastically. Don apologized for not telling us, and said he didn't want anything to throw us off or hurt us anymore. Richard and his new family entered the courtroom again, and it wasn't long before his attorney told Richard that a courtroom is not a place for a crying baby. The woman took the baby and walked out of the room. We did not see her again.

I assumed that the trial proceedings would begin right away, but I was wrong. A court official walked up to Don and said that Judge Gray wanted to see him in his chambers. Don said, "This will probably take about ten minutes."

As Don walked away, I began to feel like a new burden was placed upon my shoulders—and it was getting too heavy. Concentrating on anything became impossible. Suzanne, Patty, Laurie, and Kristin would say things to me, but it felt like they were talking to someone else. Another supporter, Nicole from the Lewis House, joined us as we waited. I felt like an observer, removed from the situation. My emotions were getting out of control, and my insides were shaking uncontrollably. A buzzing sound echoed in my ears, and my peripheral vision grew cloudy. For the next hour and a half, I fought to keep myself together.

In agony, I yearned for my parents to hold me, just like they did at the divorce trial. Unfortunately, Mom adamantly announced she would not be here today because, "I don't trust that I will be able to keep myself from screaming profanity at Richard and making a big scene. I may cause trouble that you don't need in the courtroom. I love you, my darling Deb. Please call me as soon as you get home." My siblings had difficulty getting time off their jobs, so I didn't know who would be able to come, or who would pick up Dad, since he could not drive.

After a longer-than-anticipated delay, Don walked back into the courtroom and asked Kristin and me to follow him to the conference room. This did not seem like normal trial procedure, and I became especially concerned seeing the look on Don's face. Don shut the door and the three of us sat down at a huge conference table.

"Not very good news, Deb," Don said. His words made my heart feel as if it were going to jump out of my body. "Judge Gray has informed me that he is going to impose a two-year limitation on evidence that we can present, and also on the testimony of your witnesses."

"What does that mean?" I asked.

Don replied, "It means that although you suffered abuse for many years, you can talk only about the past two years, and if we do not abide, the judge will declare a mistrial." Don's words made the buzzing in my ears turn into a sharp, piercing sound.

He continued, "This also means that we cannot bring up the ad that Richard placed in a dating magazine with your name on it. We cannot bring up the fact that the county filed charges against him for the ad, and that he was found guilty. The judge's order rules out much of what Patty and Laurie were going to testify about. Your expense to fly Patty and Laurie here from L.A. was for nothing.

"Judge Gray said his decision was partly because we brought up the incident when Richard threw you to the floor and kicked you in the back like a football, when you were eight months pregnant. The judge said we could, in his words, 'Write any amount of money on the chalkboard and the jury would award it to you.' The judge feels this would not be fair to Richard. Two years ago, your divorce was filed, and Judge Gray's limitation will now make it appear to the jury that you are just disgruntled about the divorce settlement."

Stunned, we sat motionless. My voice quivered, "Don, do you mean that nothing about the years of terror can be talked about? It took two years just to get through the divorce and the process to file this lawsuit. How does he expect that almost a quarter of a century of abuse can be erased?"

Don was angry at the judge. In fact, he was livid. He looked at Kristin and me, and we could see he undeniably understood the unfairness. Don began to pace, working diligently to figure out a way to present our case and still be within the recent limitations imposed by Judge Gray.

Kristin sat silently while Don explained the bad news. As our eyes met, my heart sank when I saw her distress. She was also feeling abandoned by the court system. Kristin had wanted to tell the world what her dad had done to us. She wanted to heal, too. The unfairness and hurt became overwhelming. The impact of Judge Gray's decision was paralyzing and we froze in disbelief. At every turn, we were being silenced. My entire emotional, spiritual, and psychological being went into overload as I tried to come to grips with yet another devastating situation heaped upon us. But it was too much—simply too much.

I can only explain what happened next this way: the world came crashing down on me. I lost control psychologically as slideshow images of the incidents of abuse flashed in my brain. The slideshow began to speed up, and I could not stop it. A floodgate opened, and I relived the abuse as images continued to flow across my mind. Suddenly my body started to go through the same contortions as when Richard would beat me. I went limp as I put my head in Kristin's lap. I began to thrash back and forth as if being hit and trying to defend myself. My hands covered my head, and I could feel Kristin hold onto me.

Don immediately stopped pacing.

"What is going on?"

Kristin cried, "She's reliving the abuse. This happened once before when she was driving a car, and she almost hit a tree. I just need to hold her." The weight of the world was on me as I slid to the floor. My legs moved as if trying to run away, and my arms wrapped around my stomach from gut-wrenching pain. Kristin was hanging onto me for my life. My body folded in half and my eyes wouldn't open. I sobbed in a voice that did not seem like my own.

"God, what is happening to me? I just want to be believed. I just want to be believed," I wailed. My eyes were shut so tightly that the muscles in my face hurt. With all of my might, I could not open them because I was trying to make the images of abuse go away. I could hear things, but I could no longer talk.

Kristin moved to the floor and put my head in her lap again. My body continued with its involuntary reaction to the immense pain of reliving punches inflicted for so many years. I was being crushed by the weight of the violence, as dreadful images raced through my mind of Kristin and me trying to be protective decoys for each other. I could hear Richard's harsh voice in his daily ranting that I was ugly, worthless, and stupid, and that no one would want me. Never good enough for him, he was masterful at ridiculing me, and succeeded in making me feel inadequate as a human being.

Terrifying memories flashed me back to our family vacation on the cruise ship when he had his hands tightly grasped around my throat. My loud gasps for breath still lingered in my memory. Images and sounds of years of abuse were bleeding through my soul.

With me not even having the strength to stand up, my head remained in Kristin's lap. My joints felt disconnected, and my muscles would not work. I was falling through the air with no bottom in sight. My body would alternate between flailing and curling up in a ball. I was exhausted, and could barely breathe.

The world abruptly shifted into slow motion. The air in the room was heavy. Even though I felt very sad and weak, anger was boiling inside me. My eyes opened slowly, and stared at emptiness. In a faint and barely detectible voice, I whimpered, "I just want to be believed."

"I know, Mom," Kristin whispered as she stroked my hair. Slowly, I began to hear the quiet conversation Don and Kristin were having that made it apparent they were very concerned, and planned to call Dr. Lund.

Softly, I whispered, "I want people to listen to us. I want people to believe us. I want my life back. I am so tired." We remained on the floor of the conference room for a long time. A second hand stroked my hair. Kristin told me later that it was Don's hand.

Don informed Judge Gray that I was having a hard time in the conference room, and that we would need to break for an hour. My friends seated in the courtroom were worried, and wanted to join Kristin and me, but Don told them it was better for us to be alone for a while. After the hour passed, the judge asked Don and me to join him in his chambers. Another attorney from Don's law firm came with us as we were led to Judge Gray.

We proceeded briskly to the chambers, and when I saw Judge Gray seated behind his desk, I was taken aback momentarily because he looked remarkably like Montgomery Burns, from *The Simpsons* cartoon. Appearing to be in his late seventies, he was a thin, bald man with wisps of white hair sprouting randomly from his scalp and a prominent chin that was chiseled to a point. Judge Gray's shoulders hunched over, and his glasses rested halfway down his beak-like nose.

I mistakenly thought that the judge would be concerned about Kristin and me. Instead, the unfairness continued as he said, "It would be better for you to settle out of court. Eighty percent of all cases do. The jury won't listen to you." Judge Gray folded his arms across his chest, as if to demonstrate his point, before he blurted, "The jurors will just fold their arms and look away from you. It's better to just get on with your life, and quit obsessing about this."

Now I was angry! My weak voice turned into a strong, confident voice that startled even Don. My survival rhythm was throbbing in my ears. I glared into the judge's eyes and said, "If Richard had done to you what he did to Kristin and me, he would be in jail right now with criminal charges filed against him. We are just as valuable and worthwhile as you. It is important to me that you hear the crimes Richard committed against Kristin and me. It is important that you hear the details of what the terror is like when a gun is pointed at you in anger, and you are placed in a position to pray that you can outrun a bullet. It is important that you understand our pain."

Annoyed, Judge Gray looked at Don a moment and next changed his focus to me.

"If you settle out of court, at least you know what you have got. You need to just get on with your life and—"

"Your honor, we need to go through this trial in order to get on with our lives. We cannot bury this inside us anymore because it will destroy us. Everything that makes us who we are will be gone. During my divorce trial, Judge Redford refused to listen to any details of the abuse and ordered my attorney, Rita, not to bring them up. He ordered, 'Not in this court. That's for another court on another day.' And now, here I am in another court on another day, only to find that all the instances of abuse that could have been talked about in the divorce proceedings are now beyond the time limitations that you have just ordered for this trial. What am I supposed to do?"

Judge Gray suggested, "Go to your congressman and have the laws changed."

Don remained in the judge's chambers, but sent me back to the conference room where Kristin had been patiently waiting. An hour passed before Don returned to let us know what Judge Gray was recommending.

"To settle this case, Richard will be asked to offer $50,000 to you, which is exactly the amount you would have received through the spousal maintenance settlement in your divorce. You therefore would get nothing more than what you are already getting from the divorce settlement. The only difference is that you will get it in one payment rather than over a period of five years as stated in your divorce document. In Minnesota, the law will work against you in that if you win this trial, your spousal maintenance will automatically end. The state will not allow you to get both the settlement from your divorce and the settlement from this trial. There has not been a trial like this before, and the court can't seem to separate the divorce trial from this trial, even though we know they are very separate issues.

"As part of your divorce settlement, Richard was ordered to continue to carry medical insurance for you for five years. In a separate attempt to settle this case, he offered to have you remain on his family medical insurance plan for a few more years if you pay him $150 per month."

I was shocked and speechless for a moment.

"Don, do you mean that because Judge Redford would not let us talk about the abuse during our divorce trial—now, when we are in court to talk about the abuse, we are really just reconfiguring the divorce settlement? What is happening is that the abuse will never be talked about. I have worked in human resource departments before and know that family medical insurance covers all family members, no matter how many dependents there are, so having me on his medical health plan has actually cost Richard nothing beyond what he is already paying for his current family. What he is trying to do is make me pay for his new family's monthly health insurance premium. Not only am I not going to receive a settlement for the abuse, I am being asked to pay for his family's health insurance. Don, you *have to understand* what a conniving snake Richard is."

The realization of what Richard was trying to do sent a wave of anger over Don.

"In the lawsuit, I asked that Richard also write a letter of apology to Kristin and me. Did he offer to do that?"

"No, he refused," Don replied as he angrily marched out of the room. Don went back to Judge Gray's chamber for another conference, returning a few minutes later.

Each time that Don returned to the conference room he seemed to be angrier and more determined to have justice done.

"The judge is adamant. He will only approve $50,000. If this case goes to trial, and if Richard loses, the judge expects that Richard and his attorney will file an appeal. The jury may award more than $50,000, but Judge Gray can rule to lower the amount back to the $50,000."

Completely puzzled, I asked, "Why is the judge saying this, and making these decisions already when he has not yet heard the facts and the testimony of the witnesses?"

"Because he is the judge," Don replied, "and he does not want any of Judge Redford's remarks on record when he refused to hear about the abuse during your divorce trial."

"So basically he is trying to protect another judge, and it really does not matter to him what happened to Kristin and me," I cried out.

Don recommended that we go along with what Judge Gray was proposing, and if Richard refused to settle, we would be in full trial in the morning. Don made another trip to Judge Gray's chamber and returned minutes later to say, "Richard and James have refused to settle in accordance with what the judge proposed." Trial was set to begin at eight the next morning.

Laurie had to get back to San Diego. Upon finding this out, Don had her testimony videotaped before we headed home for the day. As I drove Laurie to the airport, she gave me many encouraging and supportive words in her usual caring way. Patty was able to stay one more day.

Both of these women have been steadfast in their friendship, and we will be friends for life. They give me backbone when they know I need it. They pull me back on track when my emotions start to crumble. We are guided by the same spirit.

On the way home from the airport, I promised myself that for the remainder of our lives, I would take Kristin on an annual vacation to celebrate "us." Patty insisted that she be able to join us on our first trip as I told her about my desire for a Caribbean cruise. And on this one we would not be hurt.

When I arrived home, I put the key into the front door lock and realized that it would still be a while before I opened the door to a new life. Going through my usual routine of walking Misha and feeding him, I really appreciated how comforting dogs can be. Kristin also had a dog, a Doberman, and something about these dogs makes us feel safe. We are loved unconditionally, and they shared an incredible history with us.

I crawled into bed and was motionless for a long time, staring at the ceiling. During my sleep, angels in a soft blue and white glow visited me. One hovered over me while another sat on the side of the bed and held my hand.

"Everything will be fine," they said.

Calling All Angels

TRIAL DAY TWO - AUGUST 13, 1996

Today Kristin did not need a ride. She and her friend, Debra, would come together to the trial. Patty and I arrived at Don's office a few minutes apart. No one was there so we went to the downstairs coffee shop. Today I had to bring to the trial the rifle that Richard aimed at me, and walking into the coffee shop dressed in business suits and high heels, with a rifle in a camouflage case, made both of us look peculiar, to say the least. No one noticed except one gentleman who asked, "What's in the violin case?"

Earlier in the week, Don instructed me to go to my suburban police department to pick up Richard's rifle that they had kept safely locked in storage for me. Don needed the gun as evidence, and after I delivered it to his office this morning, security personnel would transfer the rifle from his office to the courtroom.

Don's office was now open, so we dropped off the rifle and headed to the courthouse, arriving at 8 a.m. A few minutes later, James and Richard walked into the courtroom. Kristin, her friend Debra, and Nicole from the Lewis House arrived and sat next to Patty and me in the observation seating. Looking around the room, I felt a presence that was very intense, but comforting.

"Patty," I said, "there *are* angels in here today."

Patty leaned over and whispered, "The angels are always with us."

Don and Suzanne entered the courtroom and motioned for me to sit with them at the plaintiff's table. As I stood up, my heart began pounding rapidly, and it was questionable whether my legs would support me. I had been waiting and praying for this day for Kristin and me to finally be able to talk about the violence and abuse Richard heaped upon us.

I walked up to the plaintiff's table and sat by Suzanne. Hearing familiar voices enter the room, I turned around and saw my dad and brother, Kurt. Their presence gave me an incredible feeling of comfort. Smiling, I nodded to thank them for being there. Since childhood, my dad had been there for me. Always my hero, I wanted to rush up to him and beg him to please make my hurt go away. Dad's Parkinson's disease was worsening, and it took a tremendous amount of energy for him to even be there. As Dad smiled and nodded back, I knew that with every ounce of strength left in his weakened body, he was going to protect Kristin and me. Dad and Kurt were holding two little African violet plants in their laps. I looked at Kristin and Patty, gave them a "thumbs up" sign, and said, "I love you."

They both whispered, "I love you, too."

Even though I was physically weak, I was confident and hopeful. Yesterday had been emotionally and physically draining, and the weight of that experience still enveloped me. Today we would be on a forward path to justice. There was an immediate distraction in the courtroom when it became filled with the chatter of voices. I glanced back and saw many unfamiliar people entering. Suzanne reached over and touched my hand to get my attention. She softly said, "Don't look back."

Richard and James walked from the corner of the room and sat at the defendant's table. At that moment, everyone stood as the bailiff announced Judge Gray's arrival.

"All rise," he instructed.

Eleven potential jurors walked into the courtroom and sat in the jury box. Judge Gray announced that seven would be selected. I couldn't help but study their faces and wonder if they would believe me. Would they understand the fear Kristin and I had lived in for so many years? Would they be able to visualize the bruises and tears? Would they hear our screams and cries for help in the middle of the night? Would they know the way of life this had become for us? Would they see through our eyes the damage that had been done?

In his monotone and robotic voice, the bailiff made more announcements to the group assembled for jury selection. The judge explained to the potential jurors the rules for selection, and that the basis for the trial was a civil suit filed for assault and battery, defamation, willful infliction of emotional stress, and false imprisonment. Oh, my! How awful those words sounded—and how awful they had been to live.

When Judge Gray read the charges, I felt sick to my stomach. I wanted to shout, "How could you, Richard? How could you?" How much hatred did he have for Kristin and me? We were two innocent human beings in court on a quest to be validated, and be heard for the first time. We needed to tell our story in a safe environment where Richard could not hurt us anymore. Judge Gray asked me to stand to see if any of the potential jurors knew me, and he did the same with Richard. No one did. The judge read the list of witnesses to see if the potential jurors knew any of them, but no one did.

Certain things stand out in my memory about the potential jurors. There was a dark-haired woman who was an attorney and a bald-headed man with big cheeks that made his glasses lift off his nose when he smiled. One was a woman with a cane who fell asleep during the selection process, and one was a young blonde law student. Other people included a woman from the Philippines, and a woman who was a psychologist and relationship counselor. One woman was a janitor supervisor who said she had no social life, and owned two cats. A young, dark-haired man said his father was an attorney, and a heavy-set man kept picking something out of his teeth. A tall, gray-haired man said his wife did artwork, and that he went to church regularly. And there was a pretty woman with shoulder-length brown hair who kept looking at me and wiping away her tears.

Richard's attorney asked the potential jurors long and tedious questions, and joked around, trying to make the people think he was a great guy. He kept making light of the situation until he asked a question to the dark-haired female attorney, "Do you feel your divorce, which you say was due to emotional abuse from your ex-husband, would cause you to be biased?"

"No," she said. "Because of my legal training I know I need to be impartial; however, I would have trouble in that I know emotional abuse never leaves you." Even if she was not selected as a juror, all of the other potential jurors heard this. My tears welled as she spoke, and I bit my lower lip to avoid crying out loud. She looked at us and sent an unspoken message of support.

The jury selection process was long, and James was taking his time on purpose to allow the potential jurors to become more acquainted with him. He also knew that one of my witnesses, Laurie, already had to fly back to California, and that Patty would have to fly back in the morning. If he delayed long enough, I would lose both witnesses. Finally, James finished his questioning.

Don approached the potential jurors and asked if certain profane language that would be revealed would offend them. No one objected. Don read the charges listed in the civil suit one more time, and asked if anyone would find it difficult to sit through the trial, given the nature of the charges. No one objected. After Don and James met privately with the judge, the court revealed the list of the seven jurors chosen for the trial. Those people not selected were told they could leave the courtroom.

The trial had officially begun. Kristin and I now had a voice, however limited.

As things started, my right foot bumped into something. Looking down, I saw the case for Richard's rifle hidden under the table.

"What is this doing here on the floor?" I whispered to Don.

"I had the security guard place the gun case there before anyone arrived in the courtroom. You'll know in a moment why it's there—I just don't want the opposing party to see it yet. Security personnel will bring the actual rifle into the courtroom as evidence when needed," he whispered back.

It was time for Don to present his opening statement. He stood quietly with a very serious and determined look. This trial was the first of its kind, and I knew that the emotional strain of its preparation, and hearing the horrible facts about our situation, had been hard on Don. He cared deeply about Kristin and me, and stated several times that every cell in his body detested what Richard had done.

As the jury watched, Don bent down and slowly reached for the gun case and laid it lengthwise on the table right in front of me. Don gazed at the jury and at everyone else in the courtroom. He didn't say a word. He quietly and slowly walked to the podium. His silence spoke loudly. But before Don could even say his first word, Richard yelled out, "That's *not* my gun. That's *not* my gun."

James approached Don and said, "My client denies that this is his gun case." Don walked over to me and said, "Your ex-husband denies this is his gun case. Deb, is this indeed his gun case?"

I answered, "Yes it is. Three police officers can attest to the fact that this is the case of the gun they have kept in safe storage."

Instead of feeling empowered at that moment, as one might think I would, I became even more afraid of Richard. His ability to lie frightened me to the core. Both attorneys were called to Judge Gray's desk. After they whispered a bit, James returned to the defendant's table, and Don began his opening statement.

****

Opening Statement

There is a house in Apple Valley, Minnesota, just off County Road 38, not far from the Minnesota Zoo. It is a gray house with a dark gray roof. The lawn is neatly kept. A mailbox sits at the end of the driveway. In the backyard there is a garden. In the garden are daylilies, geraniums, daisies, and azaleas. All in all, the house is unassuming and looks like any other suburban Twin Cities home. But there is something different about this house. This house has a secret. A dark secret about violence and pain. A secret maintained by that family because of the threats and violence of one man. A woman and her daughter's secret pain. Secrets, which as of today are no more. Secrets, which during the next few days are going to be spoken publicly for the first time.

You will hear the story of Deb, and her daughter, Kristin, who suffered physical and emotional abuse at the hands of their husband and father, Richard. You will hear the story of Deb who, despite beatings and humiliation at the hands of this man, did not leave her husband until her daughter was grown and out of the house. Much of what happened to Deb and Kristin you will not hear about due to the limits of the law as to how far back you can go. What you will hear details about are only the things that happened after September 28, 1991, until September 1993.

You will hear how, in April of 1992, Richard shoved Deb into the bathroom door-frame and, when she fell to the floor, kicked her in the back, saying, "Get out of my way. Some of us have to go to work."

You will hear how, in April of 1992, Richard hit her during an argument and said, "The problem with you, Deb, is that you don't obey."

You will hear how, in November of 1991, while Deb was sitting in a chair in the family room, she asked Richard what book he was reading. He became angry and yelled at Deb for interrupting his reading and threw his book at her, which hit her below her right collarbone, tore her skin, and bruised her.

You will hear how, in December 1991, Richard repeatedly hit her very hard with his right fist on her ribs, and awakened her from a sound sleep.

You will hear how, in March and April of 1992, he became even more obsessed with controlling her. And if she left to go to another room to sew or clean, he would often yell at her, "What are you doing, you f_ _ _ _ _ _ bitch? Get down here and quit ignoring me."

You will hear how, in April of 1992, Richard threatened her in their home with a gun and, when she fled, pursued her in a car; how when he caught up with her, he forced her into the car and back into the home.

You will hear how, in June of 1992, he harassed her in his office.

You will hear how, in June of 1992, after she obtained a domestic abuse protection order against him, it did not stop her husband. Instead, in a gratuitous act of cruelty, he took out an ad in a singles newspaper listing her as "disease-free" and "looking for romance."

You will hear how the pain of all this was made worse by the acts of previous physical and emotional abuse she and her daughter suffered at the hands of this man. How Deb, when he was hitting her, lost bladder control. How when he was hitting her she learned to go limp because it hurt less.

Richard, of course, denies all of this. But you will hear his own daughter, Kristin, testify against him.

You will hear of people who were there when some of the things happened.

You will hear from people to whom Deb went for help.

The law will not allow us to go into detail about the years of abuse Deb and Kristin suffered; however, there will be non-specific references to the past abuse when necessary to understand their pain.

But I ask you to hold on to the notion that Deb and Kristin were not abused, which is what Richard wants you to believe, as long as you can. We will provide you with enough evidence that you can no longer hold on to that notion. That I promise you.

And I ask you to hold on to the notion that Deb has already been compensated for the abuse he heaped upon her in the divorce settlement, which is what Richard wants you to believe. Hold on to that notion as long as you can.

We will provide you with enough evidence that you can no longer hold on to that notion. That I promise you.

****

With magnum force, Don reeled in the jurors' undivided attention. They did not blink, concerned that they would miss even one word. My focus was glued on Don until another sound—one that I had not heard for many years—beckoned me. Someone behind me was sobbing. Could that be Kristin? Could she finally be starting to let go of the pain?

I had not heard Kristin cry since her childhood. Because of her dad's abuse, she had built up a protective shield around her, letting in very few people. At a very young age, she had to develop coping mechanisms that would allow her to go on with her life. One was to stuff the hurt deep inside her in an emotional storage box, and hide the key. I had prayed that the trial would give Kristin the strength to open that box, and finally let the hurt that was inside escape forever.

Turning, I saw Kristin's head on Debra's shoulder, and her hands covered her eyes as she wept loudly. Don was speaking Kristin's pain, too.

"Oh, God," I whispered. "Thank you for letting my baby cry!" How beautiful it was to hear Kristin cry. It was her turn now to let the pain dissipate from her body. It was her turn to feel limp and weak as she transformed into a new person. It was her turn to have her head on someone's shoulder, and I longed for it to be mine. I wanted to leap from the table to stroke her hair and comfort her as she had comforted me.

My emotions were rumbling to a boiling point, like sap in a pine tree consumed by a forest fire. I felt heavy and light, as if floating and grounded at the same time. I was being turned inside out; up was down and down was up. Right was left and left was right. My ears were buzzing, and I felt faint. I felt simultaneously alert and sleepy. Everything was in opposition, but I felt centered.

It was finally happening to us. We were being transformed right in front of everyone, and they did not know it. Deeply buried hurt was starting to find its way out of our burdened bodies and minds. Tears fell down my cheeks as I heard the sweet music of Kristin crying. My body began to shake. My baby was finally crying, and I kept thinking, "Oh, God, how wonderful. It is working. The trial is our road to recovery and justice."

I knew Kristin was hurting as much as I was, and we knew in our hearts and in our souls that this trial was for both of us.

In a split second, I stopped crying. I did not want Richard to have the satisfaction of seeing me cry again, although he would never understand that the tears Kristin and I were shedding meant that we were healing from him—not being hurt again by him.

The mood in the courtroom was heavy and serious. Our story was being told to the extent that Judge Gray's imposed restrictions would allow. Sitting motionless, I tried to imagine that Don, Kristin, and I were speaking in unison, like a choir. Oh, those words. How powerful! I wanted the jury to see me as strong and truthful, so I stopped crying, remembering angels were in the room. They took the burden from me, and had it leave through Don's words. I remembered that my dad and brother were holding the African violet plants in their laps.

Silence filled the courtroom when Don finished his opening statement. It was not a peaceful silence, but one of amplified strength. It was the silence before a storm—a silence of anticipation that horrible things were about to be found out.

"No more secrets," I thought as Kristin sobbed. I knew there would never be any more secrets. The burden of carrying those secrets was lifted from us. The jury was visibly moved by Don's statement—some wiped tears away. As quietly and slowly as he had walked up to the podium, he returned to the plaintiff's table and sat by me.

James, sporting a goofy grin, walked briskly to the podium and tried to make light of the situation. He made a few comments, as a joke, but thankfully no one laughed at his sick humor. He began his opening statement by saying, "My client admits that he has done things that he is not proud of. He admits that he had a relationship with a woman in his office. He admits that he wrote the ad in the singles' magazine."

"What? Now Richard is admitting this after all of his lies?" I whispered to myself.

James continued, "These are normal things that people do during a divorce. People do crazy things during a divorce."

James portrayed Don, Dr. Lund, and me as collaborators in a great scheme to get my ex-husband.

"My client is not at fault here. They are all ganging up on this poor guy," he blurted. He also tried to paint me as a money-hungry litigious person who was unhappy about the alimony amount awarded during the divorce. He closed by saying that he would prove that I have already been amply compensated through alimony payments.

At this point, the jury was unaware that Judge Redford forbade any mention of domestic violence to be brought up in our divorce proceedings. The jurors also did not know that the alimony amount, set by Judge Redford, was based solely on the amount of our respective take-home pay, in which there was great disparity.

James kept dragging our divorce into his opening statement, and walked over to a whiteboard to chart out the alimony payments for the next five years. As stated earlier by my divorce attorney, our settlement was typical of divorce settlements—even without domestic violence as an issue. The alimony awarded did not even cover the house payment, and I was trying to find more work to avoid losing my home.

During James' opening statement, another floodgate opened in my mind, releasing horrific memories, and I anticipated another emotional meltdown. The slideshow was taking so much energy out of me that for a moment, my body did not have enough strength to sit up. Don looked very concerned and leaned over to whisper, "There will never be any price that will compensate you for what both of you have been through." James spoke to the jury about money. Don spoke to the jury about justice and secrets that were no more. He talked about pain. He talked about crimes against humanity.

Patty was the only witness called today. She looked pretty as she walked up to the witness stand. I was proud of her strength because she held up well and didn't fall into any of James' questioning traps. Patty disclosed the fact that she regularly saw bruises on my arms and legs, and that after Richard and I had separated, she did not see bruises anymore. Patty admitted that she did not think things were right in my marriage, and that she had had ample time to discern this because she, Richard, Laurie, and I had socialized quite often.

"I was always troubled by the way Richard treated Deb in public, but did not say anything because I felt it was none of my business. I was deeply concerned about her emotional and physical safety, and had talks with Laurie about how to approach Deb without making it look like we were prying," she testified.

The jury listened intently to Patty. She spoke the truth and held her composure in a very business-like and dignified manner. Patty added, "Over the years I saw Richard heap one hurt on top of another on her, including his affair with a co-worker."

How I wanted to go to the witness stand and explain what it was like to be systematically controlled. I wanted to explain what it was like to have the person who you are slowly disappear. The jury needed to hear Kristin's perspective about the abuse, as a child, and now as an adult.

After Patty's testimony, Judge Gray adjourned the trial for the day. A few hours later, I drove Patty to the airport for her flight back to California.

"When this is over, Deb, I want you to stay at my home by the ocean in San Clemente and relax. I'm concerned about you, and I want to know for myself that you are okay," Patty pleaded.

"Thanks for the invitation, and I agree, I will need some time to let the dust settle." Giving her a hug, I wished her a safe flight. When I arrived home, and turned the key to unlock the front door, it felt that I was a significant step closer to a new life.

I called Kristin to talk for a while, and get a pulse on how we were doing emotionally, to share supportive words of love. I called Dad and Kurt, and asked if they would please be in the courtroom again the next day. A feeling of abandonment came over me—and I didn't know why. Patty and Laurie were truly a source of strength for me, and now they were gone. My spirits lightened a little when I remembered that they undoubtedly would remind me of the angels in the courtroom. The domestic violence lawsuit was something that Kristin and I needed to face on our own, in order to heal and be empowered.

I walked and fed Misha, lit a few candles by the bathtub, and climbed into a magnificent bubble bath, taking a moment to breathe. Smooth jazz music whispered in the background as I sipped pinot grigio.

Easing myself into bed, Misha curled up by my side and we both fell asleep instantly. In my sleep, one angel hovered over me, and one sat on the bed next to me and held my hand. I remember a soft blue and white glow around the angels and heard once again, "You will be fine. You will be fine."

A Victory—Free at Last!

Misha licked my cheek to wake me. Feeling very alone, I tried to prepare myself psychologically for the day ahead. I hoped that Dad and Kurt would be in the courtroom again today. I locked the front door, and braced myself for the unknown.

Kristin and I had the most supportive and intense conversation in the car on the way to Don's office.

"We're on our way, honey," I said, meaning that we were taking our first steps to heal from many years of abuse.

"I know, Mom," Kristin answered as she reached over and held my hand. Her soft, warm hand made me feel safe. We discussed the years of abuse, and talked again about how we were coping at the moment. "Mom, I'm very proud of you. You're finally standing up to Dad. You're standing up to crimes against women," Kristin said confidently.

I gently squeezed her hand.

"I'm proud of you, too, sweetie, and I love you. We are in this together."

The car was full of the music of our newfound voices. We could not stop talking. The chatter was uncontrollable as we finally let words about the horror of the past, and a hopeful future, leave our lips. Each word made us feel stronger and stronger.

"No more secrets," I proudly proclaimed.

I had prayed each night leading up to the trial that I was teaching Kristin a good lesson in life—to be able to stand up for what she believes is right, and to help her gain strength and confidence knowing that she was part of the first-ever trial of this type. We were boldly taking steps to heal, and to hold her dad accountable for what he had done to us.

Walking into the courthouse, we remarked how the court system failed us by forcing us into silence—not once, but twice. Once we sat down, Dad, Kurt, and Mom entered the room. I knew Mom wouldn't be able to stay away this day, and the compassionate look in her eyes promised me that she would keep her cool. Richard and James walked by, and I was amazed at how strong I felt. Richard's wife (or girlfriend) was not with him today, my assumption being that he got smart and did not want her to hear the truth about his darkness. The atmosphere in the courtroom was different than yesterday, as if events would not be how I expected them to be. Now I was confused as to whether to be happy or concerned. Don walked briskly by and motioned for me to sit with him at the plaintiff's table. Kristin sat by her grandparents and uncle. Nicole, the advocate from the Lewis House, sat in the back with her notepad and pen, ready to memorialize the trial.

A desire for victory filled my heart and soul. Crimes of this type had been handled before in Criminal Court, but never in a civil trial. Don explained to me that this case was new to Civil Court, so everyone involved was in uncharted territory. Until now, attorneys had been reluctant to take on a case like this because it is not like suing a huge corporation with deep pockets. It is assumed that the abuser's ability to pay, if liable, is finite, and that the work and expense involved overwhelms the potential award amount. Instead, a case like this must be fueled by passionate resolve to see justice done, rather than by a big settlement check. Another crucial consideration is the makeup of the victim's inner strength. It must be strong as steel to proceed. Don and his entire staff worked tirelessly, often volunteering their time. This had been an emotionally draining journey for everyone, and we agreed from the onset to persevere.

The jury entered, and we rose as Judge Gray appeared. Don stood up and positioned himself in front of the jury. He was about to call me to the witness stand when James walked up to the judge and asked for a conference. Judge Gray excused the jury for ten minutes, and everyone in the courtroom rose again as the jurors followed the security person to a special waiting area.

Richard and James looked extremely tired, as though they had aged twenty years over night. James' shoulders were slouched, and he had no pep in his step. He was not in a joking mood. In fact, he walked rather slowly, without confidence. James glanced my way, and for a split second our eyes met.

"You've met your match," I thought as an inner strength took over. I had never felt this before, and it seemed very foreign.

To say that Richard looked pale and worried was an understatement. During the past two days he witnessed me as a new person, like he had never seen before. He could not control me with physical or emotional force. His body language and evil looks did not have the effect that he had come to expect. His control was no longer working. He was powerless, while Kristin and I radiated a powerful grace. This unnerved him. Perhaps, during the night, he and James realized the gravity of the situation. I was not backing down. I had witnesses. The jurors' body language seemed sympathetic toward me, and most importantly, they knew that what Kristin and I said on the witness stand would be the truth. Stress has an incredibly unkind way of manifesting itself psychologically and physically. The manifestation of truth, however, is beautiful.

Without looking at Kristin seated behind me, I could feel the energy blossoming in her. Kristin and I were experiencing a synergistic force that was connecting our growing spirit and confidence. We were healing.

The judge and both attorneys finished their discussion, and as Don walked toward me, he said, "We need to talk in the hallway."

Suzanne and I followed him, and as we stepped into the hallway, I noticed a newspaper reporter and a television journalist waiting for the outcome of the trial. Don spoke to them briefly, assuring them that he would let them know the final results. Don abruptly turned around and looked me straight in the eyes.

"Your case is settled." I was shocked and stunned. "They have offered an amount that I think Judge Gray will allow because it is within the parameters that he laid out yesterday."

My first reaction, "Do I have to accept their offer?"

"No, but I recommend you take it because it is a good offer." The look on Don's face did not match his words, as if he were saying, "Yes," but at the same time shaking his head, "No." He was unusually stern.

Up to this point his advice was always sincere, and I trusted everything he said completely. At this particular moment, however, I saw, felt, and heard a major disconnect between what he was saying and how he was looking at me. Did he really want me to accept the offer—or reject it and go on with the trial?

Strength morphed into confusion. I asked Don if Kristin could please join us in the hallway. When Suzanne returned with Kristin, it was obvious that she sensed something important was going on. Don and Suzanne explained to her what had just happened. Kristin held my hand as I turned to Don and said, "I thought you wanted to try this case. I thought that once a trial begins there is no more room for negotiating." I still had a difficult time reading Don's intense look. Things just felt so bizarre.

Don said to Kristin, "Your father and his attorney have conceded, and I recommend that your mother take the offer."

The reporters were watching very intently as I asked, "Don, what would I gain to not accept the offer, and move on with the trial?"

Don still did not seem like his usual self.

"Your day in court. You stand to get more money, or possibly less money, or a verdict that the case has no grounds, in which case you would get nothing. I am one 100 percent sure that Richard and his attorney would bring this to Appeals Court. That means you will be in court with these two swell fellows for another two years." Don added that if we did not accept the offer, we would most certainly face the wrath of a judge who clearly did not want to try this case in the first place.

"I suggest that you take it—and get on with your life to heal. You need Richard out of your life in every possible way."

Kristin held my hand tightly.

"Mom, I agree with Don. You should accept because we won. They threw in the towel!"

The strength that I had felt building up inside me earlier today totally disappeared. I truly felt that now I was being—once again—silenced. How could this be? I needed to get on the witness stand. I knew, with all my heart, that Kristin needed to get on the stand, too. I kept thinking, *Twenty-three years! Twenty-three years!*

I was in absolute agony, and much of the hurt that had left my body was now coming back with a vengeance. I longed to make a statement that domestic violence is a crime against humanity. I could feel myself slipping into living through another violent slideshow. Don instinctively knew what was happening, and what my concerns were.

"Deb, there is no gag order here. You can talk about what happened to you all you want. In the courtroom there are only seven jurors." And, as he spread his arms wide, he continued, "You need to get out there and tell seven thousand people! You can, Deb, you can!"

Suzanne broke down crying.

"Deb, you have won. You won! Get out there and start a new life. You and Kristin are free!"

But I still could not answer. The words simply would not leave my lips. I wanted to burst into the courtroom, look Richard in the eyes, and say, "No, I won't settle! You have to sit there and hear me out. You can't hurt us anymore!" And as had been happening quite frequently during the whole trial process, spiritual guidance intervened and when I spoke, it was as if someone else was talking through me.

"Okay, I'll accept the offer."

At that moment I wanted to look around and say, "Who just said that?" Don asked me to repeat what I had said.

"I'll accept the offer." I felt like I was in a zone between victory and caving in.

Suzanne repeated, "Deb, don't ever lose sight of the fact that you just won."

With each step as we walked back into the courtroom, I began to feel increasingly victorious. A chant started rolling around in my head, "We did it! We did it! We did it!" I was so proud of Kristin and, for the first time in my adult life, I was proud of me. Richard and James looked like whipped old horses. The wear and tear of the evilness within Richard revealed a vacant soul. I stood up to him for the first time. I stood up to the legal system's hurdles.

I felt united with Kristin in so many ways. Today we were able to communicate strength and confidence—again, without words—as we stood in the courtroom. We felt validated for the first time. I had a sense of hope for all battered women and children, and wanted this trial to stand for victory for anyone in a similar situation. I felt a deep and sincere responsibility to succeed for their sake.

Judge Gray asked, "Do all parties understand the settlement? We will notify the divorce court to have them immediately terminate the order for Richard to pay Deborah any further alimony, since the settlement agreed to today should be enough for her to live on." His comment totally blew me away.

Now I was faced with another weird and unfair twist within the court system. This trial's outcome affected what had already been agreed upon in the divorce trial. It was as if our divorce had been re-tried, instead of domestic violence being on trial. I experienced no financial gain from the domestic violence lawsuit. What I experienced, instead, which no amount of money could buy, was the rebuilding of Kristin and me. The building blocks were now stacking up again to reveal the women we actually were.

Both attorneys approached the judge to work out the wording of the settlement, which Don read into the record. I was still flabbergasted by Judge Gray's comments regarding the alimony, and his other remarks that just about killed me.

"I'm glad that you two settled. It would have done you no good to get on the stand and say bad things about each other. You two need to respect each other. You two need to become friends. You have a daughter in common, and you need to be friends."

From my perspective, in one stroke of incredible insensitivity, Judge Gray blurted to the world his ignorance in regard to the plight of battered women and children. In my mind, he became as evil as Richard. My moment of feeling victorious was not only stolen—the judge might as well have thrown it to the ground and stomped on it. His words were like stagnant air. Looking directly at me, the judge pointed toward Richard and said, "You need to respect him, and he needs to respect you."

Judge Gray continued with his icy remarks, resulting in me becoming angrier than I truly had ever experienced before. My body began to rock back and forth. I was a volcano about to erupt. This insult was beyond comprehension, and the years of abuse whirled around inside my body and mind, destroying in its path every fiber of my being. How did the judge expect me to respect and be friends with a man who had tried to kill me? The weight of the world came crashing down on me again.

All I could hear was Judge Gray making light of domestic violence.

For two innocent people, living in fear had become a way of life—and the judge just blew it off. He made me feel like a speck of dust in the courtroom. I felt the judge had insulted my daughter and every battered woman and child out there. How could this happen?

As our eyes met, all the color seemed to have drained from Don's face. Visibly upset, he said, "Deb, I'm sorry that the judge said that."

"Don, if I had known that the judge was going to say that, I would never have settled." Every muscle in my face felt tight as rage set in.

Don knew I was having trouble controlling my emotions, and ordered, "Deb, get into the hallway. Get into the hallway." I ran out of the courtroom, falling to my hands and knees, sobbing uncontrollably. My eyes shut tight and would not open. I didn't want to look at this horrible world anymore.

Don, Suzanne, and Kristin quickly followed me into the hallway. Kristin wrapped her arms around me, making me feel safe in our own special cocoon. I felt Don's hand on my head as he reached to help me up. Dad had a hard time walking in his frail condition, so it took him, Mom, and Kurt a little longer to catch up with us. Again I wanted to beg my parents to please make the hurt go away. Dad smiled faintly, and handed me the African violet plant that he had been carrying with him to the trial each day. Kurt gave his plant to Kristin. They knew this was the exact moment for their gifts to do their soothing magic. It is said that flowers have meanings, and the African violets they lovingly gave us symbolize faithfulness and virtue, and convey endearing admiration.

For a long time, Don, Suzanne, and my family talked in the hallway. They were diligent in trying to reinforce that we had won—and we believed the judge was a buffoon. Our group slowly walked toward the elevators. As we were waiting for the elevator doors to open, Judge Gray came around the corner carrying a briefcase, with his suit jacket draped over his arm.

"Good evening," he said. The doors opened up and all of us, including the judge, entered the elevator.

This was my moment.

"Your honor, you disrespected me, my daughter, and every battered woman and child by your comments after the trial."

Judge Gray was about to speak, but my dad cut him off, and in his frail voice demanded, "Let her finish!"

I continued, "I would like to set up an appointment with you to discuss what it was like to live in fear for so many years. You need to know the emotional and physical devastation that abuse causes to women and children."

A split second after I finished speaking, Judge Gray replied, "That would not be a good idea." The elevator doors opened, and Judge Gray walked away without looking back. We stood in deafening silence as the doors slowly closed. Stunned speechless, and confounded at the judge's response, no one even blinked until Kurt blurted, "What an asshole."

When our group reached the parking ramp, Don took me aside to congratulate me on standing up to Richard.

"Don, I thought you wanted to try the case. I was so confused and torn when the settlement was offered. I really could not tell if you wanted me to accept the offer or reject it. Your words told me to accept it, so I did, but something in your voice was telling me not to. I could only go by what you said."

"I did want to try the case. I wanted you to reject the offer. However, I knew that if the trial continued and you won, the law says that it is up to you to collect the amount awarded to you. I knew that you would be in court time and time again to try to collect from your ex-husband. He would not be out of your life. But now, by virtue of the fact that Richard made a settlement offer, the court enforces that he pays you.

"I also saw the emotional drain on you, and my concern for your well-being was much greater than my desire to continue with the trial. I desperately wanted to have Richard on the witness stand. I wanted to tear into him. But what I wanted more was him out of your life."

Don reminded me that Judge Gray was up for re-election in a few months, and we both hoped he would lose. (As it turned out, he did.)

Our family went to dinner, sitting quietly, still feeling the blow from Judge Gray's comments. Everyone knew we had just been part of the first trial of its kind, and we won. I told my family that only time would tell how Kristin and I would recover from the years of abuse, expecting many twists and turns on our healing journey.

After our dinner, Kristin and I expressed our love for each other, proudly carrying our African violet plants as we walked back to our cars. Nothing was going to stop us now.

My drive home seemed extra long. As I turned off the freeway, I realized I could not go home tonight. Was I afraid that Richard would cause problems because of the trial's outcome? Or was I afraid to be alone when the realization of my newborn freedom hit me? I am finally free from Richard's control, free from not having a voice, free from burying horrible memories deep inside, free from appearing weak, and free from the grasp of silence. I am free to love again and free to start a new life.

By filing the lawsuit, Kristin and I proved our strength and determination to stand up against evil. Now we can become the women we were meant to be. We broke free from the spinning centrifuge of domestic violence, and survived the process. We won!

Only Kristin can say how all of this has affected her. As her mom, I pray that today I sent an example of strength instead of weakness, as in the past.

At dinner this evening, I did notice an immediate change in Kristin as she beamed with self-confidence and pride in what she was doing at the university. She talked openly about what we had been through, and I knew from experience that every time words about abuse leave your lips, you heal a little more.

Knowing that a neighbor offered to care for Misha for a few days, I turned my car around, and headed back to a Holiday Inn that I had just passed. I parked and checked in. I dashed to the elevator and waited to be lifted to much-needed rest. In my deep slumber, one angel hovered over me, and one sat on the bed next to me and held my hand. As before, a soft blue and white glow filled the room. Again, they sang, "You will be fine. You will be fine."

The next thing I remember was waking up in the morning to a "tap, tap, tap," on the hotel room door, followed by a soft voice saying, "Housekeeping." I immediately called Patty in California and told her to get ready for a visitor in a few days.

After checking out of the hotel, I quickly drove home to unlock the front door. A new life was patiently waiting.

Kristin and I now had quite a story to tell. Don's words keep whirling around in my head, "You need to tell seven thousand people! You can, Deb, you can!"

Phoenix Rising

Now, two weeks after the trial, I am flying to Los Angeles for a much-needed break. As I write this I have just stowed my carry-on luggage, and am now in my seat by the window. For some reason, the Introduction to Sailing class that my friends, Patty and Laurie, invited me to join last year comes to mind. Maybe the peacefulness of that day is resurfacing because that was the last time my friends and I had been together outside of trial matters. When it was my turn to take the helm, our stocky young skipper said, "Deb, you handle the boat well. It's as if the wind is your dance partner." It was a poignant observation because I had just been reflecting on how I have had to adapt to whatever life blows my way. And, after all, I was a dancer.

An hour ago my brother, Mark, drove me to the airport, giving me a hug to wish me well on my evening flight to Los Angeles. Compassionate Mark often referred to me as his second mom. Today was different because it felt like he was the parent, and I was the child moving out of the house for the first time.

The plane charged down the runway as I thought of my long journey to get here. This will be my first vacation in a very long time where I will not be hit or emotionally terrorized. I will return home without a bruised body or a battered soul. It feels good to close my eyes and breathe. Ahhh! I love the moment when the plane's tires disengage from the runway, and I choose this moment to disengage from my past—and blast off to a new life. I am the Phoenix rising.

My heart and head are peaceful. I feel the warmth of the sun on my face as we fly west into the sunset. Uncontrollably, tears are welling in my eyes, and the blur makes it hard to see to write. I have a strong spiritual feeling that God is sending me on my next journey. Leaving Minnesota to visit Patty in California is symbolic, because the physical act of leaving will help me put closure to the past. My return trip will be a rebirth of who I am, and what God has planned for Kristin and me.

As the plane continues its powerful climb, it sways like the lead partner of a waltzing couple. Once again I am "dancing with the wind."

My New Life

Patty and her husband picked me up at midnight, and during the long drive to San Clemente, we caught up on what had transpired since the trial. I was extremely tired, thus I willingly accepted her rules for my visit.

"This is your time for some R&R, and I won't allow you to talk about Richard or the trial for the remainder of your visit. You have a whole new life waiting, and we will take plenty of time to go over planning things for your studio," she ordered. The Pacific Ocean was within listening distance of Patty's house. The sound of the pulsing waves made me fall asleep almost before my head hit the pillow.

In what seemed like an instant later, warm golden light spilled through the bedroom window as the sun heralded a new day. Waves pounded the beach like the mallet of a tympani drum while trumpeting seagulls added another layer to the mighty symphony. My eyes were open, but my body lay motionless as my senses gradually came alive to their fullest.

"Deb! Get up 'cause we are driving to Tijuana to shop," Patty shouted from her kitchen. Unfortunately, Laurie could not take the day off from work to join us, even though we would pass by her home in San Diego.

After a stop for breakfast at a favorite ocean-side restaurant, we headed to shop 'til we dropped in Mexico. Patty had always said the day would come when she would own the luxury car of her dreams, a Lexus, and she did it! Opening the sunroof, we let our long hair do a special dance in the wind as we blasted down the freeway. Her new business and entrepreneurial spirit had paid off for her. For both of my dear friends, the glass of life was not only half full—it was overflowing.

Driving along the coast, the music of our laughter echoed to eternity across the ocean. When we reached the Mexican border guard checkpoint, we debated whether to leave the Lexus parked on the U.S. side, and walk into Tijuana. However, Patty was on a mission to pick up some decorative clay pots to place in her house and garden, and knew they would be too large for us to carry around. She decided instead to try to find a safe place to park the car in Tijuana. The Mexican border guard asked a few questions before waving us through.

Patty cautiously drove around until she found a parking spot right in front of a dilapidated building adorned with a sign that we think translated to "Fire Department of Tijuana." Feeling that her car would be safe there, we shopped for hours until the setting sun painted a vibrant palette across the horizon. Exhausted and giddy from being in the hot sun all day, we were ecstatic that we had incredible shopping and bargaining successes. All of my early

Christmas shopping got done, and Patty found her large clay pots that now filled the trunk of her car.

Not wanting to be in Tijuana after dark, we drove to the U.S. border guard checkpoint. Assuming that we would be asked the same questions as when we entered, we kept our joyful conversation going and didn't really pay much attention to the guard's serious and unfriendly demeanor. The guard sternly asked, "Do you have any illegals hiding in your trunk?" Patty laughingly blurted out, "No. Just some pot." I looked at Patty as if she had just dropped in from Mars. "Oh! I meant that I have some pottery in the trunk," Patty quickly recovered. Patty's Lexus had probably never had quite the exam it did over the next several minutes, but we were eventually allowed to pass. The guard laughed and winked as we proceeded back into the U.S.

A new me was faintly beginning to emerge. During the last few days of my relaxing getaway, Patty had to go to work, so I dropped her off at her office and drove around in her Lexus until it was time to pick her up.

Return to Reality

September 6 was the last day of my visit. I walked along the beach, feeling a deep need to have some alone time to reflect on things. Even though a new life was beginning, it felt a bit scary and uncertain. After my soulful stroll, I headed back to Patty's house to pack.

Realizing that I hadn't checked my voice mail in almost a week, I reluctantly retrieved my messages. My parents called to see how I was doing, and Kristin called to say that rehearsals for her modern dance group were starting. The pet boarding kennel was checking to see if I wanted Misha to have a bath and haircut before I picked him up the next day. Lastly was a message from Gregory Hines' agent saying that he would be coming to Minneapolis to see me in two days to teach the master tap class in support of my building Heartbeat Studios. I dropped the phone to the floor.

"Oh, my Lord!" I yelled. Angels were at work again.

I must have listened to the message from Gregory's agent about one hundred times before Patty came home. I called Kristin and one of my dance friends to ask them to contact twenty-five of my advance-level tap students to make sure they kept September 9 open, because they were going to have an extraordinary experience.

My flight home arrived late that evening, and as I unlocked my front door, even though it was dark, I stepped into a house full of light. Many angels were present, and I think they were having a party.

A Wish Come True

First thing the next morning, I anxiously called Gregory's agent to confirm all details. Gregory would arrive on September 9 at 1:00 p.m., and I would pick him up at the St. Paul Hotel by 5:00 p.m. His master tap class would run from 6:00 p.m. to 8:00 p.m., after which I would give him a ride back to the hotel. The hotel's limousine service would take him to the airport early the next morning.

The dance studio in a local high school was reserved for this event, because Heartbeat was not built yet, and the school's administration had been informed that the class had to be kept quiet from the public and news media. Gregory had insisted that the focus of his visit be entirely about Heartbeat, and not about him. On September 9 at 2 p.m., my telephone rang.

"Hello, Deb. So, what are you doing right now?"

"Getting ready to pick you up, Gregory," I laughed.

"I am very excited to meet you, and look forward to the class. When you get to the hotel, have the concierge call my room to let me know you have arrived," Gregory instructed.

"I can hardly wait to meet you, too," I replied.

What does a person wear when she is about to meet her idol? Clothes flew around my bedroom like a flock of birds while I raided my closet. Rejects went one direction while possibilities went another. After all of the commotion, I finally decided on basic black dress pants, a lovely long-sleeved black angora sweater, red high heels, and red lipstick. It was very hard to remain calm—I was about to meet *the* Gregory Hines. Thoughts of, "Don't say anything stupid. Keep your cool. Don't behave like a screaming fan that has lost her mind," ran through my head.

Needless to say, the drive to the hotel was surreal. I pulled up to the entrance and, smiling from ear to ear, I asked the doorman if I could leave my car parked there, "Because I am picking up Gregory Hines!"

"Sure," he said, "Gregory already told me to expect you." Then it hit me; I knew what Gregory looked like, but he had never met me. I decided that when he arrived in the lobby, I'd walk up and introduce myself.

The hotel lobby was crowded as I made my way to the concierge desk.

"Please call Gregory Hines to let him know that Deb is in the lobby," I instructed. The concierge called Gregory's room and, after he hung up, informed me that Gregory would need about another ten minutes, and that I should just make myself comfortable. The hotel lobby was full of huge palm plants that towered above everyone. The crowd was beginning to thin out, and every time an elevator door opened, I expected to see Gregory walk out. I could hardly stand the wait. My heart felt like it was doing gymnastics. Twenty minutes had passed, and just when I thought I was beginning to calm down a little, my heart would start racing again. I worried whether I looked okay, and stopped to see my reflection in the enormous lobby mirror. My face had a very healthy glow, and for the first time in many years, I looked beautifully happy. Nervousness kicked in again, knowing that any moment Gregory would step out from one of the elevators.

Hearing the elevator bell's ding began to drive me crazy as I paced back and forth.

"He doesn't know what I look like. What if he thinks I'm a lousy tap dancer? What if he regrets coming here?" I was driving myself nuts, and wished that I could be magically beamed out of there. Only a handful of people were in the lobby when the moment arrived. I peeked through the leaves of a lush palm plant as Gregory stepped out of the elevator. He looked around to see if he could figure out where I was. Our eyes met as I stepped away from the plant. Gregory walked directly toward me, wearing the friendliest and warmest smile I had ever seen. He wrapped his arms tightly around my waist, leaned me backward as if we were doing a dip in a ballroom dance, and gave me a monumental kiss on my cheek.

Five generations: Deborah with her grandmother, father, great grandfather and great, great grandmother

Deborah at her humble Madison, MN home

Deborah and her parents

Deborah and infant, Kristin

The Lysholm family:
Standing (L to R) Robert, Jalma, Butch. Seated
(L to R) Nancie, Shirlee (holding Mark),
Deborah (holding Kurt)

Kristin starts kindergarten

Kristin at the University of Minnesota

Our new family

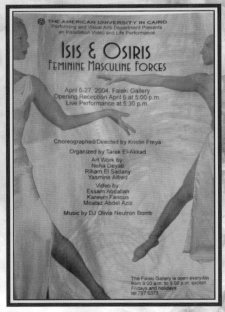

Poster for Kristin's event at the Falaki
Art Museum, Cairo, Egypt

Deborah and California friends,
Laurie (L) and Patty (R)

Deborah and Kristin prior to first-ever trial

Deborah and Gregory after his master tap class to show support of her dream of Heartbeat

Deborah, Shirlee and Heidi meet Gregory on the set of his show

Deborah and Kristin: The Phoenixes rising

*Deborah and Kristin throwing
nightmare memories overboard*

*Deborah performing at MN Orchestra Hall Hot
Summer Jazz Festival*

Kristin performance with Vox Medusa

*Deborah and Kristin at Heartbeat
groundbreaking ceremony*

One of two studio rooms in Heartbeat

Exterior of Heartbeat

Kristin and Paul get married

*Deborah in Milan about to see
Da Vinci's Last Supper*

*Guillem and the Camut Band
at the Up and Down Nightclub*

Yukiko visits Heartbeat

*Kristin is greeted by Cuban dancers
at the Havana airport*

Deborah, Kristin and Tony (center) in large conga line to celebrate their visit to Tony's dance studio in Havana

Deborah and Kristin ready to depart Havana

Heartbeat's teachers and Yukiko celebrate in Barcelona (L – R: Tona, Kristin, Levi, Deborah, Yukiko, Carlos, Stephany)

Deborah and Kristin visit Tony's dance studio in Havana

Kristin and Heartbeat dancers perform "Fire" dance in Barcelona

Standing (L-R): Deborah, Kurt, Shirlee, Mark, Butch. Seated (L-R): Robert, Jalma, Nancie

Kristin in Cairo, Egypt

Playbill cover Paul designed for Heartbeat's
show at Sadler's Wells Theatre in London

Deborah, Dianne and Yukiko and her students hold
Certificate of Friendship with Heartbeat

Deborah, Dianne and Yukiko perform during
Heartbeat's Tenth Anniversary Show

Deborah and Dianne Walker
backstage at Tokyo performance

Paul and Kristin by Mt. Fuji
during trip to Tokyo

Tokyo comes to Heartbeat

Heartbeat teachers depart Minneapolis for their
trip to teach and perform in Barcelona. (L-R:
Stephany, Tona, Deborah, Kristin, Carlos, Levi)

Deborah and Guillem after class in Barcelona

Kristin and Paul still in love after all these years

Deborah doing what she loves best…
dancing at Heartbeat

A toast to all survivors from Kristin and Deborah

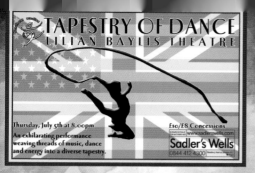

Playbill cover Paul designed for Heartbeat's show at Sadler's Wells Theatre in London

Deborah, Dianne and Yukiko and her students hold Certificate of Friendship with Heartbeat

Deborah, Dianne and Yukiko perform during Heartbeat's Tenth Anniversary Show

Deborah and Dianne Walker backstage at Tokyo performance

Paul and Kristin by Mt. Fuji during trip to Tokyo

Tokyo comes to Heartbeat

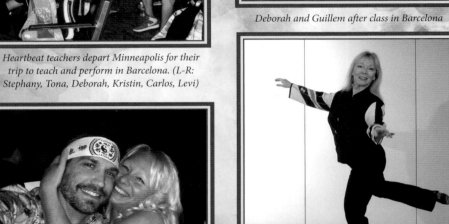

Deborah and Guillem after class in Barcelona

Heartbeat teachers depart Minneapolis for their trip to teach and perform in Barcelona. (L-R: Stephany, Tona, Deborah, Kristin, Carlos, Levi)

Kristin and Paul still in love after all these years

*Deborah doing what she loves best…
dancing at Heartbeat*

A toast to all survivors from Kristin and Deborah

Still in the dip position, Gregory looked into my eyes and said, "You must be Deb."

Without skipping a beat I replied, "No, you've got the wrong person." In an instant, a flash of panic came across Gregory's face. I started to giggle, and he began to laugh uncontrollably out of pure relief. From that moment, we talked non-stop as if we had been friends forever.

"Gregory, I was so nervous waiting for you that I had to say something to relieve the tension."

"Girl, you almost got me on that one. I like your sense of humor, and I can tell we are going to have a great time." The hotel doorman stood watch by my little Chevrolet Cavalier, and graciously opened the car door for Gregory and me. He tipped his hat as my idol and I sped away.

At the school, we were quickly ushered to the studio by the building manager who said, "Nice to meet you, Gregory. I'm a big fan." I could hear the dancers' tap shoes off in the distance, and knew they were warming up. Gregory and I stopped in restrooms by the dance studio to change into our dance clothes and tap shoes.

"Are you ready to meet my crew?" I asked.

"Yes, Deb. This is just as exciting for me. You are giving up so much to pursue your dream. You are giving up so much for the arts. You are giving so much to your students, and I hope they understand and appreciate your dedication to them."

Gregory held my hand as we entered the studio to the sound of my students and family members' thunderous applause. Kristin had postponed her dance company's rehearsal so they could attend as well. I was so proud of my dance students, and knew that they would be experiencing moments that they could only have dreamed of before. Gregory was wonderful and kind. It took a while for my star-struck students to peel themselves off the ceiling, but finally we all got down to the business of our passion—tap dancing.

The class flew by, with no one wanting it to end. We learned an incredible amount of new tap technique from Gregory, and ended the class trading steps, the part he loved the most. When the class finally came to an end, Gregory asked us to gather around and said, "I am here not to promote myself. I have people who do that for me. I have people who run almost every aspect of my career. Heartbeat Studios, that is Deb's dream, and she has done all of it on her own. No one is risking anything but her, and it is because she loves you and loves the arts. I am here to tell you that I support her dream and admire her passion. I promise to come back to see Heartbeat when it is built." Gregory turned and applauded me. Never before could I have imagined this moment, and I felt his warmth deep in my soul.

The dancers and my family members took many photographs with Gregory, and he autographed our shirts and the instep of our tap shoes (a tradition of tap enthusiasts). Gregory and I slowly made our way outside and joined my brother, Butch, for a ride in a beautiful antique car he had rebuilt. Gregory was thrilled to see Butch's artistry, and after a short while, we were headed back to the St. Paul Hotel.

"I'm hungry. May I treat you to dinner?" Gregory asked.

"Sure. The hotel actually has one of the best restaurants in the area." Gregory's wonderful and supportive conversation continued well into our dinner.

Gregory (an Aquarian), was an amazingly funny person with a dry sense of humor. We talked about our families, about raising children, and about tap dance. He was very inquisitive about the domestic violence trial because he was in the midst of rehearsals for a movie that had a courtroom scene, and he wanted to hear more about courtroom dynamics. I tried desperately not to be a typical star-struck fan asking the same questions that he probably had answered a million times. By the end of dinner, we seemed to have solved all of the world's problems during our lively conversation. My cheeks were sore from all of the laughter.

We lost track of time and didn't seem to care. When the restaurant was completely empty, our waitress stopped by to tell us, "Keep enjoying your conversation. I'm nearby if you needed anything." As she refilled our water glasses I said, "Gregory, I admire your tap dancing, and equally admire your singing."

Gregory was quiet for a moment, and in a smooth and mesmerizing voice, began to softly sing one of my favorite songs, "You Can Change the World." My tears came from pure joy. Who would ever believe this night? He was an angel sent to make me believe that life would finally turn around for Kristin and me.

After his song, everything became magically quiet. Gregory said, "Deb, you are selling your home and everything you own to pursue a dream. I don't know anyone else who has done this. From the little time that I have known you, I can tell that you do not fully comprehend the magnitude of what you are doing to contribute to the arts. Maybe the trial is still too recent. Maybe your journey to start a new life is too new. What I do know is that you are a rose ready to bloom, and I want to be there when it happens."

Gregory exuded warm, brotherly compassion, and I felt as if I were talking to an older sibling that I had never had. He kissed my cheek, and said that he admired me for the risks I was willing to take, from leaving my ex-husband, to the trial, and finally to building Heartbeat.

"Not many people are willing to pursue a dream." As he shrugged, added, "Not many people even have a dream." With that comment, the sun rose. We had talked through the night, and to this day, I still hear his words.

When the *St. Paul Pioneer Press* interviewed Gregory on January 19, 1997, he talked about our meeting. Gregory is quoted, "*She has a very pure heart…It was great to see her dance. Her life is really starting to take off now. She deserves it.*"

With regard to my initial letter to him, Gregory is quoted, "*It was a beautiful letter. It was a passionate letter. It was her passion that drew me to her. She talked about her desire to open up a dance studio in Minnesota. Her commitment to dance was really something I could relate to.*"

To do justice to the kind heart of Gregory, and to attempt to convey his admirable and compassionate soul, I need to explain a few of our subsequent meetings. On my birthday, March 1, 1997, Gregory surprised me by sending two dozen peach-colored roses and orchids to my house with a note that read, "*Happy Birthday! Good times ahead. Love, Gregory.*"

Late that year, in early December, he invited me—and my sister, Shirlee, and her 10-year-old daughter, Heidi—to travel to Los Angeles to be in the audience during the taping of an episode of his television series, *The Gregory Hines Show.* Kristin had also been invited, but had exams at the University of Minnesota. The plan was that after the show, Gregory and I would talk about arranging for his visit to Heartbeat after it opened. Shirlee, Heidi, and I stayed in a hotel three miles from the Culver City Studios where Gregory's show was produced. We rented a car, and being unfamiliar with Los Angeles traffic, decided to give ourselves at least fifteen minutes to drive the three miles. Forty-five minutes later we were still stuck in traffic and practically hyperventilating, expecting that we would not be admitted into the studio.

When we finally arrived at the studio guard's gate, he asked why we were there.

"For the *Gregory Hines Show,*" I said. "I know we are late, but we just flew in from Minneapolis, and ran into a massive traffic jam."

"Traffic jam?" he blurted. "It's always like this. I'm afraid that it may be too late, but let me make a call."

When the guard hung up the phone, he said, "Follow me," and climbed into a nearby golf cart. We wound our way around several buildings until he motioned for us to park by the entrance door of Studio Six.

Shirlee and I quickly grabbed our handbags while Heidi grabbed the Christmas gift she had secretly picked out for Gregory. At the studio door, another man with a clipboard asked, "May I have your names, please?"

"My name is Deborah, and we are very late due to traffic. I really hope we can still be admitted, and we really do not mind if we just stand in the back," I implored.

After carefully checking his list, he smiled as he said, "Follow me."

We were led to the front row where three seats were adorned with huge white ribbon bows.

"Those are your seats," the man whispered.

Fortunately, the taping of Gregory's show was off to a late start, so we had not missed anything. As we sat down, the house lights darkened as the set lights glowed. The announcer introduced all of the actors one by one. The last person introduced is always the main character, and when Gregory's name was announced, Shirlee, Heidi, and I jumped from our seats and gave him a standing ovation. Looking around a bit until his eyes focused on us, Gregory walked closer and threw us kisses.

The taping started at 7:00 p.m., and periodically throughout the evening, a comedian would come out to entertain the audience while the actors took breaks to discuss scenes or changes in the script. During one break, while lively music filled the studio, the comedian dared a group of college students in the audience to come to the front to demonstrate some of the latest moves in the dance club scene. None of the students took him up on his dare, so the comedian chided them for their lack of bravery. Without skipping a beat, before Shirlee or I could react, Heidi bolted from her seat and ran up to the comedian.

"I can show you some moves," she said.

Heidi was very small for her age, and looked like a little cherub decked out in her Christmas, red velvet holiday dress with a white lace collar, white leggings, and black patent leather shoes with bows. Her smile lit the room as she danced moves that would put any avid club dancer to shame. The audience roared with robust laughter that caught the attention of all of the actors and crew.

After Heidi's impromptu performance, it was time for the taping to resume. While the audience sat back in their seats, I noticed a woman wearing a headset handing out what appeared to be script papers to all of the actors. Gregory and his cast members returned to their positions on the set, standing with their backs to the audience as the house lights went dark. Once the bright lights illuminated the set, all of the actors, including Gregory, abruptly turned around and began to dance as they waved signs above their heads that read, "Heidi Rocks!" Again the audience roared. It took several minutes before Gregory and his cast members could regain their composure to continue taping his show.

The evening progressed with many starts and stops, and it was almost midnight before audience members were asked to leave because script changes were going to take several more hours. When the house lights went up, Gregory motioned for us to join him on the set.

"I'm afraid the taping may take until four this morning, so I will not have time tonight to talk to you about coming to see Heartbeat," he sighed.

Heidi walked up to Gregory, hugged him, and handed him her Christmas gift.

"Please open it," she giggled.

Gregory carefully opened the small box, pulling out a precious porcelain figurine of an angel playing a drum.

"Thank you, Heidi. This is a very special gift, and I will take good care of it," Gregory promised. He hugged us, and again apologized for not being able to talk longer.

After we had a quick photo taken with Gregory, he said, "Deb, I've got to leave now to discuss changes in the script, so I will talk to you about returning to see Heartbeat when I see you in Chicago in two weeks."

"But Gregory, I live in Minneapolis, not in Chicago," I replied, puzzled.

"I know. A complimentary ticket will be waiting for you at the Auditorium Theater for my show in Chicago, and you are invited to the after-party. Just call my manager to get the details." Walking away, he blew us another kiss.

Heidi got Gregory to autograph one of the "Heidi Rocks!" signs, which she has framed in her bedroom. What a memory for a ten-year-old child.

Two weeks later I arrived in Chicago on Saturday morning for Gregory's show that evening. I checked into the Congress Hotel across the street from the Auditorium Theater. His manager left a message that my ticket for Gregory's show was being held at the box office, and that I should remember to bring my tap shoes so Gregory could autograph them after the performance. The performance was a formal affair, so I spent the remainder of the day getting ready, deciding to wear a black evening dress and, of course, red lipstick.

At 7:30 p.m., I walked across the street decked out in my formal attire, with my tap shoes in a bag thrown over my shoulder. From my seat, I marveled at the enormous beautiful theater with at least two thousand seats, all filled with an audience anxiously awaiting Gregory's show. Finally, it was time. Gregory burst onto the stage, singing in his smooth voice, accompanied by many talented musicians joining forces in the song, "Rhythm Is Gonna Get You." The show progressed flawlessly, and was a huge success.

Toward the end of the show Gregory asked the audience, "Are there any tap dancers out there?" and a few voices yelled back, "Yeah!"

"Come on up," Gregory said. I grabbed my tap shoes, trying not to step on others' toes while exiting the row of seats. Only four brave souls walked up the steps to the stage to join Gregory and his band. I kept wondering why Gregory wanted to autograph our tap shoes in front of the audience instead of after the show.

"Put your shoes on, and let's get to work," Gregory laughed. Feeling insecure, I naively thought I would get an autograph and head back to my seat, but as I tied my tap shoes, it became apparent that there was a special reason why I was asked to bring them to the theater.

Our group of four did a little back and forth with Gregory much like a mini-tap class on stage. Next, he invited us to give the audience a sample of our own improvisation. One person backed down, the second froze until Gregory came to her rescue, and the third blazed a trail of impressive steps on the stage floor. Now, it was my turn.

I walked to center stage, and felt the intense heat from the stage lights. I was both ecstatic and nervous to be on the stage with Gregory. I took a deep breath as my feet began to sing a familiar rhythm—putting me in a deep, soulful comfort zone. It was my survival rhythm, one that I often danced to release my soul, and to feel alive during the many years of abuse. My smile was genuine, and I felt good. The audience clapped loudly.

The improvisation session was over, and the other dancers and I started to leave the stage to head back to our seats. As I passed Gregory, he gently grabbed my hand, whispering, "Deb, I just wanted you to see that in your life you are capable of doing things on your own. I know you can." At that magical moment, Gregory gave me the gift of confidence, the first building block to reassemble me.

After Gregory's performance, his manager and I headed to the after-party in Gregory's hotel suite near the theater. Guests included his band members and several others associated with his show. We were treated to lavish food trays, wine, and great conversation. Gregory was deep in conversation with his manager when we heard a loud knock at the door. He politely asked if I would open it so he could continue with his conversation. I happily obliged and flung open the door to see a vision that made me blink a few times. There, in complete grandeur, stood the iconic singer, Harry Belafonte.

"Hi, Harry!" was about all I could muster to say in my star-struck coma.

Gregory rushed over to greet Harry, introducing me as, "A rose ready to bloom."

Over the next several years, Gregory and I stayed in touch through my letters to update him on the progress of my studio, an occasional telephone call, or actually traveling to New York to study with him or to see him in a show or receiving an award. He made sure that at least once a year I was able to take a class from him or to see him perform.

Several times it seemed his schedule would allow time for him to visit Heartbeat, but something in his active schedule would intervene. He always let me know that he was trying to make it happen, but in his profession a person is often pulled in a million directions at once. Gregory never charged me for any of the tap classes that I had taken from him. And for every show, a complimentary ticket was waiting for me at the box office. The essence of Gregory touched the tap dance community worldwide.

Miracles Happen

Now, getting back to the fall of 1996, in addition to meeting Gregory, I was able to connect with a banker, Tim, who was willing to help me finance my studio. I taught dance to his daughters for a few years, and never knew his profession until one day when he overheard me talking to another parent about my desire to build a performing arts center.

"Deb, stop in my office on Monday. You do not have to convince me about the wonderful effect you have on the lives of your students, because I have seen you in action with my own daughters. You're a great teacher, and I like your vision," Tim remarked.

Tim was the fifteenth banker I had talked to—apparently my magic number. I dropped off my business plan at his office on Monday, and within a month, after a long application process, I had a banker and the Small Business Administration willing to work with me.

"You are selling your home to help finance your dream, and that tells me you want it to succeed. You are definitely showing commitment," he added.

Prior to this, one banker after another had turned down my loan application because businesses in the arts were considered too risky. My meetings with the bankers always ended with, "We're sorry we cannot help you. By the way, your business plan is one of the best and most comprehensive I've seen. Who prepared this for you?"

"I did," I responded, after which the look on the bankers' faces said, "You're kidding me, right?"

One banker actually blurted, "You have three strikes against you; you want a loan for a risky business, you are female, and you are divorced." Another banker said he would try really hard to help me qualify for a loan on the condition that I would date him. Immediately I marched out of his office. It became very tiresome to have to put double the effort into everything to prove that I was not a ditsy blonde dancer, and, unlike the scarecrow in the *Wizard of Oz*, I really had a brain.

Now in November 1996, my long "to-do" list became even longer. I had to quickly find and buy a piece of property for the building, and have soil, water, and environmental tests done. My plan required city council, city planner, and zoning approval. To qualify for the bank loan, I had to go in for a medical exam in order to get life insurance. Endless forms needed to be filled out, and questions answered. My friend, Barry, and his architectural firm had completed the blueprints and, through a bidding process, singled out a construction company for the job.

The odometer reading of my car increased substantially in my quest to find the right piece of land. One day while I was running errands, my eye caught a tiny handmade "For Sale" sign on a piece of land that I had not noticed before. Even better, it was located in a prime section of the business district in Apple Valley. I parked my car and carefully walked through tall grass to the center of the lot. Majestic trees lined the rear of the property, and I peeked through to a lovely pond filled with geese planning flight details for their migration south for the winter. Just then, a gust of wind rustled the leaves, and I heard the chatter of angels everywhere, like the background noise of another class reunion. Maybe it was a reunion of all the ancestors that came before me. Closing my eyes, I was immediately transported back to my grandma's farm. The warm Indian summer sun cast a comforting and reassuring glow on the land.

I sat cross-legged in the center of the lot and breathed slowly to inhale everything that this piece of earth was trying to tell me. I reached down and grabbed a handful of the rich black soil.

"This is it," I said out loud. I stretched out on my back and stared at the sky. At that moment, a cloud formation in the shape of angel wings momentarily hovered over me before it gently sailed on.

As I lay in an altered state on the land, I heard the screech of tires, followed by a car door slamming. Pounding footsteps got louder as a gasping young man ran up to me.

"Lady, are you okay?"

"Never been better," I replied. "I'm pretending I'm a building." The young man walked away, perplexed.

I drove home like a crazed race car driver to call the realtor who was helping me sell my house.

"John, I've found a piece of land for Heartbeat. Please come over right away." On November 2, I made a down payment. The seller agreed to hold the land for me, contingent on the sale of my house. Also, I would have to close on the property no later than July 31, 1997.

A Ceremonial Respite

Time marched along at a turtle's pace. Completing mountains of paperwork for the loan approval was coupled with endless weeks hoping my house would sell. The home market was not good, and on top of that, I did not have much negotiation wiggle room because I had to net a certain amount to qualify for the mortgage loan.

To get a brief break from the doldrums of trying to sell my home, I decided it was time to take Kristin on the Caribbean cruise that I had promised her to celebrate our freedom and survival. In addition, as part of our healing process, we planned to have a secret ceremony one night on the ship, and throw court documents overboard that listed all of the instances of abuse we had suffered.

On January 14, 1997, Patty flew in from California to join us on the cruise, a much needed respite from Minnesota's long winter. The cruise was just what the doctor ordered: sunshine, beautiful scenery, and hours of laughter. On the last night, while the ship was midway between Aruba and San Juan, we decided we were in the perfect location for our secret ceremony.

As planned, Kristin and I had brought copies of the court affidavits, and proceeded to tear the documents into little pieces before we left our cabin. Next, we'd throw the court document confetti overboard to sink into the ocean—never to be seen again. Patty grabbed a bottle of champagne from our cabin, and I grabbed the envelope containing the confetti, and at 2:00 a.m., the three of us gleefully strutted off to the ship's stern.

Frantically I began to rip open the envelope. A black, velvet sky diamond-studded with millions of stars was the ceremony's backdrop. Moonlight served as the spotlight for our secret endeavor.

"Here we go," I said as Kristin and I held overflowing fistfuls of nightmarish memories.

"Wait!" Patty yelled, "I want to get a picture of this moment. I'm so proud of both of you. On the count three, let them go." Her camera captured forever us flinging the horrors of the past upward.

Hundreds of tiny shreds of paper flew into the air and lit up like more stars against the dark sky. Unfortunately, a mighty ocean breeze spit them right back at us. Covered in confetti, we were aghast.

"Well, that didn't work," I blurted matter-of-factly.

Quickly, we gathered the pieces and shoved them back into the envelope, this time hoping the envelope's weight would help us accomplish our mission. Once again the stage was set.

"One, two, three," we yelled. Patty's camera flashed as the envelope departed forever to its burial at sea.

"Champagne, anyone?" Patty laughed.

From the deck above us, a ship's officer yelled, "What are you doing down there? What did you throw overboard?"

We felt like kids who had just been caught with their hands in a cookie jar. Before I could explain, Patty looked up at him and yelled, "We just received the bill for our cabin, and don't want to pay it—so we threw it away." The three of us toasted a new life and gulped down our glasses of bubbly.

Moving On

When I returned home from the cruise, I sat down and studied my calendar to get a realistic grasp of how little time remained to try to sell my house— now on the market for almost one year. Each day my dream of the studio became fainter. February, March, April, and May plodded along. On June 1, 1997, I was served with legal papers from the owner of the property that I wanted to purchase for my studio. Basically it said that I had until June 30 to buy the property or it would be sold to a higher bidder. *Someone else* wanted my land. Even if my house sold today, there might still be contingencies. I had the blues—and the blues never felt so bad.

My logical mind told me to just give up and get my earnest money back from the down payment on the land, but my passionate heart told me not to give up hope.

One week later, while I was busy housecleaning, I received a call from my realtor.

"Are you sitting down, Deb?"

"I know my dream is pretty dim right now. Should we just take the 'For Sale' sign out of the yard?" I said, anticipating that he would lecture me to call it quits.

"Yes, that would be a good idea, because your home is no longer for sale. We just received a purchase agreement from a couple who is paying your asking price in cash, and they need to close on the house no later than June 30!" John's voice sang into the phone.

"Wow! My dream is coming true!" I couldn't even begin to count the number of angels dancing around me at that moment.

Three weeks was a very short time in which to sell my furniture and all of my belongings to put toward the studio's construction costs, and I had to search for a place to live that would allow me to have Misha. On June 30 at 10:30 a.m., I closed on the sale of my home, and four hours later, I closed on the purchase of the land for my studio. It literally was the very last day before I would have lost the piece of land to someone who had offered to pay double my offer. The property's seller was not happy at the closing because he believed that I was in a very hopeless situation, and would certainly have to withdraw from purchasing the land. Another building block of me had been planted firmly into place: Perseverance.

Within three weeks, thanks to the help of many friends, my belongings were sold and anything remaining was placed in storage. Moving out of the house was a bittersweet moment because I was proud of the fact that I had maintained it on my own, and in the past few years had developed many new memories there. The house, however, had closets full of many horrible memories. It was time to leave them behind. Those were my caterpillar years, and I was now morphing into my cocoon phase.

As I drove away from the house for the last time, I headed down the very same street on which I had fled for my life that rainy April night five years prior. I drove past the cluster of bushes that I had hidden behind when I believed that I would be shot—and at that point, realized that I did not know that woman anymore. That scared, frightened woman in a nightgown was fading away, and a new woman was emerging. I knew that the layers of the cocoon would peel away the day construction began, and at that moment, a magnificent butterfly would be set free.

My plan was to find a place to live until the studio was built, and fashion a temporary living arrangement for me in the studio until I could afford to move back into a home—hopefully in about six months. The only temporary living situation I could afford was a small hotel near the building site. The main attraction to this hotel was that the manager allowed Misha to stay in my room while I was at my day job in the human resources department of an insurance company.

I could not sleep very well during the first few weeks, due to the noises inherent in a hotel: children running up and down corridors, televisions and vacuums blaring, the tap, tap, tap on the door from the housekeepers, and elevator bells. At least once a week I was awakened from a deep sleep by a fire alarm pulled by pranksters, and on one occasion, the alarm was real, and I awoke to firemen banging on my door to usher me outside in my nightgown. Luckily, the fire did not affect my wing of the hotel. After a month at the hotel, cracks in my cocoon were beginning to appear. Could these be from a restless butterfly? The Phoenix had risen; the butterfly was emerging.

The Dream Manifests

I truly believe it was God's gift of dance that brought Kristin and me to the triumphant place of personal and career success. He gave us the gift, and it was up to us to know what to do with it. I was also blessed with parents who nurtured my interest in dance. I put on my first dance shoes when I was four years old, as did Kristin. Dance saved us from succumbing completely to Richard's abuse, and gave us the ability to connect with and feed our souls. Stepping into a dance studio and teaching dance gave us a feeling of being safe. In this sanctuary we felt worthwhile, whole, and pretty. It kept us going and gave us purpose, and we hung onto it with our lives. During those violent years, I would put on my tap shoes every night because they made me feel alive. I could pound out my frustration, and momentarily awaken from the paralysis of fear. Tap dance became my voice—a voice that no matter how hard Richard tried, he could not silence.

For Kristin, dance gave her a release for her creative intellect. She was obviously very much at home in the studio and on stage. She explains that, in her years at the university, dance was a way for her to express the fear and rage that had built up since her childhood. She purged the darkness inside her and proceeded to study women's mythology, in addition to dance. This opened a world that also helped her heal. Rather than being cowed by the constant abuse when it was happening, she would simply disengage from this man in her home. She no longer thought of him as her dad, but devised clever ways of getting around the abuse and its effects. Kristin concluded that her dad just did not have it in him to be a kind person.

As a teen, she began to study the mythology of the goddesses, which helped her more deeply understand the strength a woman could demonstrate in the face of tribulation—something she had already experienced. When Kristin founded her own modern dance company, she chose the name, Vox Medusa, in honor of the goddess, Medusa, who had been so misunderstood.

Expanding her dance theater work studies in her mid-twenties, she adopted the elements of fire, earth, air, and water represented by the goddesses Kali, Freya, Isis, and Aphrodite, respectively, and, in fact, decided to change her last name to Freya. In Norwegian mythology, Freya is the goddess of death and rebirth. Taking on the mindset of the goddess, expressed through the medium of dance, helped give Kristin the strength to continue to overcome her childhood abuse. Maybe by coincidence, or pure premonition, it was a Nordic goddess that I envisioned Kristin as on that crisp November day when she was born.

From the beginning, we both responded to our passion for dance, and we possessed natural gifts as performers, instructors, and choreographers.

And now that we were free of my ex-husband and the abuse, we were even more inspired to devote our whole lives to dance, and to create something that would give other victims of abuse, especially women and children, the courage and the tools to survive and thrive. Our choreography changed noticeably by becoming less confined, and instead it invoked, evoked, and provoked passion.

Doubters and Believers

After the sale of my house and the purchase of the land where Heartbeat Studios would be built, the remainder of the summer was filled with more meetings with Barry, my architect friend, to secure last-minute permits, variances, and approvals from the city before construction could begin. I worked at top speed to get Heartbeat's administrative systems set up and registration materials prepared. I announced to my students that my house had sold, and that Heartbeat would be a reality. Working full-time, plus starting a business, was all-consuming, and it felt like I had to make an appointment to set aside time to sleep. I was running on pure adrenaline.

Mom was worried about the pace I was keeping, and insisted that I relax and attend a family gathering in our small hometown. My parents and I rode together for the three-hour drive to Madison, as we had so many times before during my childhood. I talked non-stop about the studio and my excitement for a new life. Dad was bursting with pride. Even though Mom was also proud, she expressed her concern that I was without a man in my life.

"Don't you ever get lonely?" she asked. Even though I knew she loved me and asked this out of concern, I quelled her anxiety by reminding her, "Mom, I felt more alone and abandoned while I was married. There is no match to the loneliness I felt back then." Now she would see that the person her daughter was meant to be was finally emerging, and her dream was about to come true.

"Do you think you will ever be able to forgive Richard?" was her next question. The ability to forgive, embedded since childhood, had been exhausted, temporarily or maybe permanently. The right to be angry, and stay angry as long as needed, was more important to me now, and at this point, I anticipated the end result will be that I'd have no feeling toward my ex-husband. No love, hate, sympathy, or forgiveness—just a black hole, void of any emotion.

A hot, dry spell vaporized the normal August humidity when we headed to Madison. Dust billowed and plumed behind our car like a rocket burner as we sped down the rolling gravel country road. I was anxious to see my many aunts, uncles, and cousins to tell them that dreams do come true. I was living proof. White church steeples and red barns still dotted the landscape—not many changes happen over time in this part of the world. A crowd had already assembled at the family gathering, and I paused to inhale the aroma of honest-to-goodness home-cooked food. Living in the hotel meant that I had to eat in restaurants more than I should, and in short order, restaurant food lost its charm.

As I parked the car, Dad asked, "Deb, I'd like to be the one to tell everyone about the studio. Is that okay?"

"Of course," I laughed. He was in such poor health, and his showing pride in me brought great pleasure to both of us. Dad and I eventually caught up with Mom and the other family members. Dad said he really admired my ability to take an enormous risk to pursue an enormous dream.

"It shows you have gumption," he beamed.

Near the door, a distant cousin ran past, yelling, "Deb, you're young enough so there is still hope for you. Don't worry; you'll marry again someday."

My parents saw how exasperated I looked, and Mom said, "Chin up, Deb. I can tell now that this is going to feel like a very long day for you, so don't worry; we'll head back home earlier than planned."

Rather than stressing about the untimely comment, I realized that perhaps none of our extended family knew all of the details of my marriage. They could not yet understand how far I had come from whimpering behind a bush on a rainy April night to opening my own performing arts school. Shortly, I would own a commercial building—and parking lot.

Shadows in the Sunlight

When the word first got out about my endeavor, some people thought I was crazy and irresponsible to risk so much for what was often termed "a silly dream." I was bombarded with many patronizing comments of, "Oh, good for you, Deb. You just keep working at it." Those remarks quickly changed to, "Wow, I didn't know you had it in you," along with an assortment of other disbelieving remarks.

It is often said that when people succeed in pursuit of a dream or a passion, they do not change—the people around them do. To paraphrase an old Chinese proverb, *"Shadows are always darkest where the sun is brightest."* Unfortunately, a handful of acquaintances revealed an unpleasant side of their nature as the studio construction became imminent. Their relentless insistence to be co-owners ruined our relationships. They were also unsuccessful in their attempt to sabotage my student base by spreading disparaging and skeptical comments about my ability to run a business.

Whenever I encountered these disappointing situations, rather than recoiling in hurt, my new reaction was to analyze the situation and learn from it. A new building block was emerging—turning a negative into a positive.

Love is in the Air

By this time, a year had passed since Kristin began dating a strapping young man who would eventually become her husband. Paul (another Aries like my dad) was strikingly handsome and towered at six foot three. His perfectly tossed dark hair, intense brown eyes, and warm smile made it seem that he was peeled off the pages of a men's fashion magazine. What was the most impressive about Paul was his intellect and sincere interest in Kristin's passion for dance.

They met quite by accident in May 1996, in a situation where one might say fireworks were flying in opposite directions. It was a sunny Sunday afternoon when Kristin and her friend, Debra, were at work, moving Debra's things from the apartment she had lived in with her soon-to-be-ex-boyfriend. At the same time, it just so happened that the soon-to-be-ex-boyfriend called his friend, Paul, to help in the moving-out process on his behalf.

Kristin and Paul met and fell in love at the same time that their good friends were falling out of love. While sparks flew like daggers between the breakup couple, Cupid's arrow zinged Kristin and Paul. The day ended with the breakup couple still arguing over the fate of their CDs, while Kristin and Paul sealed the beginning of their relationship with numerous kisses in the back of a moving van.

Birth of a Butterfly

September 1, 1997 was a momentous day. I closed on the mortgage for my studio, and was informed that construction would begin on September 9, exactly a year from the date of Gregory Hines' visit. Knowing that a construction worker's day starts at the crack of dawn, I woke up at 4:30 a.m. and drove to the lot where Heartbeat would be built. I wanted to be there the exact moment the first scoop of earth was taken for the birth of Heartbeat. I parked my car and walked to the center of the lot. Cool dewdrops covered my shoes, and I stopped to inhale the fresh intoxicating air of the time when summer is almost gone, and fall is almost here.

I faced east and waited for the sun. The world is quiet in those early hours until the faint glow of a new day awakens birds from their slumber. Sitting cross-legged on my land, I fixed my gaze to the rising sun, and let its warmth soak into my bones. My soul was being fed the nourishment it needed to at last break free from the cocoon. Suddenly, far off in the distance, I could hear the rumble and roar of husky diesel engines approaching. Minutes later, huge silhouettes of semi-trucks hauling heavy-duty equipment were cast against the fire-gold sun. The throaty engines shifted to a deeper growl as the trucks turned the street corner to witness a mighty butterfly spreading her wings.

The pain of being birthed from the cocoon was excruciating, as a thousand cries from a horrific past turned into cries of a new life born. My tears fell to the ground and sparkled with the morning dew while my wings opened wide, spreading across the length of my land. The earth vibrated beneath me as the semi-trucks drew near, and I sprang to my feet to gasp my first breath as a newborn.

"I am a survivor!" I cried out in splendor. Another building block was in place: Hope.

Four semi-trucks lined the street, and the chatter of construction workers accompanied the creaks, clanks, and moans of equipment being unloaded. I begged one of the workers, "Please let me know when you are about to take the first scoop of earth, because I want to take a photograph of that moment."

His eyes squinted from the bright morning sun as he sipped his coffee. He paused, "Who are you?"

"This is my building that you are constructing, and as you set each block into place you are helping rebuild me!"

He took another sip of coffee and peered at me over the rim of his thermos.

"It's a long story. I'll explain later," I added.

At 7:15 a.m., the first scoop of earth was moved for Heartbeat. I snapped some photos, ran quickly to my car, and headed into work. From that morning on, my daily routine included an early-morning stop at the site to greet the construction workers, bring them freshly baked pastries from the corner coffee shop, snap another photo of their progress, and bid them good day as I headed to work. In a few days, they accepted me as one of their crew.

One day the lead construction worker took me aside saying, "We've never met anyone like you before; you're always so cheerful. In this business we have to deal with some bad tempers, and I want you to know that we are making sure we do an especially good job on your building."

And they did!

The Celebration

A few weeks into the construction, on October 5, 1997, an official groundbreaking ceremony was held on a perfectly clear and warm fall day, attended by over one hundred dancers, friends, family members, construction workers, and city officials.

Many caring friends made supportive and hopeful speeches. My attorney, Don, announced to the crowd that he was reminded of the play, *Finian's*

Rainbow, and its main character, Susan, who could only communicate through dance until she uttered her first words, "I love you."

He continued, "The return of hope is the undertaking of a hopeful act, and Heartbeat is Deb's hopeful act. We live in the land of the free and the home of the brave, and Deb is free; Deb is brave; Deb is back."

A pastor from my church led us in prayer, and blessed Heartbeat and its future. My friend, Mary, exclaimed, "Deb is following her dream. She has given many of us the gift of dance, and because of that, we are following the dream with her."

A dozen high school students sang hopeful tunes as three Air Force jets coincidentally flew over at that exact moment. Clusters of pink balloons in the shapes of hearts and ballet slippers lined the piles of bricks, lumber, and construction equipment. The construction company owner handed shovels adorned with pink bows to Kristin and me, and as we turned over another scoop of earth, love, cheers, and applause surrounded us.

Both Kristin and I struggled to give speeches of thanks, but couldn't get past our tears of joy. Through those tears I promised, "Heartbeat will be a studio where dancers feel good about themselves. We will give them not only the ability to dream, but also the skills to pursue those dreams. It is out of love for my students and my love of dance that Heartbeat is built. There was a flame inside me that helped me get through those terrifying years, and now I know that flame was dance. Heartbeat is now the flame that I hope will launch a thousand dreams."

A large bold and beautiful sign announcing, "Future home of Heartbeat Studios—Opening January 5, 1998" now replaced the small "For Sale" sign once staked in the corner of the lot.

The Best Christmas Ever

Weeks passed quickly, and it was time for Christmas. This year the holiday season would be particularly happy because the studio was in its final construction phase, with a promised completion date of January 3 and an opening date of January 5.

Christmas Eve, Kristin and I were bubbling with energy in anticipation of the grand opening of Heartbeat. It was easy for my parents and siblings to shop for us that year as we discovered office supplies, desk sets, briefcases, desk lamps and more, wrapped in festive paper and bows. Dad gave me a crystal paperweight engraved, *"Some people make the world special just by being in it."* Mom gave me an angel figurine that would be one of many angels finding a home in the studio over the years.

My family's tradition was to spend Christmas Eve together, and always Christmas Day was spent with our respective in-laws. I no longer had in-laws, so Christmas Day became a day for me to spend quiet time alone. For a few years after my divorce, it was hard to be by myself on Christmas Day, but I began to look forward to having that day to privately reflect and give thanks.

This particular year on Christmas Day, I received a surprise call from Judy, a co-worker at my insurance company day job.

"Deb, I know you are sitting alone in your humble hotel-home, and I am on my way to pick up you and Misha for a picnic."

Just to clarify the situation, I reminded Judy that there was snow on the ground.

"Doesn't matter," she said.

About twenty minutes later, Judy arrived at the hotel. She did, indeed, have a picnic basket in her car.

"Don't worry about the snow," she giggled. "I made cold-cut sandwiches, and we won't have to be concerned about the champagne losing its chill."

A few minutes later we pulled up to my studio, and I thought she had just wanted to take a peek inside. I unlocked the door to show her the studio and lobby areas, still full of doors and other woodwork yet to be installed, as well as scatterings of scaffolding, ladders, and paint cans. The carpeting had not been installed, and the wood flooring had not been polycoated. Sawdust was everywhere, along with the aromatic scent of cut wood; everything smelled new and fresh—definitely a work in progress.

"Wait here a minute," she said and ran outside to retrieve the picnic basket from her car. Within minutes she had a red-and-white checkered tablecloth spread out in the middle of the studio floor, a vase full of red poinsettias, three lit candles, a bottle of champagne, and an abundant assortment of deli food arranged on lovely serving platters. One place setting was a dish full of dog treats for Misha. She poured champagne into paper cups, and raised hers with a cheerful toast, "Merry Christmas and a Happy New Life!" A delightful Misha dashed around the studio.

Misha and I spent New Year's Eve watching television in our small hotel room. After getting my fill of festivities from around the world, I decided to take us for a midnight walk through the new blanket of glistening snow. Heading toward the studio, it seemed as if we were the only creatures on earth. Steam from our breath sparkled as it froze before it twinkled away. The only sound we heard was the crunch of my boots pressing into the snow. Along the way, I imagined hearing a choir of young voices as children entered the studio to begin their dance lessons. I imagined the synergy of music in the lobbies—classical, jazz, modern, voices singing, pianos playing, actors reciting, and tap shoes punctuating every beat. The studio would have a life of its own in just a few days.

Moonlight illuminated the front of my studio, providing just enough brightness through the large windows so I did not have to turn on the lights when we entered. We meandered slowly through the building to check out every detail, and came to rest by the large rear windows. We stood motionless for several minutes, gazing at the frozen pond. Suddenly, I fell to my knees and sobbed—my dream finally had a home. I held Misha close to me as a multitude of angels filled the studio to bless... and to welcome. I could feel their presence and their love, and they are still there to this day, protectively watching and joyfully laughing.

On January 3, 1998, I met with Barry and the city building inspector for Heartbeat's final inspection. The front windows were decorated with an assortment of inspection notices for various phases of the construction, and all were officially approved and signed by the inspector. Our anticipation of passing with flying colors came to an abrupt halt when the inspector said, "You cannot open for business until the men's restroom is widened by two inches. There is not enough room for a wheelchair to maneuver."

Barry retorted, "Why didn't you say this at the last inspection when it would have been easier to correct? The restrooms meet Minnesota building code, and Deb has classes scheduled to start day after tomorrow!"

The inspector peered over his glasses to correct Barry, "Apple Valley's codes are different. This has to be fixed, so call me when you are ready. As of now, Heartbeat cannot open on the fifth." With that, the inspector walked away.

I lamented, "Barry, what am I going to do? The dancers have already paid for their classes, and how am I going to let everyone know? This is unfair; he should have mentioned this to us last inspection!"

Barry informed me that it was useless to try to argue with the inspector, and that his order meant that all of the restroom's plumbing, ceramic tile work, wall framing, sheetrock, and painting would have to be worked on steadily over the next 24 hours to make sure that Heartbeat could open on the fifth. We would also need another visit from the building inspector.

"Who pays for this?" I asked.

"You do, unfortunately. This correction would have cost nothing extra if the inspector had brought this two-inch change up earlier."

Overhearing our conversation, the construction company foreman walked over and said, "Don't worry. I'll find a crew who will get it done on time for you. You can sleep tonight knowing that we'll get it done." On January 4 at 4:00 p.m., Heartbeat passed its final inspection.

We Have a Pulse

Early in the day on January 5, 1998, I hung a heart-shaped chime on Heartbeat's door to announce the arrival of every dancer. Heartbeat's design for the nearly 6,000-square-foot space was welcoming, and our intention was to make anyone entering immediately feel at home. The richness of the birch and maple reception desk in the lobby beckoned visitors. The interior of the building had the appearance of a soft-contemporary loft home with exposed ductwork that lined the perimeter of the fourteen-foot-high ceilings like a silver necklace. The south wall had three eight-foot square picture windows that overlooked the city's business district. The north wall had four picture windows that overlooked a lush tree-lined pond. The east wall had ninety feet of glorious mirrors, with fourteen small glass block windows above them that sparkled like diamonds in the morning sun. The west wall was lined with display boards and a photo gallery. The main event, however, was the huge expanse of maple wood dance floor, polished like glass, in each studio room—a dancer's dream!

Heartbeat's lobbies were furnished with comfortable chairs and sofas, some of which I had salvaged from my home. The ladies' restroom came equipped with a shower, and the teachers' lounge had a small refrigerator and microwave oven. Observation windows in the lobbies and doorways allowed parents to enjoy the classes in progress. A thick acoustic folding wall divided the two dance studios, and opened to create a massive dance space for master classes and in-house performances.

The building's exterior was simple and unassuming: a black shingle A-frame roof with terra cotta-tinted stucco siding. The building looked grand positioned among the thick clusters of mature oak, maple, pine, and apple trees that stood watch over rows of Japanese evergreens and lilac shrubbery. During the warm months, an assortment of burgeoning daylilies and coral bells welcomed all who entered.

From a distance, Heartbeat resembled a precious citrine jewel, cradled in dark green foliage. It is said that the citrine promotes creativity and helps personal clarity; it is also Kristin's birthstone—an observation of coincidence that probably only the woman who gave birth to both would appreciate. Modest as the exterior of Heartbeat seemed, the vastness and beauty of the interior made you pause as you entered.

Kristin met me at the studio to set up the front desk and do final decorating touch-ups. At 4:00 p.m. the door chimes began to ring—and didn't stop. Dancer after dancer filed into the studio accompanied by their smiling parents. Kristin and I helped new students enroll, and directed them to the appropriate studio room. Both lobbies were humming with the excitement. At the stroke of 4:30 p.m., music flowed as Kristin taught Heartbeat's first dance class. Another building block of me emerged: Pride.

I was blessed to be able to watch my first baby teaching dance in the heart of my second baby, and I deeply loved them both. All of the terror of the past vanished at that moment, and I felt fulfilled as I admired my daughter and her flawless talent. We were survivors, and we now had a new, large family comprising talented teachers, dancers, and their parents. Heartbeat had come to life. It was indeed a special place with its own strong pulse.

At 4:45 p.m., I began teaching my first class at Heartbeat, to four-year-olds eager to become ballerinas. A wide grin flashed across my face as I observed fourteen bodies looking like a perfect row of newly hatched little chicks with their round tummies and short legs. They exuded incredible innocence, dressed in pink leotards and tights, with ribbons adorning their hair. Their twinkling eyes beamed their dreams to be stars someday, and I was honored to help them on their journey. I looked forward to the responsibility, as their dance teacher, to be another parent to them to guide the growth of their self-esteem and confidence. The joy of dance is like no other, and once it is in your system, it becomes an integral part of you, no different than your arms or legs.

I could hardly control my emotions on Heartbeat's first day. There were moments when I felt I was walking around in a surreal world, and other moments when tears of joy flowed without warning. At the end of my first class, one little dancer brought me back to my newfound purpose in life when she whispered in my ear, "Miss Deb, thank you for making me feel pretty today!"

As she cheerfully skipped out of the studio, I softly whispered, "Thank you for making me feel pretty, too." Deep in my soul I knew that I had to look at the years of violence and emotional abuse as the universe's training ground for me to be able to help others develop healthy self-esteem and self-worth. I could put this into perspective in many ways; yet I chose to believe that I had to know what it was like not to have it, in order to nurture it in them.

Living in the Studio

When Heartbeat opened, I moved from the hotel into the studio because all I had left was $200. I had poured all my financial resources into the construction costs. Yes, my life was changing for the better, but obviously I had a little ways to go before I would have my own place to live. Living in the studio provided many unforeseen humorous, and sometimes frightening, experiences, and a period where privacy was nonexistent. Here are a few of the realities of the situation: a laundromat was two blocks away. I used the studio's shower, microwave oven, and refrigerator. I stockpiled paper plates, cups, bowls, and basic utensils for the minimal amount of cooking I would be able to do under the circumstances, and I washed dishes in the restroom sinks. One of the storage cabinets became my makeshift closet, and cardboard boxes became my dresser.

It took several weeks to figure out my sleeping arrangement. My office was too small for a hide-a-bed sofa, so I slept on the lobby sofa until my back started to ache. I tried sleeping on a folding chaise lounge, but it would not recline perfectly flat. An inflatable air mattress proved to be too cold on the floor, and would often deflate during the night. I ended up placing a thick piece of plywood under the sofa cushions to support my back; however, it was a love seat, and not long enough for me to completely stretch out.

For that, and other reasons, a good night's sleep was rare. The last people leaving the studio for the evening, most often not until 10:30 p.m., were the singing instructor's adult students. When I locked the door after they left, the studio immediately transformed, in my mind, to my home in order to feel like I was not always at work. I would clean the building, catch up on bookwork, go to the laundromat, or work on choreography. Not having a kitchen was the worst thing. Being a gourmet cook, I desperately missed my personal "chemistry lab."

My usual bedtime was 1:00 a.m., and standard procedure was to cover the sofa with sheets and a comforter, call Misha from whichever studio he was playing in, and both of us would squirm about on the sofa until we found our sleeping position for the remainder of the night. To finish the nightly routine, I would set the alarm clock and hope that I would wake up before Karen, the piano teacher, arrived at 7:30 a.m. for early-morning students. More often than not, I would be startled awake by the sound of Karen unlocking the front door. Shifting into high gear, there would be a blur of sheets and blankets snatched from the sofa as Misha and I made a dash for the ladies' restroom, where I would shower and get ready for the day. Six hours of sleep each night was about it.

I had to keep my living arrangement as confidential as possible, concerned that I would be evicted by the city. Only my family, friends, and Heartbeat's teaching staff knew my whereabouts. I became adept at warding off curious people, including the local police. I was essentially homeless, and became diligent in trying to keep a roof over my head. One evening, shortly after I moved into the studio, loud knocking on the front door at 3:00 a.m. awakened me. I tiptoed to the window and saw a police car in the parking lot. Quickly, I grabbed a mop and pail before I answered the door.

"Hello, officer. May I help you?" I asked.

Looking around, he replied, "Is there any reason you are here at this hour?"

"Sure, I'm the cleaning crew, and the owner is really fussy about keeping the place spotless."

I really was telling him the truth. A few weeks later another police officer stopped by at 2:00 a.m., and I told him that I was the owner but was putting in long hours on some bookwork. After that, I parked my car behind the dumpster at the rear of the building to make it appear that no one was in the studio.

Again, a few weeks later, a third police officer stopped by during the day. I recognized him as the person who finally put me in touch with the women's shelter when my ex-husband had threatened me with a gun.

"Deb, how are you doing? I'm just making a friendly stop. I often think about you and heard that you built this place. It is incredible! How's business?"

"Things seem to be off to a good start, and I want to thank you for helping me. You are actually the first person who listened to me, and pointed me in the right direction to get help."

The officer whispered, "I suspect that you are living here, and I don't want you to worry. I want to confirm that you do live here so if we see the building on fire, or some other emergency happening, we know there is a person in the building who needs rescuing. It's for your safety."

After that wonderful conversation, I slept much more calmly. I was committed to my dream and, considering what I had been through for so long, it wasn't nearly as dangerous as what my daughter and I had survived.

Misha and I moved into the studio expecting to be there for no more than six months, but ended up living there for three years before I felt financially able to move out. The main advantage to living in the studio was that I had shelter, which in turn kept me off Heartbeat's payroll as I tried to establish solid financial ground for Heartbeat before my own.

And—I was *never* late for work. I used a post office box number for my personal address to avoid disclosing my place of residence to anyone who may have the authority to evict me. When I tried to vote during the next presidential election, I found out that you couldn't give a post office box number as your address when you are at the polls, so the voting officials sent me on my way. Whenever I became too sick to teach, I had to check into a hotel to recover because I had no private place to rest at the studio during the day.

My office had only enough electrical outlets to accommodate the refrigerator, microwave oven, computer, and other office equipment, so early in the morning I would plug the toaster or my clothes iron into an outlet in one of the dance studios. A few times I forgot to put the iron and toaster back into my office before young students arrived for dance class. They would ask me quite directly, "Why is there a clothes iron in the studio?" It was easy to come up with an excuse like, "Oh, I was ironing costumes." The presence of a toaster sitting on a stereo speaker was a little more difficult to explain, however.

Occasionally, some of the teachers would return to the studio late in the evening to retrieve something they had left behind and, forgetting that I lived there, would scare me out of my mind as they unlocked the front door and woke me from a deep sleep. My ferocious little guard dog, Misha, would simply run up to them and want to play.

One evening was particularly scary when I woke to a repetitive whirring sound. The emergency exit door in the back studio had been propped open just a crack for ventilation by one of the teachers who forgot to shut it after classes ended for the evening. The glow of security lights illuminating through the door ajar became an attraction that a local high school boy took as an opportunity to see what was inside. Not knowing that I was asleep on the lobby sofa, he proceeded to take his bicycle into the building and ride in circles at high speed in the back studio. Waking up in terror, I don't know who screamed louder, me or the boy fleeing out the back door.

Severe weather in the summer months made life in the studio action-packed, to say the least. Minnesota is a tornado state, and living in the studio meant I had no basement to go to for shelter. Whenever severe-weather sirens blared, I would take Misha and hide in a restroom stall. Hail hitting the expansive roof sent echoes throughout the building, sounding like hundreds of machine guns. High winds made the roof trusses vibrate, creating eerie creaks and moans.

The first summer that I lived in the studio was particularly stormy. Late one afternoon, the pond behind the studio became a lake from pouring rain that brought the water level up to within four feet of the building. I watched as the overflow eventually surrounded the entire building. I was trapped on an island called Heartbeat. I called the police department, asking for help with sandbagging, but was informed that they did not provide that assistance. However, they would drop off a pile of sand and empty bags for me to fill. Kristin and a few of Heartbeat's teachers came to the rescue as we worked diligently to save our precious wood dance floors.

Living in the studio, and, for that matter, running a business, have challenges, to be sure. But I have gained the gift of putting challenges into perspective by looking back at the dark years when I had worse days as an abused wife. The trial was the best tool to groom me to face these challenges head on.

My Voice is Heard

As I settled into my new life at the studio, news about the domestic violence trial and my journey to build Heartbeat flowed in directions that I would never have imagined. During Heartbeat's first year, its story became a featured article in major local newspapers and television news reports. The *St. Paul Pioneer Press, Minneapolis Star Tribune,* and several smaller newspapers gave it the front page. The CBS affiliate television station, *WCCO Channel Four,* devoted their entire March 10, 1998 *Dimension Report* on the story behind Heartbeat and Gregory's visit, and again on September 25, 1998, when jazz singer, Bobby Caldwell, gave a mini-concert at Heartbeat to promote his new CD, *Love Shouldn't Hurt,* in regard to child abuse awareness. The local talk show, *The Minnesota Experience,* invited me to be a guest.

The late Senator Paul Wellstone and his wife, Sheila, contacted me to be a co-presenter at several domestic violence awareness rallies. In addition, a number of police departments, churches, colleges, medical and legal organizations, as well as women's groups, invited me to give presentations regarding violence in the home.

Among the groups and organizations, two proved to be the most challenging and rewarding. First were about a dozen men court-ordered to get counseling from a psychologist for their violent behavior toward their wives or girlfriends. Second was a group of immigrant women from the Middle East, who were raised in a culture where violence toward women was acceptable. After their initial resistance, both groups listened intently to what I had to say. Their questions and comments afterward made it apparent that they were taking a serious look at their circumstances.

An attorney in Don's office asked me to present my story to the State of Minnesota House Research Civil Law Committee and the State of Minnesota House of Representatives (House File No. 47, a bill for an act relating to civil actions, providing a cause of action for victims of domestic abuse, and proposing coding for new laws in Minnesota Statutes, chapter 611A), in her effort to have laws changed in Minnesota regarding domestic violence, including that domestic violence should be identified as a basic human rights violation. My words were heard, and aspects of the laws were changed.

Phone calls and emails arrived from women around the U.S. and Canada who wanted to congratulate me, or to get advice on how to get out of a violent relationship. A new responsibility had been placed in my hands, and I felt ready to work. I have a soft voice but my words are powerful, and they are the truth. Domestic violence *is* a crime against humanity.

As time progressed, more noted dance professionals visited Heartbeat. My friendship with Dianne was rock-solid, and I was honored that she was on our board of directors. Through her connection, I met other world-renowned tap dance sensations like Savion Glover, Jason Samuels-Smith, and Henry LeTang, to name just a few of the luminaries who graced Heartbeat's floor. Members of the Paul Taylor Dance Company, Alvin Ailey Dance Company, and the Broadway hit, *Fosse*, also took time from their busy schedules to teach at my studio. The students at Heartbeat were receiving an education in dance that they could have only dreamed of before.

Through our passion for dance, with a lot of support along the way, our dream of a dance studio had manifested. My next task was to take it global.

A Heartbeat Heard 'Round the World

After Heartbeat opened for business, I started an outreach effort. I had this passionate belief that dance is a universal language, and that we can gain much from sharing this art form with dancers in other countries. I emailed letters introducing Heartbeat to dance studios across Europe, explaining my desire to establish travel study and cultural exchange programs between my studio and theirs, and the benefits this would have in furthering the art of dance for our students.

In their responses, three studios stood out as like-minded in this endeavor, and I began to correspond regularly with El Timbal Studio in Barcelona, Spain; Encore Studio in Geneva, Switzerland; and On Stage Studio in Milan, Italy. After several months of getting to know each other via email, I was invited to visit them to both take and teach classes, and begin talks in earnest regarding relationships between our studios. With the supportive words from my dear dancer friend, Dianne, I began planning my solo trip to Europe, which would help another building block of me develop: An adventurous spirit.

Kristin's Wedding

At this point in their relationship, Kristin and Paul were also developing adventurous spirits in the local arts and entertainment community. The news media and public loved the multi-medium arts' parties and events they produced in order to give new artists venues to become better known. They had paid their dues in order to reach this level of admiration and deserved every minute of it. It was at one of these events, a special New Year's Eve arts' party, when Paul proposed to Kristin precisely at the stroke of midnight while the world advanced from 1998 to 1999.

Kristin's dance company, Vox Medusa, and the events she and Paul produced, formed a unique and natural synergy with Heartbeat in that there was an unending flow of talented dancers being trained at Heartbeat who were available to perform at their events. In turn, Vox Medusa comprised some of the best dancers in Minneapolis/St. Paul who, along with Kristin, were available to teach dance at Heartbeat. We found ourselves in frequent collaboration using our respective talents, and we spread our artistic wings beyond what we could have ever envisioned just a few years earlier. We were respected, a feeling that had seemed foreign to us because of my ex-husband's expertise in crumbling our self-esteem.

Kristin and Paul got married on September 25 in a ceremony that made the evening news. Television film crews lined the interior of First Avenue, the popular Minneapolis nightclub, to capture a wedding unlike any other. To make it even more unique, the entire ceremony would be danced. Kristin had choreographed her own wedding to emanate more passion than words could convey.

In honor of her newfound wings, Kristin chose a wedding gown design that leapt from the pages of a fairytale book. It was an elaborate fairy goddess-style gown in red and iridescent gold fabric, complete with sheer red butterfly wings. Her waist-length blonde hair was curled in ringlets that cradled a veil of cascading red rose buds. The bridesmaids wore gold iridescent gowns with gold butterfly wings, and rather than carry traditional flower bouquets, they held large glass mirrored balls that reflected light in every direction. Paul and the groomsmen wore floor-length tunic vests over their wide-legged silk pants. Paul wore red, and the groomsmen were in gold. All the men held lighted torches. The entire wedding party, even the justice of the peace who officiated, was barefoot with fancy henna designs painted on their hands and feet.

My elderly relatives were speechless, and thought it quite objectionable to have a wedding in such a place—that is, until the beautiful event transported all of us to a magical world that nobody wanted to leave. To start the wedding procession, a percussionist pounded huge conga drums in the rhythm of a human heartbeat. The bridesmaids and groomsmen, with their mirror balls sparkling and torches burning, danced down the aisles and onto the stage. Drum beats intensified as Kristin and Paul entered. The drum chorus was infectious, triggering the hearts of wedding guests to beat louder. Suddenly, the drums stilled as Kristin and Paul reached center stage. The justice of the peace broke the silence with words that made Kristin's and Paul's union official. As they kissed, flash-pots hurled sparks into the air while the wedding party and guests erupted into spontaneous cheering. Drums that I think could be heard on the moon pulsed again. My skeptical elderly relatives looked at me and said, "Uff da, this was great. Is this on video? I want to see it again."

In Pursuit of Cultural Exchange

A few weeks after the momentous wedding, hands finally reached across the Atlantic. On October 12, 1999, I packed my bags and headed to the airport to visit Guillem Alonso at the El Timbal Studio in Barcelona, and Peter and Maggie King at the Encore Studio in Geneva. The fruits of my labor had blossomed. I had never traveled alone before, and had only been on vacations typical of Midwesterners in the winter: Mexico and Caribbean cruises.

At the airport, Kristin gave me a big hug and kiss, and assured, "Mom, don't worry. I'll make sure things run smoothly at the studio while you are gone. Good luck and be safe."

Having read as much as I could about Spain and Switzerland, I wondered if they would be as beautiful as in the travel books. The first four hours of my flight were filled with lively conversation with passengers seated near me as I spoke fondly of my two children, Kristin and Heartbeat. I was the proud, confident parent of both, and had hopeful dreams of cultural exchange programs with studios overseas. I was having dreamy visions of Kristin and me teaching master classes and my students performing in a theater in Europe.

Hour five in the air brought on an unforeseen anxiety attack, with me wishing the pilot would turn the plane around and head back to Minneapolis. The fear was real, and I had a hard time breathing and keeping from shaking. An Italian gentleman seated next to me said, "Just breathe slowly, my dear. Everything will happen as you planned." He asked the flight attendant for another blanket and tucked it around my shoulders. I fell asleep and woke up when we landed in Amsterdam for the connecting flight to Barcelona. Feeling groggy, I gathered my carry-on bag and book, and followed the other passengers off the plane in a very obedient single-file line.

A vibrant multitude of languages greeted me as I tried to find someone who spoke English to help me with directions to the gate for my connecting flight. Amsterdam's airport is huge; that's all I can say. A classic deer-in-the-headlights look was plastered on my face for several minutes until I saw an information desk with signage in English. When I opened my mouth to ask for directions, nothing came out. Honest-to-goodness, worst-case-ever laryngitis had settled in somewhere over the Atlantic while I was sleeping. The two women behind the counter spoke very broken English, and I could not speak at all except for weird chirps and barks.

Out of desperation, I placed both of my hands around my neck, stuck out my tongue and swayed back and forth in an attempt to pantomime that I was sick, and could not talk. This feeble display only made them laugh, and made me look like I was trying to strangle myself. It finally dawned on me to simply show them my ticket, point to the gate number, and look puzzled. One of the women pulled out a map and highlighted the route. I curtsied gracefully and went on my way.

My connecting flight was at the opposite end of the Amsterdam airport, and I had one hour to get there. After a quick stop at the restroom, I grabbed some bottled water and hot tea, and made my way through shoulder-to-shoulder pedestrian traffic. Passengers were already boarding by the time I arrived at the gate. I settled into my seat next to two women from Amsterdam who were going to Barcelona for a holiday vacation. They spoke very good English, and tried to initiate a conversation with me. I did not want to seem rude by not answering them due to my laryngitis, but I was afraid of what strange sound would erupt if I tried to talk. After sipping the hot tea, I was able to emit a very deep and soft whispering voice if I spoke slowly.

"You sound so sexy," they kept saying. The same Italian gentleman from my earlier flight was seated in front of me and leaned over his seat to say, "Oh, you sound so sexy!" Next in line was a flight attendant who, upon asking me if I wanted anything to drink, said, "Oh, you sound so sexy!" A fellow from Greece seated behind me tapped me on the shoulder to ask me my name, which was followed by, "Oh, you sound so sexy!" And so went the remainder of my flight from Amsterdam to Barcelona.

Beautiful Barcelona

Barcelona and I fell in love the moment we met. The city is a haven for people in all genres of the arts, and its culture openly respects the artists. Never before had I been in a community where going to live theater is the norm (rather than watching television). Fortunately, my taxi driver spoke enough English to help me learn the Catalan language basics of "Please" and "Thank you" as we drove to the hotel. The Hotel Majestic lived up to its name, and when I walked into the lobby, it was as if I had been transported to an art deco movie set. After quickly checking in, I took a shower and put on a lovely dress that I had bought specifically for my first meeting with my email-dance pals in Barcelona. I called Guillem to let him know that I had arrived, and told him I already knew that I sounded sexy. After much laughter, he said to meet him in the lobby in one hour.

Guillem was a dark-haired, handsome young fellow with a lean dancer's body and a contagious smile. His tap dance partner, Roser, was pixie-cute with sparkles in her eyes. Immediately we started to talk about dance; it was as if we had known each other for years. Any feelings of anxiety or concern immediately disappeared. We wasted no time, heading right to the El Timbal Studio located in the Gothic part of Barcelona. The narrow streets and wrought-iron walkways made me feel like we were on the set of *Romeo and Juliet*. Grand cathedrals and ancient buildings lined the cityscape. Buildings and parks designed by the eccentric architect, Antoni Gaudi, decorated the city like charms on a bracelet.

We walked for several minutes through a labyrinth of streets too narrow for cars to drive through, and stopped to face a tall, thick dark wooden set of double doors with dinner-plate-size iron rings for handles. The doors creaked as they opened, and we stepped over a high threshold into a lush Spanish courtyard filled with exotic plants and palm trees. My eyes could not take in Barcelona's beauty fast enough. It was breathtaking—I longed to live here.

Guillem and Roser led me to the second floor, where I heard the familiar sounds of a tap dance class. One wall of the studio lobby was nearly floor-to-ceiling stained-glass panoramas. The studio floors were wide slats of wood that had darkened with age, and smelled of ancient varnish. Guillem introduced me to the teachers and administrative staff, and invited me to a tap jam later that evening.

"Tomorrow you should go on a bus tour of the city, because I do not have a car. And later in the evening, I have a surprise for you."

I strolled back to the hotel, guided by music of flamenco guitars along the way. The pulse and rhythm of the city were captivating. After I changed into my dance clothes, I leisurely walked under a canopy of tall Oriental plane trees lining Las Ramblas, the main boulevard. Artists set up shop along this enchanting thoroughfare: painters, dancers, musicians, poets, puppeteers, singers, sculptors, photographers, and more. It was a feast for the eyes and ears—and the soul.

A clearing in the distance drew my attention, and I picked up my pace to see what it was. My pace turned into a sprint propelled by the magnetism of something great—and I saw it in its splendid glory—the Mediterranean Sea. I kicked off my shoes and ran to the water's edge to let it lap at my feet. I never dreamed that someday I would be standing in this body of water rich in history and mythology. Looking out across the expanse of turquoise water, I tried to imagine Columbus sailing away in a tall ship to an unknown world. I tried to imagine the tall ships carrying traders and conquerors before his time. I closed my eyes and listened patiently to hear if any of their voices still echoed.

Wading along the shore, I let every drop of water touching my feet tell me its history. I wanted to absorb all of it, but it was time to head to the tap jam. I stopped along the way at a tapas restaurant for dinner, and became hooked on the taste of Spanish olive oil. To this day, the tasty Spanish gold is a staple in my diet.

Guillem's tap dance friends welcomed me with many hugs and kisses, and once introductions were completed, we traded tap dance steps. First I learned their style, and next they learned mine. I firmly believe an instinctive sense of camaraderie is born into every tap dancer worldwide. I knew I was doing something good for Heartbeat and its students. The travel study and cultural exchange program stands to be life-enriching at the least, and life-changing for those amenable to the opportunities presented. This evening was life-changing for me, and nudged my young studio forward, shaping its future identity. More building blocks of me were set into place: Leadership and purpose.

As Guillem suggested, the next morning I toured Barcelona in order to get my bearings. The tour lasted most of the day, and filled my mind with more beautiful images as well as a thorough history lesson. Looking at the La Sagrada Familia Cathedral, you can understand why Guadi is now my favorite architect.

Guillem had left a message at the hotel instructing me to take a taxi to the Up and Down Nightclub where Roser and he would meet me at 9:00 p.m. I grabbed a bite to eat, freshened up, and jumped into a taxi that the doorman beckoned with one sharp whistle.

"You want window up or down, miss?" the driver asked.

"No. I want to go to the Up and Down Nightclub," I clarified. The knuckles on my hands turned white as I hung onto the door handles out of sheer terror while the taxi driver rushed me to my destination. My body jolted to the right and to the left as he gleefully made his turns.

Up over a curb and down again, "I save time," he said.

His attempt to have a conversation with me was punctuated by horn honking, and what I think was profanity in Spanish as he glared at other motorists. He spent most of his time looking at me in his rearview mirror instead of looking straight ahead. Screech! Panic stop. Screech! Jackrabbit start and full speed ahead. Barcelona's city lights at night were a blur as my taxi whizzed its way through the maze of streets. Guillem and Roser looked concerned meeting me curbside as I stumbled out of the taxi and tried to walk upright in a straight line.

"Oh my gosh," was all I could say—but it was in a sexy voice.

"So, you experience our taxi drivers," Roser laughed. Guillem smiled and presented me with a complimentary ticket to see his tap dance company, Camut Band, perform that evening.

Nothing prepared me for the excitement that would follow. Five male tap dancers and percussionists, in black pants and shirts, exploded onto the stage. Two percussionists played the Udu and a Djembe drum, while Guillem and two other men tap danced on top of huge wooden drums. The dancers traded surfaces to tap on by simultaneously leaping from one drum to the other, or down to the floor and up again. The music they created with their instruments and tap shoes blended flamenco and African rhythms, a combination that makes you weak in the knees and unable to hold still. It was not long before I joined the other audience members in our own improvisation fueled by the vibration running through our bones.

I could not wait to tell Dianne about what I had seen, and about Guillem and his tap dancing friends. They were a best-kept secret. Nor could I wait for my students and teachers to experience Barcelona with its open respect of their artistry. Professionals in the arts are as revered in Spain as sports figures are in the U.S. Momentarily, I was sad when I thought of how arenas back home would fill to capacity for an event like a tractor pull or demolition derby, but for tap dancing? If only everyone back home could experience what I did tonight.

After the show, Guillem, Roser, and the men in the Camut Band invited me to join them for a glass of wine and wonderful conversation under the stars by the Mediterranean. When I remarked that I would love to know how to play the Udu and Djembe, Guillem whispered something into one of the percussionist's ear.

"We have another surprise for you tomorrow night," Guillem laughed.

The next day I toured a Picasso museum and a glass-blowing studio. One cathedral housed the actual baptismal font used for the natives Columbus brought back from the New World. The natives had to be baptized before they were allowed to enter the cathedral to meet the king and queen of Spain. The abundance of history in Barcelona is mind-boggling and hard to comprehend, because buildings in the United States that are two hundred years old would be two hundred years young in Europe. I was saddened that I had so little time to experience Barcelona before I had to leave, as I suddenly craved history and wanted to absorb as much as I could.

I dined on delicious Catalonian delicacies before heading off to El Timbal for more tap classes. When the classes were done, Guillem and Roser said to follow them. Their smiles and giggles told me they were up to something. We walked down Las Ramblas again to the shore of the Mediterranean, and veered to the left to a pier with hundreds of sailboats. A few minutes later I saw the dancers from the Camut Band, and heard the familiar sounds of the Udu and Djembe drum. There, under the stars and moonlight on a Mediterranean beach, I learned how to play these fine percussion instruments. With each beat of our hands, the drums sang incredible tales of their history. We ended the evening by going to a local jazz club where I met several of Guillem's musician friends, including Rene, an upright bass player.

My final day in Barcelona included more tap lessons followed by a meandering solo walk through this charming city, to reflect on my odyssey. I yearned to come back someday. As the sun was setting, I reluctantly returned to the hotel to pack my bags for my flight to Geneva in the morning. Rene had left a message that said he would drive me to the airport in his car. He was originally from Switzerland, and gave me names of not-to-miss jazz clubs in Geneva. After many hugs and kisses from my new Spanish friends, and a promise from Guillem and Roser to travel to visit Heartbeat, I was off to meet Maggie and Peter.

Glorious Geneva

Having recovered from laryngitis, my voice was no longer sexy. The few-hour flight to Geneva was over noble, mountainous terrain. On this leg of my trip, I would actually be staying with the owners of the dance studio. I felt grateful that Maggie and Peter insisted that I stay with them in order to save the expense of another hotel, especially since hotels had doubled their prices because of an international technology convention there.

The Geneva airport was easy to navigate, but the baggage claim area was thick with conventioneers. How would I ever find Maggie and Peter, and how would they find me? I wandered around a bit, and out of pure exhaustion from delayed jet lag, sat on my luggage, closed my eyes, and pretty much fell asleep sitting upright. I woke to someone shouting, "Deborah. Deborah." There was Maggie, a woman who looked to be in her mid-fifties, with curly gray hair. She was dressed in tight, flaming-red leggings, neon-green shoes, and a canary-yellow shirt. Holding a sign with "Heartbeat" printed on it, Maggie joyfully explained, "I wanted to make sure you could see me so I wore this bright costume."

Maggie was an enigma. Originally from England, she now lived in Geneva with her daughter, her granddaughter, and her second bit-younger husband, Peter. First impression of Maggie could be that of an eccentric, absent-minded woman who perhaps was a friendly waitress in a small town diner. Instead, Maggie was an intelligent and gifted woman—a computational linguist who had studied at Oxford, as well as taught at the University of Geneva where she was responsible for Certificate of Specialization in Machine Assisted Translation. She held many professional offices, and wrote for many professional publications.

Maggie was also involved in research projects in machine translation, semantics of natural languages, and evaluation of language engineering products and systems. In her spare time, she owned Encore, a dance studio, which was her passion. Peter's main job was managing and teaching at the studio. He was originally from New Zealand, and I never did quite understand how he ended up in Geneva, except that he had lived in several parts of the world over time, due to his finesse and award-winning talent in Irish Highland dancing.

First stop was Maggie and Peter's flat to get settled into my living quarters for the next two days. Their apartment had a lovely sunroom where Peter rolled out a futon mattress on the dining tabletop. "We don't have a spare bed, so I hope this is alright for you," Peter lamented.

"This is perfect. I love the view, and the plants on your terrace are lovely."

After I was introduced to Maggie's daughter and granddaughter, I was instructed to take a little nap because they had a big evening planned. The nap was luxurious and badly needed.

A few hours later we piled into Maggie's car and headed to their dance studio, Encore, where a large group of adult students anxiously awaited the American visitor. Spontaneous, thunderous applause surprised me as I entered the studio, and the genuine warmth of their welcome was overwhelming. The world tap dance community's camaraderie was again apparent. I was very humbled and a bit choked up, and expected that Peter would proceed with a formal round of introductions when he boldly announced, "This is Deborah, our guest from America. She doesn't smoke, doesn't drink, and isn't part of a cult or strange religion. She is normal. You can breathe a sigh of relief now. One caution, however—she does chew gum."

Peter, it turns out, was also a comedian, a bit wild-spirited, and openly and charmingly rebellious against the notoriously conservative Swiss culture. I didn't know quite how to respond to his introduction, but before I could say anything, one of the female students spoke up, and with mischievous fervor said, "Peter, in anticipation of the arrival of our lovely guest from America, we, your Wednesday night students, prepared a list of instructions for you."

She proceeded to unroll a scroll of parchment from which she read: *"1) Do not talk about body parts, 2) Do not use profanity, 3) Do not drink from the whiskey bottle during class, 4) Do not fart, 5) Do not belch, 6) Remember to take a shower this week, 7) It would be nice if you shaved, but if you forget, that's okay, 8) Do not smoke the stinky cigar, 9) Do not wear the pants that show your butt crack, and 10) Do not run up and slobber kisses on the women every time we get a step right; save that for the men instead."*

Peter and I were speechless for a moment, but immediately the entire room, including me, doubled over in uncontrollable laughter. It was hard to get the tap class started after that, but eventually it began, and eventually it ended, at close to 10:00 p.m. The entire group of twenty people agreed to keep the night young so we headed to a popular restaurant that featured an array of French cuisine and fine spirits. The roaring-with-laughter tap dancing crowd livened up the place, entertaining the other patrons.

During the course of the evening's conversations, I found out that the entire class was made up of doctors, physicists, lawyers, professors, and scientists, who used tap dance as a stress release from their professions.

"Our robustness in dance class is not the norm for Swiss people, so I hope you were not offended," the physicist explained.

"Not in any way. I had *so* much fun. And thank you for making me feel very welcome. I love the feel of sore cheeks and ribs from laughter. It's one of life's best gifts." After one more glass of wine, the brainy group departed for the evening.

Maggie woke me early in the morning to say she had to attend a meeting at the university, and gave me a bus pass for the day.

"Geneva operates on the honor system, so you can use the pass to go on any bus anywhere in Geneva. No one will ask you to show them the pass; people in Geneva just trust each other. You do not have to lock the door to the flat when you leave, either. There simply is no crime around here," she explained.

"Do you have a map of the bus routes? And where is the nearest bus stop?" I asked.

"This is my challenge for you today," Maggie continued. "I want you to find out for yourself how well planned Geneva is, and how easy it is to go from here to there. There is a placard on the corner with basic instructions, and the best and most fun way to visit Geneva is to strike out on your own. I will be home around 6:00 p.m., and you can tell me about all of your discoveries over dinner. You will have a great day." Maggie's challenge stirred my interest and I sprang from my tabletop bed, showered, and headed out to discover Geneva.

The bus service was frequent and timely. I simply jumped onto the first bus that came along just to see where it would go. If something looked interesting, I got off, looked around, and caught the next bus that would take me in a different direction. I spent the day riding through neighborhoods to study the quaint architecture, strolling through museums, shopping in the Swiss watch and wine district, following the aroma of the fine candy stores, and taking a moment to sit by the shore of sky-blue Lake Geneva. A huge fountain spurting lacy white water high into the air was the only thing blocking my view of the stately, snow-capped mountains of the Savoy Alps—a picture postcard come to life.

Relaxing by the lake, I realized in my excitement to explore Geneva, I had paid no attention about how to get back to Maggie and Peter's flat. I did not have their address or phone number with me, having forgotten to take my address book out of my luggage, but I remembered the intersection of the streets by their studio. I crossed the street and found another placard, and searched until I saw the bus that would take me to the studio. I did not want to fail Maggie's challenge, and to save face, I would just tell her that I lost track of time and thought it best to catch up with them at the studio, where I was already planning to take another class that evening.

On my way to catch the bus, I passed the charming store where earlier that day I had purchased a decorative decanter of exquisite pear liquor. The storekeeper spoke French and very little English, and while shopping, I had tried to remember some of the French I had studied in high school decades earlier. He seemed to appreciate my effort; however, about all that I could remember was *Hello. Goodbye. What is your name? What time is it? Where is the White Horse Inn?* and *What is the matter with you?*

I waved at the storekeeper as I walked by again. When I was a few shops past his store, the storekeeper, in a white apron, bow tie and ear-to-ear smile, caught up with me. In his limited English, he said, "Thank you, madam; this sweet for you." He handed me a bag full of pear-shaped chocolates, and kissed me on both cheeks. I smiled, expressed my appreciation, and mentioned that I was trying to find a bus to take me to the Encore Dance Studio.

"You friend of Maggie and Peter? I know, too. Come, come," he said, as he held my hand and led me to another placard. He traced his finger over one bus route and said, "Encore," and from that location, traced his finger over another bus route, and said, "Maggie and Peter."

Now I could confidently complete Maggie's challenge. The route back to their flat would take me past their studio, giving me the opportunity to see it in daylight, since it was already dark when I had arrived the night before. Residents of Geneva speak many languages, a skill that I greatly admire and envy. Maggie and Peter would often switch between English and French without skipping a beat during our conversations, and it wasn't too long before I could understand what they meant.

Maggie was correct; I did have a great day. The bus motored through the commercial district, and eventually came to the traffic light at the intersection by the studio. When the bus stopped, my eyes glanced upon a vista that took my breath away. I quickly got off the bus and ran to the side of the bridge to gaze down the winding, dark-blue Rhone River. I had no idea that the studio was located on the riverbank. Trees, plump with intricate blue-green leaves, spilled over each bank of the river, their reflections meeting in the middle. Hundreds of clumps of purple, pink, and lavender flowers peeked through wisps of white fog dancing above the water. The view reminded me of a Pierre-Auguste Renoir landscape. I stood motionless for a moment to let my body and my mind absorb the beauty.

It was too early to head to the studio so I caught the next bus and arrived at the flat by 5:30 p.m. The door was not locked, and everything inside was still there. The only other time in my life that I remember people not locking their doors was when I was a child visiting the farms of my extended family. Maggie returned a half-hour later and said, "I trust you had a lovely day."

"Maggie, it was enchanting. Thank you for your challenge. I would never have experienced what I did if I had gone on a group tour. Here is your bus pass back."

"Keep it as a souvenir of having the courage to strike out on your own," she whispered and winked. Maggie understood and knew much more about me than I thought, which I found comforting. Her challenge helped me rebuild myself much more than I think she will ever know.

Later that evening I attended one more tap class with Peter, and had another episode of side-splitting laughter. After the class, the group headed to a new jazz club with incredible musicians taking turns on the stage. The guitar and bass players passionately caressed their instruments as saxophone, trombone, and trumpet players blew their notes into the stratosphere. The pianist hit the keys with soulful clarity, and the drummer created perfect rhythms in perfect time. Some of the musicians played jazz standards while others took a musical trip outside the charts—and back again. It was all so magnificent.

A few glasses of wine later, I bid adieu to my new eccentric, brilliant friends and made the trip back to the flat to pack my luggage before I climbed into my tabletop bed. Maggie had to be at work very early, and left a beautiful friendship card on top of my luggage. Peter brought me to the airport, only he wasn't his usual jovial self.

"I met you only three days ago, and I will miss you very much. I feel like we have known each other for a long time," Peter lamented.

"Tap dance has a way of doing that," I whispered.

For the first four hours into the flight home, I pondered my amazing experiences over the past eight days. Hour five in the air brought on another unforeseen anxiety attack, and I wished the pilot would turn the plane around and head back to Geneva and Barcelona. Again, the anxiety felt real, and as before, I had a difficult time breathing and keeping my body from shaking. At that moment, I remembered the gentleman from Italy who was seated next to me when we departed from Minneapolis. In his heavy Italian accent he had said, "Just breathe slowly, my dear. Everything will happen as you planned." And, of course, he was right—even better than I could have imagined.

The Ripening of Courage

Heartbeat and I were a match made in heaven. I adored each student, and my studio became a family full of families. If at this point I had decided to start dating, any relationship would have ended quicker than the flap of a tap shoe, because I had no time to devote to it. My good friend, Dianne, continued to introduce me to other luminaries in the professional tap dance community, and I felt the warmth of that unique family. This truly was all that I needed.

A Parliamentary Encounter

In April 2000 I traveled to Europe again. This time I revisited my new tap friends in Barcelona for three days to further the development of a travel study program, because they seemed most receptive to the idea. I also planned a three-day side trip to Italy to meet Alfonso and Donatella, owners of On Stage Dance Studio in Milan.

In contrast to the joy of again dancing with Guillem and my Barcelona tap friends during this second visit, my days in Barcelona were also spent dealing with a stuffy nose. One afternoon I decided to bake the sinus problems away by relaxing in the sun by the hotel's courtyard pool. The warm sun felt good, and I hoped I would be breathing normally again. High above pool level was a deck full of men and women dressed in business suits, and to my astonishment, not only were they speaking English, their accent was very familiar. It was the unique Midwestern/Minnesota accent—the land of *Ya sure, Ya betcha,* and *Uff-da.* In an effort to be sociable to fellow Minnesotans, I excitedly yelled out, "Hey, are you guys from Minnesota?!" After a long pause, a handsome gentleman leaned over the deck railing and hollered, "No. We are from Norway, and we are practicing speaking English. May we come down and converse with you?"

Six men and one woman marched down the steps from the upper deck, and joined me by the pool where we talked for about an hour. Most of the conversation consisted of their questions about my Norwegian heritage, why I was in Barcelona, and general questions about Minnesota, its school system, and state government. I thought they just wanted to practice speaking English until I finally asked, "So, what do you guys do for a living?" This time their pause was very pregnant.

"We are members of the Norwegian Parliament," the handsome gentleman answered. "My name is Torbjorn Andersen; these are six of my colleagues."

He further explained that he was reluctant to let me know who they were, thinking that I would be uncomfortable talking to them.

"We appreciate your time with us. We are having dinner, if you care to join us. We will meet you in the hotel lobby at six."

Torbjorn's invitation was sincere and happily accepted. At six, I found myself walking arm-in-arm down the Las Ramblas in Barcelona, Spain, with seven members of the Norwegian Parliament. All the while the lyrics to the song, "If My Friends Could See Me Now", whirled around in my head.

After dinner, the Norwegian Parliament and I continued to stroll Las Ramblas until they, one by one, departed for the hotel to pack bags for their flight home in the morning. Torbjorn encouraged me to continue walking with him for a while longer. He had the classic Scandinavian blue eyes, sandy-blonde hair, and a handsome Nordic face. Fueled by non-stop conversation, we wandered aimlessly around Barcelona. At 1:00 a.m., we realized that we were lost, and I suggested that we ask for directions back to the hotel.

"No. I will find the way. No need to stop for directions," he assured me.

"That is exactly what most men back home would say," I laughed.

Another hour passed, and we were still lost.

"Torbjorn, I must leave for the airport very early, and it is now two, and I still haven't packed. Perhaps we should get a taxi," I urged.

At that moment both of us turned to see if any taxis were around, only to find out that our hotel was actually across the street.

"See, I told you I would find our way back," he joked.

When we got to the hotel entrance, I thanked him for a lovely evening, and wished him a safe trip back to Norway. Torbjorn gently held both of my hands, pulling me closer to him, and whispered, "I am the luckiest man in the world tonight to have had the company of such a beautiful woman." He kissed me on both cheeks, smiled, and waved goodbye as we bid adieu. I still have daydreams about how this day unfolded.

Majestic Milan

Guillem left a message at the hotel that his friend, Rene, would take me to the airport, and that he would come to Heartbeat when possible to make the travel study and cultural exchange program come true. Thanks to Rene, I caught my flight to Milan to meet Alfonso and Donatella at their dance studio, On Stage.

My lovely hotel in Milan was situated near the Milano Centrale Train Station, considered to be one of the most beautiful in the world. Originally built in 1864, its massive structure and architectural design made it look like the set of a movie starring Humphrey Bogart, complete with rows of platforms, steam rising from the massive engines, and many bustling passengers dressed in long trench coats and carrying briefcases and black umbrellas. Outside the station were numerous avenues boasting high-end designer shops, which are synonymous with Milan.

After freshening up, I caught a taxi to meet Alfonso. On Stage Dance Studio was grand. Its wood floors were polished to the point of appearing liquid, and three enormous chandeliers made it seem like a ballroom for royalty. One wall was floor-to-ceiling stained glass panoramas, one wall was solid mirrors, and the other two walls were draped with white fabric that cascaded like snow on a mountainside. I was invited to observe a few jazz dance classes before joining Alfonso in his tap class, where we traded steps with the other dancers. It was very apparent that On Stage was more ballet, jazz, and modern-dance-oriented.

"Unfortunately, tap dance in Milan is not quite as popular as ballet," Alfonso lamented at dinner, adding, "I take a train to Switzerland to get the more challenging tap classes." Donatella, Alfonso, and I realized that a travel study program would not be feasible for their studio, so we decided instead that we would be welcome at each other's studio if we happened to be in town, and would stay in touch.

For the remainder of my time in Milan, Alfonso was a gracious host, making sure I toured the city and ate in magnificent restaurants.

"Deborah, there are two more stops we will make today, and you will remember them forever," Alfonso assured me. Huddled under an umbrella, we walked briskly through the rain and a maze of narrow streets until we came to a plaza. Across the plaza was the world-famous La Scala Opera House.

"My friend works here, and said to bring you at this time to hear the rehearsal."

I followed Alfonso into the opera house and up a flight of stairs. In a barely audible whisper, Alfonso instructed me to slowly open the red velvet drape that covered an entrance into the main hall. We quietly maneuvered through the drape and sat in the back of the theater to watch and listen to the opera in rehearsal. Angels should be so lucky to have voices like those. We were two quiet mice afraid to breathe to avoid being found out, and we did not want to interrupt the enchantment we were hearing. A sparkling crystal chandelier graced the ceiling of the opera hall, every inch decorated with red velvet and gold trim. The grandeur of the interior, however, was no match for the grandeur of the voices.

We stayed only a few minutes, as Alfonso reminded me that we really weren't supposed to be in there, but he had found a way to give me an experience of a lifetime. Next stop was a visit to the Santa Maria delle Grazie, "to see a painting masterpiece known around the world," Alfonso noted, which kept me guessing as to which painting we were about to see.

Under the shared umbrella, we splashed through puddles as we quickened our pace. We came upon a building that was not as large as the Duomo Milan Cathedral, but beautiful nonetheless. I followed Alfonso to the end of a long line of people waiting to see a recently restored masterpiece. Suddenly I realized that in moments my eyes would behold the original Leonardo da Vinci masterpiece, *The Last Supper*. When it was our turn to quickly pass in front of the painting, complete reverence filled my body, and my mind took a snapshot to forever remember its stunning beauty. Throughout my life, I had seen copies of *The Last Supper*, and now I was standing right in front of it, feeling humbled and blessed.

My trip to Milan went much too fast. In the morning, Alfonso treated me to breakfast before taking me to the airport. We promised to stay in touch, and as true to form with tap dancers, we felt as though we had known each other for a long time. We gave each other a kiss on the cheek and waved goodbye.

Unbeknownst to me, I was about to be treated to yet another masterpiece as the plane lifted off, but this time the artist was God. Majestic snow-covered Alps rendered all passengers in awe as we marveled at the view. Fixing our gaze at the heavenly creation, the plane's windows were covered with hundreds of faces pressed against the glass. The amazing mountainous panorama will forever be burned in my brain.

The flight home seemed to go by extremely fast while I basked in the glow of knowing that the travel study and cultural exchange program I dreamed of for Heartbeat was one step closer to reality.

Home Again

While I lived in the studio, I had to do my laundry at the local laundromat, usually late at night because of my teaching schedule. Most often I was the only English-speaking person there, and would show others how to use the machines. My other laundromat buddies were Harley Davidson biker guys. The day that I observed local pet grooming staff washing their shop's towels in the same machines the public used, I knew it was time to get a place of my own. Oh my.

In December 2000, I moved out of the studio and into a townhouse. At long last I was able to cook in a real kitchen again. My hands shook excitedly, and I became euphoric over the littlest things, like pots and pans and measuring spoons. It was culture shock for me to shop for a clothes washer and dryer, and just three years later, gaze in wonderment at all of the new bells and whistles now available on these appliances. I was elated to have a garden and yard for Misha to enjoy. I was no longer homeless.

Gifts in Many Forms

Throughout the next few years, whenever Heartbeat was on break from classes, either I would travel to study dance with master teachers, or they would be guest master teachers at my studio. The amazing events that kept accumulating made me understand one thing: my future was not entirely under my direction, but was also being guided by a higher, loving spirit. Or, another way of looking at it was that I finally understood that opportunities, challenges, and just ordinary things would happen in my life, and the gift given to me was the growing knowledge and courage to know what to do with them. My decision-making skills were finely honed.

On July 25, 2003, my Barcelona friends, Guillem and Roser, made their first trip to Heartbeat to teach master tap classes and to perform with my dancers at an event held in their honor. We now had the travel study program on more solid footing, and during the next few years, they visited Heartbeat two more times.

Wrenching Heartaches

On August 10, 2003, Dianne's phone call woke me. She could barely get her words out, "Deb, I wanted to tell you this before you saw it on the news. Gregory died yesterday."

For all of the jabbering we usually do on the phone, the complete silence said more than words. Tears flowed, and the realization that the world had just lost a one-of-a-kind weighed heavy on our broken hearts, as it did for the entire international tap dance community. We will always miss Gregory, and I will always remember his kind and supportive words when I needed them most. Gregory died at age fifty-seven of cancer.

My dad's disease had totally incapacitated him by now. He could no longer talk, eat, stand, sit, or any of the basic things humans do. Parkinson's disease is one of the world's most hideous diseases. I hate it. My dad's stiff and rigid body no longer worked, but his mind functioned well. He was trapped in his own torture chamber. I often wonder now how many times he wanted to tell his children that he loved them, but the disease would not let his voice be heard. He loved to give hugs, but the disease would not let his arms reach out. After a while, my siblings and I were saddened when we realized that we were beginning to forget what his voice and laughter sounded like. We knew he could still see and hear us, so we read and talked to him during our visits to the nursing home. On December 2, 2003, I popped in to visit my dad and said, "Hey, Dad, guess what? Next week Kristin and I are going to Cuba!" He gave me a look that spoke louder than if he could talk.

"Be careful!" his eyes said.

Captivating Cuba

Our eight-day trip to Cuba, licensed by the State Treasury Department, came about when I happened to stop for lunch at a curious little aqua and purple-painted restaurant advertising Cuban cuisine. It was one of those places that you knew the food would be either really, really bad or really, really good. Colorful signs around the front door warned, "Forbidden Food" and "Eating With the Enemy." How could I not go in? The aroma was spicy and delicious, and when I stepped inside, vibrant photographs and memorabilia from Cuba intrigued me further. The restaurant owner had come to this country from Cuba when he was only eleven, and still had ties to family in Havana. After a brief conversation, during which he found out about my dance background, he handed me information about an official state-licensed trip to Havana that departed December 8. The trip was planned for literary, visual, and performing artists, and clergy, to study the Afro-Cuban religion and its relation to Cuban music and dance. Several people signed up for the trip, but no one yet to represent dance. He was particularly excited to introduce me to Tony Menendez, owner of a well-known dance studio in Havana. I quickly called Kristin about the opportunity, and the next day we helped the travel group reach its maximum number of twenty people.

Kristin and I flew to Miami on December 7, 2003, for our flight to Havana the next morning. We met all of the travelers and made sure our official documents were in order to enter Cuba. We also attended a brief presentation on what to expect upon our arrival in Havana. Everyone seemed nervous, and I am sure had the same thoughts Kristin and I had during the night; "Should we just cut our losses and head home?" By sunrise, however, no one had abandoned ship, and all were questioned and processed through the official checkpoints in the airport.

Kristin and I grabbed our luggage, plus a duffel bag full of fifty-five pairs of ballet and tap shoes that were donated by Heartbeat's students to give to the dance studio in Havana. We boarded a Continental Airlines airplane on a flight that had no number, nor did it appear on any register because we were heading to Cuba. We were on a nonexistent flight, and as the signs on the colorful Cuban restaurant in Minneapolis proclaimed, "To eat forbidden food with the enemy." My heart pounded the entire flight.

Kristin and I listened intently as the flight attendant explained how the pilots must follow exact landing procedure to avoid getting shot down.

"See those red barges lined up in the ocean? We must follow those as our corridor to land."

We really hoped the pilots had had a good night's sleep. I looked out the window as we approached, and saw a few pickup trucks and cars from the 1950s zipping along a dirt road that cut through lush tropical foliage. Something seemed very odd as I studied with wonder this outlawed island trapped in a time capsule. As far as I could see, the surrounding shoreline had no boats. I woke from my Havana daydream when American tires touched the Cuban tarmac.

Our plane was the only one in sight as it slowly rolled to a stop. All passengers sat motionless while we looked out onto a tarmac void of people. About fifteen silent minutes passed, until Kristin exclaimed, "I see people coming!" A woman plus two men rolled a set of stairs to the plane. They were dressed in navy blue suit jackets and tan pants. I think all of us expected to see military types, with red stars on their hats and guns slung over their shoulders. Instead, as we descended the staircase, we were hugged and welcomed by a nicely dressed trio.

Our group of twenty entered the airport terminal to be questioned and processed once again—now on the other side. All went smoothly until the inspector saw our duffel bag full of donated ballet slippers and tap shoes. Kristin and I were called to the side, causing me to immediately break into a sweat.

"What is this for?" the guard asked.

Before I could speak, one of the organizers of the trip interrupted and answered in Spanish, "These young ladies own a performing arts school in the U.S., and their students would like to donate these shoes to the Tony Menendez School of Dance in Havana."

"These shoes must be divided equally and given to all dance studios in Havana. That is how it is done here," the guard insisted. Our trip organizer proceeded to argue with the guard, and said that we specifically collected these shoes for Tony's school, and if we had to divide the shoes up, each studio in Havana would receive only one pair.

We were delayed for two hours over our dance shoe-stuffed duffel bag, and just when I was about to faint from nervousness, loud excited chatter and a flurry of commotion rescued us from the stressful situation. Unbeknownst to me, Tony Menendez and the Cuban minister of culture were supposed to meet us upon our arrival to officially approve that only Tony's studio would receive the donated shoes. As luck would have it, they were in a minor traffic accident on their way to the airport, arriving just in time to save the day. Tony apparently is a revered dancer in Cuba, and the guard became very apologetic when he realized who was involved.

Tony stared at Kristin and me for a moment, slowly looking us up and down. In charming flamboyancy he sang, "I can tell you are dancers, my princesses—you stand so regal. Follow me."

Tony dramatically tossed his long red chiffon scarf over his shoulder, made an about-face, and led us out of the terminal to a huge crowd of cheering young dancers holding signs that read, "Welcome Minnesota." The unexpected welcome committee moved me to tears. Without hesitation, Kristin ran over to the crowd of dancers standing behind a security fence and reached through to hug them. I took a picture of the Cuban dancers' beaming smiles that surrounded Kristin's beaming smile, and when my camera flashed, I knew that Kristin and I would go home very different people than when we arrived. This was a trip for both of us to overcome fear and strengthen our courage.

We stayed at the Riviera Hotel, a hotel and casino formerly run by the infamous Meyer Lansky before the Cuban revolution in 1959. The hotel's expansive lobby was decorated in 1950's vintage blonde furniture, just like my grandparents had had in their farmhouse. Affixed to the wall behind the check-in counter was the same clock my grandmother had in her kitchen during my elementary school days. Most of the vehicles in Cuba dated back to the 1950s as well—and they were *still* running. The smell and fuzzy feel of the upholstery, along with the split windshields and stiff suspensions of the taxis, sent me back to my childhood when we rode to the country church in my grandfather's car. The autos were spotless with no rust—a collector's dream. Cuba must certainly have the most resourceful auto mechanics. Kristin and I laughed with excitement when we sped around Havana in another version of a taxi, the little CoCos, which were yellow, egg-shaped, three-wheeled vehicles with no windshields, and resembling something from a Weeble toy set.

Our mornings were filled with history classes regarding the Afro-Cuban religion and its arrival on the island with African slaves. We observed their sacred drum and cleansing ceremonies, while poetic chants rang out, and our gazes rose from the earth to the sky. We toured galleries of Cuba's top artists, and strolled through street markets full of delightful artwork and displays of rare books. Hanging racks of hand-crocheted and white linen clothing performed their own dance in the ocean breeze. Ornate woodcarvings were spread out on blankets that dotted the market's earthen floor. Jazz music pulsed day and night, punctuated by the aroma of fine Havana Club rum and Cuban cigars.

Our group of twenty woke each morning to the sound of ocean waves and drum ceremonies off in the distant hills. We went to sleep each night hearing the evening tide accompanied by trumpet and trombone players improvising enchanting melodies while perched on El Malecon, Havana's famed ocean-side wall. We went to the famous Copacabana Club and the Hotel National. We attended a gathering of three thousand people in the courtyard of the historic fort overlooking the Havana Harbor, and danced under the stars to a hundred jazz musicians and conga drums. Cuban music is addicting and mesmerizing. I came to the conclusion that, to most Cubans, every song and every dance is a prayer, whether performed in a ceremony or a jazz club. Their music, dance, and religion are one and the same, and the combination arouses unequalled passion. It is this passion that needs to be intrinsic in every dancer because without it, dance cannot come from the heart or be real.

One of the women in our group was a former actress, and this was her first trip back to Havana since the 1959 revolution. At the young age of eighteen, she was cast in Erroll Flynn's movie production of *Cuban Rebel Girls*, which, unfortunately, had its filming interrupted by the Cuban revolution—a minor inconvenience. After lunch one afternoon, she took Kristin and me on a walking tour to all of the places where she hid for three days with another young actress until they could be rescued and brought back to the U.S. This trip was very melancholy and emotional for her because she realized that the horror from her past had changed to pride in her ability to survive.

Later that day, I decided to venture out on my own and take a brisk walk back to the outdoor art market. Halfway to my destination, I was sidetracked by the sight of four women in long white ruffled skirts, dancing to the percussion of four conga drummers dressed in their sacred drum attire: white shirt, white pants, and a red scarf around the neck. The women were joyous in their dance, and held long sticks with colorful feathers attached to one end. A large crowd of tourists gathered around, and began to clap their hands to the heart-pounding rhythms. Being a tap dancer, I couldn't help but start to move my feet and contribute my own percussion to the festivity. This prompted the lead dancer to snatch me out of the crowd and pull me into their ceremonial circle, where she began to teach me their dance on the fly. All I could do was smile and move right along with her. Excitement welled up inside me, because the more she challenged me, the more I kept up with her.

Meanwhile, the other travelers in our group happened to be passing by in taxis on their way to the art market. They abruptly ordered their taxi drivers to stop when they saw me in the distance with my hair wildly tossing about. By this time, the lead dancer had also given me a stick with feathers on one end. Our travel group anxiously poured out of the taxis and ran up to the crowd to join in the celebration. Suddenly, the conga drummers stopped playing and started to laugh hysterically. I thought for a moment that it was because I looked ridiculous dancing with them—and I became very embarrassed. When the lead dancer noticed my reaction, she quickly pulled me toward the drummers while conversing with them in Spanish. She smiled and said, "Please do not feel bad. It is not what you think. The drummers want me to tell you they have never seen a white woman dance like you do. They did not expect you to keep up, and they are laughing at the situation—they are laughing at me because I cannot give you a dance movement that you cannot do. They laugh because you dance well for a white woman."

I thanked them, and continued on my brisk walk, followed by the other members of our travel group who made comments like, "Go, Deb!" and, "Boy, am I glad I got this on my camera!" I will forever be at their mercy to keep their footage of this event confidential.

The next evening was our scheduled trip to visit the Tony Menendez Dance Studio to deliver the donated shoes. Tony was very proud of his school, which at one time was a movie theater. It had been given to him by the Cuban government to convert into a dance studio. The interior was dimly lit by bare light bulbs dangling from extension cords randomly strung around the perimeter of the room. The cement floor was crumbling, and the dancers were taking their classes barefoot, causing cut and irritated bottoms of feet we could see as they stretched their legs. In the makeshift studio space, one corner had a ballet class, one corner a flamenco class, one corner a jazz class, and one corner a modern class. At least two hundred students in the big open space were trying to hear the instructions and music for only their particular class. It was a difficult learning environment because the collision of music echoed throughout the room. The students were very disciplined, and stood in rigid military-style attention whenever their instructors gave directions. Kristin and I smiled at the dancers as we walked around, and occasionally would get a secret smile back.

After we had observed the classes for thirty minutes, Tony suddenly jumped on top of a table and starting chanting and clapping a conga rhythm. He announced to the students that Heartbeat had donated the shoes, causing the students to explode into a joyful cheer. Tony executed a magnificent leap from the table, grabbing me with one hand and Kristin with the other, starting a huge conga line with his two hundred students, and the remainder of our travel group following behind. The dancing spilled out into the street, and passersby spontaneously joined in the conga line that had now doubled. Shouts of "Thank you, Heartbeat" filled the air while we danced into the night. I had never anticipated that tears of such joy and compassion would flow during this trip.

Our planned midweek trip to the interior of Cuba to experience a lush rain forest that our guide said resembled scenes in the movie *Jurassic Park*, was cancelled due to the U.S. military capture of Saddam Hussein in Iraq. As a result, the Cuban government prohibited all visitors and tourists from venturing inland.

"This is for your safety and security," they said. As a result, we changed course and spent the day relaxing in the San Francisco Plaza surrounded by Baroque architecture dating back to 1600. Kristin and I fantasized that we were fine ladies from days of yore, standing on the ornate balconies, dressed in white long flowing gowns, while gazing at the ocean in anticipation of first sight of tall ships on the horizon.

"My darling, I do believe that I see a ship in the distance. My love is returning, just like he said he would." Kristin sighed as she placed her hands over her heart.

"But look! Is that another ship? My hero is coming home, too. We shall dance in the moonlight and drink fine wine," I gushed while twirling in the courtyard.

The day arrived when we had to fly home. Kristin and I packed our bags, and with some time to spare before our bus arrived, walked to the beach and looked across the short stretch of ocean that separated Cuba from the U.S. We were different now. We felt our already deep-rooted and spiritual passion for dance intensify further. We had seen people confined to this island find joy in simple things because that is all they have. Unlike the freedoms we are blessed with in the United States, the only avenues for self-expression on this island ruled by communism were religion and the arts. Cubans are the combination of their spiritual and artistic voices.

During our bus ride to the airport, I thought about our taxi ride two days prior to a performance of the Cuban National Ballet. The taxi driver asked, "I hope you are enjoying Cuba. Where are you from?"

"We are from the U.S.," I replied from my front passenger seat.

The driver reached over to touch my left shoulder with the tip of his pointer finger, and through a wide grin sarcastically said, "Oh, you are the enemy, and I am so scared." He asked us to roll up our windows as we drove along El Malecon and proclaimed this was, "To protect you from waves that might splash through the windows."

He continued, "We want to know you, and you want to know us. We would like each other. It is sad politics get in the way."

After pausing, he said, "You can roll your windows down now because the ocean is quiet tonight."

All politics aside, Cuba is a preserved and rare glimpse into the past. I "saw" my grandfather's car, and I smelled and felt the upholstery. I heard the familiar motor, and looked through the split windshield of my youth. I saw my grandmother's farmhouse kitchen clock and the blonde furniture. Among the many gifts that I experienced with Kristin in Havana was the opportunity to let her see, smell, and feel some of my childhood. Havana forced us to step outside of our comfort zone. Havana let me be a little girl again.

Cairo Meets Kristin

Upon our return from Cuba, Kristin took our quest to demonstrate our newfound courage a step further—and put both of us out of our comfort zone—when she accepted a month-long residency position at the American University in Cairo, Egypt. A professor from Egypt, who taught occasionally at the University of Minnesota, befriended Kristin and Paul over the years because he was a true fan of Kristin's dance company, Vox Medusa, and never missed a performance when he was back in the States. Through diligent work, he was able to get funding from the American University to sponsor Kristin's residency from mid-March to mid-April 2004, where she taught the first modern dance classes ever held in Egypt, and choreographed the first multi-medium installation for an art exhibit at the Falaki Gallery, which became its most-attended event ever.

During her month in Cairo, Kristin encountered a culture where abuse and violence toward women were widely accepted. She had rude awakenings when she tried to walk down the street without the accompaniment of a male, or not wearing a headscarf. Dance students in her classes were slow to warm up to her due to cultural differences that also caused her to make several choreographic and costume design changes. Kristin was persistent, though, and by the end of March, peeled away the students' initial resistance until they also fell in love with her.

The female students often asked her, "You mean you can step outside your house and go for a walk if you want to, and use the telephone without asking permission first?" These concepts amazed them. Unfortunately, a scare for Kristin's security happened on March 23, while she was teaching one of her classes. Sheikh Ahmed Ismail Yassin, co-founder of Hamas, was assassinated by an Israeli helicopter gunship, and because of our country's relationship with Israel, the sheikh's death prompted a massive demonstration of more than ten thousand people around the American University building, with Kristin and her students inside. Officials informed Kristin that it was too dangerous for her to walk outside, concerned that the demonstrators, upon seeing her as an American, would kidnap or kill her. Several hours passed before university guards were able to hide Kristin in a van to whisk her back to the hotel.

Fortunately, Paul had already booked a flight to Cairo to be with Kristin during the last week of her residency because we wanted at least one family member to attend her incredible production at the Falaki Gallery. Kristin waited until she got home to tell me about her frustrations and triumphs, and about the dire situation during the demonstration at the university. The mother in me shouted, "Why didn't you call me? I would have found substitute teachers for my dance classes at the studio and caught the next plane to Cairo!"

I was extremely shaken hearing her talk about her adventures.

"Mom, I didn't want to alarm you, and I knew you would have done exactly that—catch the next plane to Cairo. I handled it myself, and I knew Paul was on his way."

I am very proud of her accomplishments at the American University, and her ability to soften the attitude of the students toward her. I am thankful beyond belief that she and Paul came home safely, and hope someday she will write about her time in Egypt. Maybe when she sees the events as they unfolded staring at her from the page, she will understand why I fell apart that day. A mother's heart beats loudly when she fears for her child.

Up to this point, Kristin and I had experienced events in our lives that not many others had. As the universe propelled us through the domestic violence trial and the blossoming of our dream to build Heartbeat, our courage was now like colorful and delightful ripened fruit basking in the sunshine.

A Heightened Awakening

15

"Dianne, my dad's doctors say that he only has a few months left," I sobbed to my dear friend in Boston. "He taught me how to waltz when I was twelve years old, and he is the only man with whom I have ever waltzed. My dad has never missed a performance of mine, and the hospice staff said that my family could hire a medical van to bring him to the theater so that he could see me dance one last time and—"

"Deb, Deb, don't worry. When I visit your studio in a few weeks, we will work on a tap waltz for you to dedicate to your father," Dianne assured me.

In April 2004, Dianne taught me an intricate tap waltz that I rehearsed every spare moment until it came effortlessly from my heart.

On June 22, 2004, I waited anxiously at the theater's front door as hundreds of families and friends of my dancers filed past, offering wishes for a good show.

"Break a leg, Deb!" they would say. My mind, however, was focused on the arrival of one audience member—my dad. At last, the medical van pulled up, and behind it, cars filled with my brothers, sisters, many nieces and nephews, and Mom. The driver carefully lowered the lift that held Dad in a recliner-type hospital bed on wheels. Dad's frail and stiff body and the frozen expression on his face masked the excitement I hoped he felt. He could not talk, and I prayed that he was aware of what was going on, and that he would be able to see me dance, and understand that it was dedicated to him. I walked with my family to the back of the theater where a special space had been made for him. I kissed and hugged Mom and Dad before rushing backstage to be with the dancers.

The opening of Heartbeat's show was flawless, and my pride radiated like a beacon from the stage wings. This was our sixth annual dance concert in a theater filled to standing room only. Now it was my turn to dance. The theater was dark, the audience silent, as I stood out of view and read aloud a dedication to my dad. A recording of Oscar Peterson playing "Jitterbug Waltz" filled the air, and I lifted my arms to waltz center stage as if Dad were dancing with me.

Photo images of Dad and me, from my infancy to the present, appeared larger than life across the huge screen behind me. One slide faded into the next slide as the years passed by. I poured out my love and respect for Dad while I danced. My tap shoes crisply sang a melody that made me feel removed from the stage and audience. I truly felt that it was Dad dancing with me one more time. As my dance came to an end and the music softened to a whisper, I walked to the edge of the stage, blowing a kiss toward Dad. I sobbed uncontrollably while more than 600 people gave a standing ovation. They, too, felt the respect and love for the only person in the audience who was unable to stand.

My sister, Shirlee, noticed that Dad struggled in an attempt to try to hold his arms up as if dancing with me, and to clap his hands. His tears flowed as he knew that this dance was for him. I know in my heart that he felt he was on stage with me.

Two months later on August 1, while I was busy doing bookwork at the studio, Shirlee called, "Deb, this is Shirlee. Dad is now in heaven."

They say that when a loved one dies, part of you dies, too. My dad's death affected me differently. I certainly felt an emotional weight and sadness that was unbearable for several months. Without warning, in places I least expected, I broke down, but I also felt a rebirth of my dad because every cell in my body that came from him suddenly awakened. I could hear his voice and laughter again. I feel his presence every day, and he truly steps in during the ups and downs of directing a performing arts school.

Dad is now the leader of the angels who have resided in Heartbeat from its first day. I feel his protection and pride. When I teach, and when I dance, he is teaching and dancing with me. Whenever I visit his grave, I hum a little tune and hold up my arms to waltz with his spirit again. My dad's spirit is alive and free from that wretched disease. He can clap his hands, sing and dance—and smile. Once again, he is a wise man with the innocence of a child.

Dancing for Joy

That October, guided by the entrepreneurial spirit of my ancestors, I cold-called several professional athletic associations and prominent performance venues around the Twin Cities area. Heartbeat was fast developing seasoned performers of all ages who were deserving of high-profile gigs. My calls proved productive.

The first long-term gig scored was for our youthful break dance and hip hop crew, when I received a callback from the Minnesota Timberwolves professional NBA basketball team. Coincidentally, the team had been looking for a group of young hip hop and break dancers to entertain Timberwolves' fans at home games. Heartbeat's "Beat Squad" soon became a fan favorite, and for the next several years, was rated the best youth dance team in the entire NBA.

Performing opportunities soon filled Heartbeat's calendar and included several corporate events. In addition, Heartbeat's dancers thrilled audiences at Minnesota Orchestra's Hot Summer Jazz Festivals, St. Jude's Children's Hospital benefits, special dance productions at the prestigious Guthrie Theater, gala events for the American Heart Association and Juvenile Diabetes Association, and performances at other major athletic events such as the University of Minnesota Gophers Men's Basketball games.

Heartbeat's dancers appeared on local television talk show, *Twin Cities Live*, when they were booked as featured entertainment for Minneapolis' annual summer parade. Our Beat Squad made it to the final cut when they flew to Los Angeles to audition for the national television show, *America's Best Dance Crew*. Heartbeat's youthful performers exuded professionalism beyond their age when they were featured in a music video for the band, Apollo Cobra.

At one gala event, it became apparent how much joy Heartbeat's dancers bring to all ages. An elderly gentleman approached me while I stood in the back of the ballroom watching my young students perform.

"Are those your dancers? They are very talented, and I'm sure they will carry the skills you give them well into their adulthood," he commented.

"Yes, they are students at my studio, Heartbeat. Thank you for your compliment."

Handing me a small sealed envelope, the gentleman leaned in to whisper, "I am not going to tell you my name. I just want you to use this to buy new uniforms for them when needed. Kids grow so fast, you know."

The gentleman quickly disappeared without giving me time to ask questions. I slowly opened the envelope and found one thousand dollars inside.

"Thank you, mister. I'll make sure they get new uniforms."

Gazing across the ballroom, I searched for him, but it was like he vanished into thin air.

Quest for Cultural Exchange and Travel Study

My quest to establish cultural exchange and travel study programs for Heartbeat shifted into high gear. In January 2005, Heartbeat's teachers and dancers were invited to be the opening act for tap dance sensation Jason Samuels-Smith's show on Carnival Cruise Line's excursion along the western coast of Mexico.

A few weeks prior to our departure, Dianne had suffered a heart attack. After the cruise, I flew to Boston to visit Dianne and her husband, to help out any way I could.

While making dinner for them one evening, Dianne suggested that I should someday meet Yukiko Misumi, a studio owner in Tokyo, whom she believed would be very receptive to a cultural exchange program. As luck would have it, in April 2005, Dianne was asked to teach master classes at Yukiko's studio in Tokyo. I accepted Dianne's invitation to travel with her to Tokyo, partly to meet Yukiko, and partly because I was worried about Dianne's health.

The flight from Minneapolis to Tokyo is beyond what some call, "Extremely long," and comes close to, "This is humanly impossible!" Dianne and I frequently headed to the back of the plane to do our own version of aerobics behind a small panel wall. Thirteen hours, three meals, and three movies later, we landed in Tokyo. Our first stop after we deplaned was the airport's ladies' restroom where we had our initial encounter with Japanese high technology. Neither of us had ever been in a bathroom stall where the toilet was computerized, and we couldn't figure out how to flush it, and once we did, how to turn it off.

While I sat in my stall, I could hear Dianne in her stall having great difficulty.

"God, Deb, every time I stand up water squirts straight into the air!" she yelled. "I have to stay seated on the toilet seat. Otherwise I am getting all wet!"

I could hear her banging around and making all kinds of racket in her stall and wondered what other women in the restroom thought of us.

"Deb, I don't know what to do. How do I stop this?" she laughed.

Our audible concerns of, "Help, how do we get out of here?" eventually turned into loud giggles that rolled into side-splitting laughter. After several minutes had passed, a quiet and polite Japanese voice said, "Push blue button."

We made our way out of the restroom stalls looking like we had been in a water-balloon fight.

"God, Deb, I have got to get this on my camera." So, the first image on Dianne's video of our trip to Japan is the Tokyo toilet.

Yukiko and her daughter, Tiffany, met us in baggage claim. Dianne was correct—Yukiko and I were on the same wavelength as far as what direction we wanted to take our studios, and we immediately became good friends. Yukiko drove us to our hotel, and assured us that someone would meet us in the lobby in the morning to help us find our way via subway to her dance studio, Artistic Rhythm Tap Network (ARTN). The sea of humanity in Tokyo is vast, to say the least—yet you really never feel crowded, due to the cultural politeness of the Japanese people.

Our first evening, we wandered around the stores in Tokyo's massive electronics district, marveling at futuristic cameras, computers, and other gadgets that might take many years before reaching U.S. consumers. Strolling around the streets of Tokyo at night makes New York's Times Square look tiny. It was sensory overload to try to take in all of the billboards several stories tall and flashing lights of every color in the spectrum. The modern architecture of Tokyo's skyscrapers neatly intermingled with ancient temples, shrines, and Japanese gardens. I had youthful flashbacks to my favorite animated cartoon series, *The Jetsons*, when I saw how the numerous multi-level freeway bridges and on-and-off ramps were intricately braided around hundreds of towering modern skyscrapers. I fully expected to see George, Jane, Judy, and Elroy with their dog, Astro, zooming by in their space-mobile. Tokyo is a revered glimpse of the ancient—and a blast to the future. The city is a science project in which opposing particles are placed in a collider to create honorable coexistence.

Our eight days in Tokyo were filled with daily dance classes, shopping, sightseeing, and trying to find restaurants where food did not have eyes staring back at you. Green tea ice cream and freshly made honest-to-goodness ginger ale were addicting. The Japanese have healthy diets, and walk to most of their destinations. When I returned home, I felt much healthier and more energetic than when I left Minneapolis.

Yukiko was an amazing host, and I adored her students and teachers. Every day Dianne and I received little gifts from the dancers, which is their custom, as sincere gestures of friendship. All of us took joy in dancing together, and once again, dance, especially tap, proved to be a universal language.

Our final two days in Japan culminated in a trip to Hakone, a traditional Japanese spa, and a stop at a winery on our way back the next day. While we traveled through Japan, I felt completely absorbed in its beauty and serenity. Lush dark green foliage covered jagged-tooth mountains. Little puffs of whisper-light clouds danced around like images I had seen many times before in Japanese silk screens. The gardens were alive with exotic flowers and neatly trimmed trees and shrubs. Even the moss was luxurious. My first view of Mt. Fuji silenced me, and I stood in awe. I found myself without enough words to describe its majesty as I peered at it through clusters of pink cherry blossoms. All I could do was stand still and hope that my mind's eye would never lose this vision of perfection.

Upon our arrival, the Hakone spa director asked us to remove our shoes before entering, and instructed us to change into the traditional Japanese robes left in our room. A young woman led us up a winding staircase and down a narrow hall with woven grass-mat floors. When she opened the door to our eight-by-twelve-foot room, I was a bit surprised at its tiny size. I assumed that large rooms were not needed because they slept on the floor, and assumed a shared bathroom was on each level of the spa.

Curious, I looked around the miniature windowless room, asking in a hopeful tone, "Will they bring us mats to sleep on?"

The young woman departed from her quiet demeanor, and let out a roaring laugh, "Oh, this is not your room. This is the entrance!" She quickly slid open the bamboo door to reveal an enormous, stunning suite, complete with a private outdoor hot spring tub carved into the mountain side. A thatched-roof balcony overlooked a waterfall that was lavished on each side with cascading blue and pink flowers and tree branches laden with leaves of every imaginable shade of green. A sliding paper wall separated the sleeping area from the living room, plus a second indoor tub filled with water from the hot springs. The furniture was of simple, exquisite, and traditional Japanese design.

The scent of floral perfume and green tea filled the air, while the music of falling water put us in a trance. I was in heaven. With only a few minutes before dinner, we quickly donned our Japanese robes and gazed at the view from the balcony.

"Deb, look at what this sign says," Dianne cautioned. At the end of our balcony was a little wooden sign with carved letters in English, "Beware of wild monkeys. Do not feed." All of a sudden the paper walls did not seem thick enough.

Our dinner was in a private room for Dianne, Yukiko and her daughter, Tiffany, and her husband, Masa, and me. We sat cross-legged on the floor as dish after dish of traditional Japanese haute cuisine was presented. Even their food was beautiful—*and* entertaining! One delicacy was a live abalone still in its colorful, iridescent shell. Our hostess carefully topped each abalone with a pat of butter, and lit the Bunsen-type burner under each shell. Dianne and I heard a strange hissing sound, and in amazement moved our faces closer to study the plump, beige sea snail at close range.

"AHHHH!" I yelled and Dianne screamed, as we recoiled from long abalone tentacles suddenly thrashing out in our direction. This lengthy display is what an abalone does, apparently, as it succumbs to the heat.

"I should take a video of this and use it as my computer screensaver," Dianne exclaimed.

After dinner, Yukiko insisted that we visit the public hot spring bath, which required that we quickly get over our modesty. Hakone boasted a women's spa, a men's spa, and a family spa. We went to the women's spa that just happened to be empty at the time, which made my first experience in a public bath easier. The warmth of the water and its natural minerals were very comforting, and are believed to be healing.

Cool night air kissed the bath's hot water and filled the room with enchanting fog that made every object seem soft and mystical. I had never felt so peaceful, and in an instant came to understand and respect the importance of the hot spring baths to the Japanese. After soaking for about ten minutes, I climbed out of the hot water and headed to the hair-washing area.

Puffs of cool fog clothed me as I walked, guided by moonlight to another pool of hot spring water. Using a wooden ladle, I poured the healing water over my head, and lavished my hair with fragrant silky lather. Water slowly and delicately trickled from each full ladle, therapeutically washing away every bubble of shampoo.

After one more dip in the bath, all of us retired to our rain-forest-style suite, and found that our spa hostess had rolled out traditional floor sleeping mats. Contrary to the discomfort I expected, I have never experienced such a comforting sleep.

Singsong melodies of sprightly birds, perched amid dainty cherry blossoms, served as our alarm clock. Sleeping on the floor must have stretched my body during the night because I felt about two inches taller when I stood up. Reluctantly, we packed our bags to head back to Tokyo. Along the way we filled our day with hikes around Japanese gardens and visits to more temples and shrines. For dinner we stopped at a mountainside winery to experience a succulent Kobe beef barbeque. Our happy chatter echoed as we sat perched on the side of a mountain, looking down to a lush valley of abundant vineyards. After dinner we decided to visit the hot public baths in the winery to luxuriate a final time in the healing water. Part of the bath jutted outdoors, which presented a magnificent view of the valley below. The golden glow of the setting sun silhouetted the jagged mountains and caught my attention so much so that I swam to the very edge of the bath's outer wall. I could not avert my eyes from the sun, and became paralyzed while cloud formations like huge pink and purple wings surrounded it. I was humbled.

We arrived at Yukiko's apartment late in the evening and had to do our packing at lightning speed. However, once complete, we took time for a glass of fine Japanese wine to toast our newfound friendship. We held a little ceremony for the joyous occasion, and signed an official certificate that now hangs on the walls of ARTN, Heartbeat, and Dianne's living room, and states in both English and Japanese:

"May it be known that on this date, April 29, 2005, Heartbeat Studios Performing Arts Center of Apple Valley, Minnesota, USA, and ARTN Tap Dance Studio of Shibuya, Tokyo, Japan, have entered into a special friendship and relationship. All students and staff of one studio shall be welcome to the other studio in the spirit and furtherance of friendship and partnership between the two."

Finally, another dream came true. An overseas partnership came to be. The possibilities and benefits for our dance students and teachers seemed endless now. Upon my arrival back in Minneapolis, I received an email from Yukiko, "Me and some students visit Heartbeat in November. Get ready!" Let the exchange begin.

Tokyo Comes to Heartbeat

Seven months later, in November 2005, Yukiko and five of her students traveled to Minneapolis to study dance at Heartbeat, and work with dancers from my studio to collaborate on the production of a dance concert. The dancers from Japan stayed with Heartbeat host families to avoid hotel expenses. Each host family planned its own special events for their guests, and learned much from each other in the process. Their eight-day visit included daily dance classes, followed by tours of the area and, of course, shopping.

Yukiko and I had decided before their arrival that two of her best tap dancers, Mika and Sayaka, would work with two of my top tap dancers, Stephany and Sonja, to choreograph their own dance to perform in the dance concert celebrating their visit. All four dancers were extremely nervous when they heard about this, and had expected that Yukiko and I would guide them in their project, since they did not speak each other's language.

On day one, Yukiko and I met our foursome in the studio and explained to them, "You have one week to create a dance that is performance-ready as the featured dance in our show. You will also need to come up with a name for your quartet." Stephany, Sonja, Mika, and Sayaka had a deer-in-the-headlights look that reads the same in all languages, as Yukiko and I waved goodbye and walked out of the building. In reality, Yukiko and I were more nervous than they were, but knew the magical communication properties of tap. And this, after all, was the purpose of the exchange program—getting to know and understand each other through dance. The lives of everyone involved would become infinitely richer.

On day five, Yukiko and I watched as our four dancers revealed to us, for the first time, their masterful creation. The happy tapping quartet wore shirts embroidered with their newfound title, "East Meets West." Dianne traveled from Boston to see the dance concert, and was moved beyond words when she saw Heartbeat's and ARTN's collaborative production. I truly believe this experience was life-changing for Stephany, Sonja, Mika, and Sayaka, who have remained friends.

Heartbeat Goes to Tokyo

On a reciprocal visit to Tokyo in July 2006, Kristin, Paul, and I, plus seventeen of Heartbeat's dancers, teachers, and parents, spent eight days exploring the same wonders of Japan I had already experienced. Dianne joined us in Tokyo to teach at Yukiko's studio and see, firsthand, the continued development of the cultural exchange program. Again, the dancers spent their mornings taking classes, and their afternoons and evenings touring and shopping with the Japanese dancers. Our cultural exchange this time became multi-generational, because parents of Heartbeat's students had a chance to meet some of the Japanese parents.

Kristin taught a master jazz dance class at Yukiko's studio, and it made me feel like the mother of triplets: Kristin, Heartbeat, and the cultural exchange program. While watching Kristin teach her class, my thoughts kept drifting to how far we had come from our imprisonment by domestic violence. We had been on full speed ahead since the trial, and instead of becoming bitter, self-pitying people, we were taking huge steps to shed our fear, and embrace a world that we for so long believed did not care about us.

Our week of dance classes in Tokyo culminated with a Heartbeat and ARTN collaborative performance at a popular jazz club. Yukiko scheduled two performances that were sold out, and each show ended with the Tokyo debut of the dance piece by our happy tapping quartet, followed by thunderous applause that propelled the audience to their feet.

Our final two days in Japan were again spent at the Hakone spa and the mountainside winery. From experience, I knew how much this would impress Heartbeat's travel group, and I longed to visit each splendid place again. Heartbeat's group gasped at Hakone's beauty, and quickly agreed to traditional Japanese massages followed by a dip in the hot spring bath.

Our dinner was adorned with a constant parade of Japanese delicacies. Topping off the night, we shed all inhibitions and sang karaoke. Under the influence of a little Japanese sake, the mothers in the group were the star performers. My heart filled with love, and I spread my caring wings further as I watched the evening's events unfold. As the music of song and laughter faded, one by one we retreated to our rain forest hideaway with paper sliding doors, woven grass floors, and sleeping mats. A new music resonated throughout the spa as Heartbeat's happy group fell into a deep, peaceful sleep accompanied by various tones of tranquil snoring and a cascading waterfall.

Lively London

Heartbeat's trip to Tokyo was just the beginning. In September 2006, I saw an ad in a dance magazine that promoted performance opportunities for dance groups on a cruise ship. Even though the description for the event seemed more appropriate for a studio that focused primarily on dance competitions, which artistically rub me the wrong way because they make dance seem a sport rather than an art form, I called anyway to see if there were cruise ship performance opportunities for a non-competition studio.

Their representative, Joan, asked many questions about Heartbeat, and encouraged me to send her a DVD of Heartbeat's dance performances. Joan agreed that, "The cruise ship events are more competition-oriented, and

I completely understand your objection to them. There is a very remote possibility of a different and much better performance opportunity for your dancers, but it may be too late. I need to take a look at your DVD before I say anything more."

The next morning, I dropped the package in the mail, and simply forgot about it because the woman did say the chances were remote, and probably too late.

One week later, Joan called, "Deborah, I have received your DVD and packet, and having reviewed it, I would like your permission to go further with this other opportunity. I am not at liberty to say what it is yet, but I need your permission to send Heartbeat's information overseas. It is past the deadline for audition material submission, but I understand the event planners are not happy with what has been received to date. So there is still a slight chance. I assure you the event is not a dance competition."

"Please, go ahead and send the DVD overseas," I urged.

As before, I decided not to get too excited. On October 10, 2006, Joan called again.

"Deborah, I can now tell you what is going on. My agency was contacted last year by an entertainment group in London to help organize a huge event to celebrate the four hundredth anniversary of the settlers sailing from Kent, England, to Jamestown, Virginia. They are planning quite a large event at Leeds Castle at the same time that Queen Elizabeth will be visiting the U.S. next summer to commemorate the anniversary. The people in London want musicians, dancers, and singers from both the U.S. and the U.K. to be represented in the Leeds Castle July 4th Celebration Performance.

"During the past year, the event planners in London have been accepting audition videos from dance groups around the U.S. They want a variety of dance forms and a wide range of ages included, from children to adults, from ballet to break dance. They want a captivating show. The deadline they gave to submit an audition DVD has passed and they have not yet found a dance group that suits them—that is, until they saw your group.

"The event planners in London are offering your dancers the opportunity to be the *only* dance group to represent the United States at this historic celebration. And, in addition, Sadler's Wells Theatre would like your show to appear there, too. I should let you know that Sadler's Wells is London's counterpart to Carnegie Hall."

"Oh, my goodness!" popped from my mouth. "Please quickly send me all the details. I want to get rehearsals started by November. Thank you so much for connecting us with this once-in-a-lifetime opportunity!" Then I squealed.

Hardly containing my excitement, my shaking hands quickly dialed Kristin's phone number.

"Kristin! I am heading to your house right now. Get ready because we have a lot of work ahead of us."

"What's going on?" was her worried reply.

"Something wonderful," I cried.

From November 2006 to June 2007, Heartbeat's twenty-six-member dance company divided its time between rehearsing and holding several fundraisers to help defray travel expenses to London. Kristin's artistic vision helped create a theme for our production, titled, *Tapestry of Dance*. Heartbeat's instructors set choreography to music from British classical and pop artists, and American jazz and contemporary artists. The genres of ballet, tap, jazz, hip hop, modern, and break dance were choreographed to smoothly transition from one dance piece to the next, while Heartbeat's youth dancers held long lengths of billowing red, white, and blue fabric, maneuvering through each other as they ran across the stage. The flowing fabric created a full-stage visual image of threads weaving and unweaving to reveal the next dance piece.

The dance pieces were the body of the tapestry, and the lengths of fabric represented the common threads that bind the United States and England. Our costumes were also red, white, and blue, the shared colors of the American and British flags.

During our months of rehearsal, Paul put his admirable artistic talents to work and created promotional poster, flyer, and playbill designs for our concerts in London. The folks in London, of course, found Paul's work impeccable, and used his designs. News of our impending trip hit the headlines of one of Minnesota's largest newspapers, the *Star Tribune*, and Minnesota Governor Tim Pawlenty penned a letter of goodwill and acknowledgment of the historic event for me to present on his behalf to the head of the city council of Kent, England.

At last, July 1 arrived and forty dancers, parents, and teachers, decked out in their official Heartbeat warm-up suits with our logo emblazoned across their backs, boarded a plane.

It wasn't until all forty of us were nestled in our seats and the plane taxied to the runway that we grasped the honor of what awaited us. I had been so busy preparing for this trip, plus day-to-day studio operations, that I hadn't had time to reflect. When the plane lifted off, I looked out the window and whispered, "Thank you, God." The baby steps Kristin and I had been taking to separate from our old and troubled life to our new life had advanced to a full-fledged sprint.

London's Heathrow Airport is a city unto itself. Crowds of travelers nudged shoulder to shoulder through the tangle of hallways to get to the immigration and security gates.

"Deb, I am so glad we are all wearing Heartbeat's jackets, because it will be easy to find each other if we get lost," remarked Barb, a parent chaperone.

The sight of Heartbeat's logo jumped out from the mass of humanity. In about thirty minutes, however, the logo would spark gut-wrenching stress among Heartbeat's travelers.

Paul's long legs made it easy for him to move ahead of our group to scout out how long we would wait before we would finally get to the baggage claim area to meet our London contact, Christian, who was patiently awaiting our arrival. At the opposite end of the long hallway, I could see Paul jumping up and down and excitedly waving his arms overhead, "Deb! Take a left when the group gets to this point because we can go through the large group processing."

Thirty minutes later, Heartbeat's group reached the left-turn point, and as we rounded the corner, we saw Paul grinning with pride that he found a solution for our journey to vacate the airport.

"Everyone waits here," the official said. "We only need two of you to process the entire group." Paul and I followed the official to his station, and handed him our group's travel documents.

The official's expressionless face was a little unnerving as he thoroughly read the information. He looked up and studied the group dressed in their Heartbeat jackets.

"Are you a professional company? Will you be working in London?" he asked.

Paul proudly answered, "We're not a professional company per se, but we have been given this great opportunity to..." Paul stopped talking when he saw the intense look on the official's face.

"Both of you, give me your passports now!" the official ordered. Paul and I obliged, and the official walked away. Everyone in Heartbeat's group stood like wide-eyed frozen statues. During the next agonizing hour, Heartbeat's group went from standing in complete numbness to one by one sitting on the floor. Their expressions were that of lost orphans. A unified sigh of relief was heard from Heartbeat's forty-member group when the official returned with his supervisor, who said, "We believe you intend to work in London, and you do not have a work permit. We are going to send your group back to the United States if we do not get to the bottom of this!"

The supervisor turned to Paul and me and said, "We are going to confiscate your passports until we know what is going on."

In moments like these, my psychological and emotional states slip into another dimension, something like floating in outer space. Many people have quizzed me about this.

"My goodness, how can you be so calm?" they would say.

I have found that since fleeing my abusive marriage years ago, when faced with mind-boggling dread, rather than losing control and letting the situation short-circuit my brain, I become abnormally calm and silent. To some, it may appear that I do not have a grasp of the seriousness of the moment or that I don't care. But in reality, I have developed a fine mechanism that helps me step into a protective bubble to provide me with the space and tranquility I need to maintain logical and rational thinking while assessing my options, decisions, and choices. I'm glad this coping mechanism, another building block of reassembling me, is part of me now. Or, simply having lived in a state of terror during my married years, I am quite tired of that feeling. It could also be that no fear can compare to having a gun pointed at you by a very angry husband.

"Officer, you are mistaken in your assumption of the purpose of my group's performances in London. We are volunteering our time and talent to participate in the four hundreth anniversary celebration between our two countries. We paid for our own travel costs to come here," I calmly informed him. "If you go to baggage claim, you will find a gentleman named Christian, who has other documents pertaining to our visit here."

"I don't care who has documents!" he shouted. "I want to talk directly to your travel agent in the U.S., and since it is now four o'clock on Sunday morning in your agent's time zone, you will just have to wait until he and I connect either by telephone or Internet." He did a masterful about-face and marched off into parts unknown.

"How can you be so calm?" a cacophony of my students' voices cried.

"If I was all hysterical and nervously crying, how would that make all of you feel?" I replied.

"Just know that things will work out, and I will definitely confront the person at the travel agency back home who dropped the ball on relaying important information about our trip to the officials here. Relax now and take advantage of this down time because we have a heck of a busy schedule once we get to the hotel."

Not only did I feel the need to verbally calm them, I wanted to demonstrate calm to my students. So I pulled out a book, sat on the floor, and slowly turned the pages as I read. The scene played out just like the dynamics of the student/teacher relationship in my studio. One by one, the dancers dug out books from their carry-ons, sat on the floor, and began reading. It wasn't too long before some were spread out in a deep slumber on Heathrow's floor.

Three and a half hours later, we were released and received gushing apologies from the security officials.

"No worries," I said, "you were just doing your job. By the way, can Paul and I have our passports back?" The official handed us our passports and the entire forty-member entourage was on its way to do what we do best: dance.

London lived up to its reputation—foggy and rainy the entire week. Fortunately most of our activities were indoors. Dance classes, Shakespeare acting classes, rehearsals, and performances filled our trip calendar. We did have windows of time where we could sightsee on our own, and hit the pubs at night.

Our performance at Sadler's Wells Theater was a once-in-a-lifetime experience for us because of its stature in the world's theaters. The main purpose for our trip, however, was our show at Leed's Castle in Kent.

The stage at Leed's Castle was similar to the Hollywood Bowl in shape and size, and had outdoor seating. Prior to the start of our show, the City Council President of Kent called Kristin, Paul, and me to center stage to present us with gift bags full of jars of honey, for which the area is known. I had the youngest dancer in our group join us during the pre-show ceremony, so that she could present the City of Kent official with our reciprocal gift bag full of boxes of Minnesota wild rice. In addition, we presented him with the letter from Minnesota's governor:

June 30, 2007

Greetings!

On behalf of the State of Minnesota, it is with great pleasure that I thank you for the generosity you have shown to the Heartbeat Studios Performing Arts Center by inviting them to participate in the 400th anniversary of the sailing of settlers from Kent, England, to Jamestown, Virginia.

This group of talented dancers and dedicated parents are especially excited about this opportunity. During this week they plan to share their love of dance, form lifelong friendships, and make priceless memories.

Perhaps someday you will have the opportunity to come visit our great state. We have much to offer from our beautiful parks' and trails' systems to our *diverse metropolitan area.*

Again, thank you for the kind hospitality you have shown these citizens of Minnesota. Best wishes for a wonderful celebration.

Warmest Regards,

Tim Pawlenty

Governor of the State of Minnesota

To sum up our London experience—I had never before felt the intense, warm-to-the- bones surge of pride that I did during our shows, which were the culmination of the many sacrifices Kristin and I made to build Heartbeat, the only studio selected to represent the U.S. at this honorable event. Wow! Now I can shout to the world once again, "We are survivors, and on top of that, we're pretty cool!"

Dancing to My Heartbeat

16

In bold print across the front page of Thisweek, our local newspaper, was the headline, "Heartbeat: A Success Story." The article began, "*Deborah Lysholm was overwhelmed by the turnout January 15, 2008, as Eastview High School Theater filled with friends, family and community members. They were there to help celebrate more than just the ten-year anniversary of Heartbeat Studios, which Lysholm owns and directs. They were there to celebrate Lysholm and the dream she had built for herself and her daughter, Kristin.*"

Further into the article, Kristin is quoted about her mother, *"Once she had divorced, it really seemed she made a choice for herself to go out and not be afraid to build her dream. She turned that around to be fearless instead of more afraid. It is very inspiring."*

Kristin's statement underscored the fact that she understands the power and gifts that are within each of us, gifts which no one has the right to minimize or beat into extinction. Another building block of me settled into place: Self-respect.

"Time flies," became an understatement when I realized that a decade had passed since Heartbeat opened for business. Underlying that astonishment was the euphoria that Heartbeat's mortgage was now 50 percent paid. Young children that I had taught dance to during my pre-Heartbeat years were now grown with families of their own, and several of them successfully pursued dance majors in their college careers. Some received full scholarships or were on tour with professional dance companies, while others still danced with me for pure enjoyment. Proudly, I can say that some are now part of my teaching staff.

All view Heartbeat as, "Our home away from home." A new generation of dancers arrives at my studio each fall as we begin another session of classes. Delightful giggles, layered with the click-clack of three-year-olds in tiny patent leather tap shoes, is still my favorite music.

Ten years is quite a milestone, and it was only natural that we would want to celebrate. Preparing for Heartbeat's tenth anniversary celebration performance was a year-long project. With each added check-off mark on our to-do list, we inched closer to fully comprehending what had been accomplished and experienced in just a decade. It also became apparent that my quest to reassemble the building blocks of me had no end in sight, and that is a good thing because it meant that I would be in constant discovery mode. I find beauty and vitality in that, and it goes hand-in-hand with dance training. There is always more to learn, and it is forever changing.

The day of Heartbeat's tenth anniversary show arrived and so had our guest artists, including Dianne, Yukiko and her dancers from Tokyo, Jason

Samuels-Smith from New York, and local show band, CBO. Kristin's Vox
Medusa Dance Company graced the stage and filled my heart with warmth
only a mother knows. Heartbeat's dance companies, instructors, and college
dance-major alumni joined the guest artists to celebrate and create an evening
to remember.

As a surprise to me, Kristin had invited a number of students and their
parents to write letters explaining what Heartbeat meant to them. An acting
student read the first letter to the audience at the start of our show.

*"Joy, talent, commitment to excellence, and quiet strengths are precious gifts
that Deborah and Kristin impart to their students. These gifts are assets their
students will carry with them throughout their lifetimes. Deborah and Kristin
are special people in our lives who we look up to as heroes. They experienced
tremendous hardship and pain, and through dance, found a way to become
stronger and inspire other people. We love them and love sharing their passion
for dance. Thank you for Heartbeat! Congratulations on your tenth anniversary!
Dance on!"*

From my preferred theater seat, a wooden stool in stage-left wing, I
watched our celebration performance, and through the prism of my tears, an
aura like the rising sun radiated from each stage light. As the letters were read,
I fell more in love with all of the students I'd ever taught.

Vox Medusa electrified the audience with their performance of *Fire,* one of
Kristin's many spellbinding masterpieces. In this exquisite modern piece, nine
dancers in flowing red gowns executed bold and fluid movements that were
in stark contrast to the intricate dance of the flames flickering high from the
palm torches strapped to their hands.

For my dance solo, I chose to do the tap waltz that Dianne had taught me
a few years ago in tribute to my dad. A minute into my dance, I could hear
another pair of feet tap dancing from my right, and immediately a second
pair joined in from my left. The audience began cheering and applauding as
two incredible women, Dianne and Yukiko, danced their way toward me. Our
trio became a special moment of improvisation in honor of our friendship
within and outside of the dance world. Three delicate rhythms harmonized

effortlessly, and we graciously invited the audience to share in our happiness. I was humbled to be performing with these two renowned professionals, and their gift that night will remain with me always.

Our celebration, bursting with music, dance, and acting, progressed until the final bow, and the audience, dancers, and actors sang, "Happy Birthday to Heartbeat." As we hit our last note, the audience jumped to their feet in standing ovation, and Kristin sweetly whispered, "We did it, Mom." A deeper love from a mother to her child does not exist. Throughout the entire evening, I felt the love and warmth from Mom and my siblings sitting in the audience. The spiritual presence of Dad, and the guiding presence of my ancestors, gave me strength. The supportive words from Gregory Hines lingered in my mind, "I just wanted you to see what you are capable of doing on your own."

The Heartbeat Connection

Three weeks after Heartbeat's tenth anniversary celebration, I received confirmation that Kristin and I, plus Heartbeat instructors Levi, Carlos, Tona, and Stephany, would be included in the lineup of master dance teachers at the first-ever international tap dance festival held in July 2008 in my beloved Barcelona. In addition, Heartbeat's dance company members were invited to be guest artists in the festival's grand performance at the Sant Andrieu Teatre. It had been eight years since I first traveled to Barcelona to meet with Guillem to establish a cultural exchange and travel study program with dancers in that part of the world. Guillem put me in touch with a fellow tap dancer named Basilio, the festival's founder and director. We became email pals writing back and forth to work out details for Heartbeat's upcoming trip to Barcelona. To make the magic of this trip more profound, Yukiko flew in from Tokyo to also be part of the master teacher lineup in the festival. Something I dreamed of years ago was about to happen—tap dancers from the U.S., Japan, and Spain getting together to celebrate our common bond.

Yukiko and I really hoped Dianne could join us, but her schedule was already full. For orientation purposes, Basilio asked that all master teachers arrive in Barcelona a few days before the start of the dance festival. The remainder of Heartbeat's adult group of dancers, and a few teenage dancers accompanied by their parents, planned to arrive two days after us. This arrangement gave Heartbeat's teachers time to wander through beautiful Barcelona before our busy teaching schedules commenced. Basilio met us at the airport, and had taxis already lined up to whisk us away. It became apparent how impeccably organized and sweet Basilio was. He made us feel at home, and as with most tap dancers around the world, a close camaraderie developed. I knew it wouldn't be long before Kristin would exclaim, "Oh, Mom, Barcelona is beautiful! You were right!"

In the taxi ride to the hotel, I closed my eyes and breathed in the fragrance of Barcelona's summer. Familiar sights brought back memories that I had been clinging onto for all these years. I felt that I belonged here, and was joyful that Kristin and Heartbeat's teachers and dancers would now understand my constant rambling about this city and its people.

Yukiko had already arrived from Japan, and after Heartbeat's teachers checked into their hotel rooms, the seven of us dashed to the swimming pool and poured down world-famous sangrias.

"You guys, Barcelona comes to life around midnight, so you have many sangria-drinking hours ahead of you!" I joked.

Carlos and Levi gazed at women sunbathing poolside, while the women in our group ogled bare-chested men who were choreographing opportune moments to flex their muscles for our entertainment while they did construction work on an adjacent building.

The Mediterranean sun and sangrias got the best of us, so we returned to our rooms to freshen up for a big night ahead that included a welcome party at the Bailongu Studio, where the dance festival would be held. An hour later we met again in the lobby, but this time we were dressed to impress, and very hungry.

"To Las Ramblas," I directed. "You are about to see the most lively and lovely boulevard with twenty-four-hour entertainment by street performers." Off we went with pep in our step.

Purposely, I walked a few steps behind my group of teachers, who were full of excited chatter and pointing like kids in a toy shop. I wanted to witness, firsthand, their reactions to Barcelona as I thought about my first stroll down this street that led me to the Mediterranean; how quickly my pace increased when I felt the sea beckoning me. Flower stands erupting with bold color dotted the boulevard that was bursting with a mass of humanity. The surroundsound of a plethora of languages added to the music of the night. Our first tapas dinner was at an outdoor restaurant on Las Ramblas where our food was spicy, tasty, and addicting. Our sangria glasses were never empty. Our smiles glowed as much as our sunburned faces.

"Do you guys want to try the subway or should we take a taxi to the welcome party?" I asked. Levi and Carlos insisted that we try the subway, something I had never done on my previous trips.

"You lead the way," I urged. The subway was extremely hot with many zigzagging staircases for us to descend. Most of the women in our group wore high heels, not good walking shoes, which made the excursion quite interesting. Our exit was at the La Sagrada Familia stop by the landmark cathedral designed by the masterful architect, Gaudi. As we ascended the final staircase, I anticipated my crew gasping when they would first behold La Sagrada Familia. Unfortunately, we were looking in the opposite direction of the cathedral.

"Where's the church?" Levi asked.

"Turn around slowly," I whispered.

One by one, the seven of us turned around to a breathtaking sight.

"Oh, my God," was about all they could say. "Oh, my God, oh, my God, oh, my God," they sang in unison. Gaudi was simply a genius architect with passion not many humans possess. Slowly we worked our way down the street toward Bailongu Studio, periodically pausing to turn around in awe at the sight of the cathedral.

Due to my teachers' first encounter with majestic La Sagrada Familia, we arrived a little late. Bailongu Studio was a four-block walk from the subway, and as we got closer, we could hear music and many happy voices.

"Well, you made it!" Basilio exclaimed from the studio's entrance.

Bailongu was a magnificent studio with three levels, six classrooms, and wide-planked wood floors, like the deck of a tall sailing ship of old. Bailongu had its own bar complete with wine and beer—something you would never see back in the U.S.

The party progressed with many hugs and kisses on each cheek from all of the master teachers based in Barcelona.

"Is Guillem here?" I asked. I was anxious to see him again after so long.

"Deborah!" I heard in a familiar Spanish-accented voice. When I turned around, Guillem and I literally ran to each other, embracing with a big, long hug. We talked endlessly, catching up on life. I proudly introduced him to Kristin and my teachers. All of us agreed that this week would be another once-in-a-lifetime experience for everyone, no matter which country we came from.

Around 2:00 a.m., my group and I decided that we had already had a full day and evening, and jet lag was draining us. We bid, "Goodbye until tomorrow," to our Spanish friends, and began our four-block walk back to the subway station.

At the top of the staircase I said, "You guys go on ahead. My feet are so sore from these shoes that I simply cannot take another step. I'll catch a taxi back to the hotel."

Levi had a concerned look on his face and said, "I'll worry about you. Are you sure you will be okay this late at night? I don't see any taxis."

"Yes, I'll be fine," I assured them. "Remember, I have been to this city twice already by myself, and I suggest that tomorrow all of you just explore Barcelona on your own. Make it your own discovery. It will draw you in forever." I watched as they disappeared into the depths of the subway.

Sore feet were not the only reason that I excused myself from the subway trek. I needed a moment alone to collect my thoughts and feelings of being back in the city that I so dearly loved. This was my moment to realize this trip to Barcelona meant that my dream had come full circle. I had reached a milestone in my quest to open a dance studio of my own, and establish relationships with studios overseas. I marveled at La Sagrada Familia, and said a thankful prayer as I stood under the dim street lamp. For several minutes, tears of happiness streamed down my cheeks, and I breathed deeply to keep grounded.

In that wee hour of the morning, I was the only person on the street. My time to reflect, however, was abruptly cut short by the sound of screeching tires from a car jumping the curb and stopping at my feet. Ah, yes, the crazy taxi drivers of Barcelona.

"Miss, my name is Enric. You need taxi?" asked the young handsome Spanish man. Popular classics of the music artist, Prince, boomed from the yellow vehicle encircled by a narrow band of white-and-black checkers.

"Sure. Thanks for stopping," I said while stepping into his taxi, "Take me to the Catalonia Ramblas Hotel, but go the scenic way. I love Barcelona at night."

For thirty minutes the energetic fellow and I sped around Barcelona with the windows down and my hair streaming in the wind. Enric cranked up the volume of his CD player and snapped his fingers in rhythm with the tune. Being the tap dancing percussionist that I was, I joined in the finger snapping, which led to us belting out at the top of our lungs Prince's classic songs, "Little Red Corvette," "Purple Rain," and "Let's Go Crazy." We were spur-of-the-moment rock stars giving a flawless performance, except twice when he spontaneously inserted the lyrics, "Oh, sheet!" as his taxi jolted up and down curbs while turning corners at the speed of light.

"You have a nice voice," I said, wishing we had not yet reached my destination.

"So do you," Enric replied. "This is my pleasure. You do not pay."

Before I could say, "Thank you," Enric sped away into the night, taxi tires squealing.

Unfortunately, the six teachers took the wrong subway train and had to circle back, so I actually arrived at the hotel a few minutes before they did. Standing in the hallway outside of our rooms, we briefly discussed the next day. While I inserted the key to our hotel room door, Kristin asked, "How was your taxi ride back? We were so worried about you, Mom."

"I'm tired, honey. I'll explain in the morning."

Completely exhausted, we crawled into bed, letting our heads sink deep into fluffy white pillows. Kristin's bed was next to a large window that framed a masterpiece—a star-studded, moonlit sky. The silhouette of Kristin's motionless body began to blur as my eyelids could no longer stay open. At the last moment of consciousness, a curious thought infiltrated my mind, and I erupted into uncontrollable giggles. I imagined Kristin's expression and response when the opportunity came for me to explain my escapade with Enric. In an effort to subdue my laughter, I joyfully began singing Prince's masterpiece, "Baby I'm a Star."

Kristin's silhouette bolted upright and ordered, "Mom! Go to sleep."

Mediterranean Magic

Heartbeat's six teachers, plus Yukiko, spent the next day exploring the hustle, bustle, and history of Barcelona. We set out in different directions, knowing that at the end of the day we would share our adventures. Eagerly we filled each minute of the day, taking in the sights of the Gothic quarter, art museums of Picasso and Miro, shopping markets, and more of Gaudi's storybook buildings. An occasional stop at a sidewalk café to partake in decadent gelato refreshed us for the next leg of our exploration. We were like little kids in a wonderland, anxious to see what fabulous experience awaited us around each corner.

All roads in Barcelona eventually find their way to the shore of the Mediterranean Sea, and so did we. Our meeting point was an expansive boardwalk area full of fine restaurants and lively nightlife. With sunburned faces and windblown hair, we gazed contentedly across the beach and watched as each turquoise wave kissed the white sand. Locals and tourists played sand volleyball, while seagulls and Spanish guitars accompanied their laughter. Every cell of my body absorbed the beauty of this moment as we stood statuesque, like ancient explorers searching for what lay beyond the horizon.

"Mom, it is getting late," Kristin reluctantly noticed, so we headed back to the hotel to swim, down a few more sangrias, and freshen up for our last night out before we would begin our week of teaching at the dance festival.

We much preferred to wander around the Gothic area of Barcelona, because what was delightful during the day was even more charming at night. Our dinner was at another sidewalk restaurant on the Las Ramblas, where many elaborately costumed performance artists entertained us.

Barcelona is a mecca for artists of all genres, and its residents view the arts as their lifeblood. We felt at home here. In a minute, we knew that we would be night owls while in Barcelona because there was too much to see and do to waste time sleeping. Our stroll back to the hotel was leisurely, again at 2:00 a.m., and along the way we came upon an establishment called, The Irish Pub.

"Let's check it out," Carlos insisted. Immediately we designated that pub as our late-night meeting place for the remainder of our week in Barcelona. We became pals with the bartender and waitress, and took dibs on the seven bar stools. At each late-night arrival, the bartender knew he would have a full house full of laughter and spirited conversation. We loved our pub.

We're Here!

Complete chaos filled the lobby of the hotel the next afternoon as the remaining twenty-six members of Heartbeat's group of dancers and parents arrived. Hotel staff had mixed up room assignments, the airlines had lost luggage, and patience was nowhere to be found. One by one, the travelers became victims of jet lag and dozed off in lobby chairs while the concierge and I discovered and corrected the reservation mistakes. Lost luggage was eventually delivered, and before long, all was calm. Once settled, the new arrivals from Heartbeat hurriedly set out to swim, explore, and down sangrias. In contrast, Heartbeat's teachers had already spent two days getting into the groove of Barcelona, and we smiled as we observed another group of kids in a wonderland.

How can I adequately explain how proud I was of Kristin and Heartbeat's teachers when we taught our master classes? During breaks between my classes, I stopped by their classes, marveling at their ability to capture the respect and attention of their students. The dance students in my class comprised tap dancers from England, Brazil, Spain, France, and Switzerland.

Language difference is not a problem in a tap class because we all speak tap, and are skilled observers and listeners. Kristin's students were mostly from Barcelona, as were those of Heartbeat's other teachers. Yukiko's students were literally from all over the world. Heartbeat's dancers jumped right in to study with teachers from Barcelona.

When I was their age, I could have only dreamed of having an experience like this. Heartbeat's dancers did very well, and their master teachers complimented me on their advanced skill and focus. I was a proud dance-mom of many. Later that evening, Heartbeat's teachers were invited to a celebration to commemorate the end of the festival's first day. Basilio, Guillem, and other festival teachers met at the Harlem Club for a reception and tap jam with a local jazz trio.

In the midst of the merriment, Basilio invited Yukiko and me to join him on stage to tap dance together in recognition of the relationship and friendship between our respective studios. An eight-year effort blossomed as dancers from Japan, Spain, and the United States made music together in their common language: tap.

Earlier in the day, while classes were in session at Bailongu, Spain's main television news station sent out a camera crew to report on the festival for a featured news segment to air later that night. The news crew filmed me teaching, but I didn't think anything of it because I was focused on my students. At one point the television reporter entered Guillem's class and asked, "What inspired you to produce Barcelona's first international tap dance festival?"

A few members of Heartbeat's group and I overheard Guillem say, "There was this lady from Minnesota who has a studio called Heartbeat, and she kept sending me emails. I did not know what she meant by partner studio and culture exchange program. She kept sending me emails for a long time, until eight years ago I invited her to come to Barcelona to meet and find out what she was talking about. Her inspiration helped us organize Barcelona's first international tap dance festival, *Tap On Barcelona*, which will become an annual event."

When I heard Guillem's comments, I was speechless—and felt the solid snap of the building blocks of me lock firmly into place. I felt humble, thankful, and respected on a personal and professional level, while angels' wings warmly hugged my shoulders. Kristin and I were walking the path God wanted us to take, and our heartache and fear in years past were experiences nudging us to navigate the right course. Both of us were natural explorers all along—it just took a while to survive the obstacles before the wind could catch our sails and send us on our odyssey.

Nothing But Blue Skies

The next morning, when I caught a taxi to Bailongu, the driver glanced at the rearview mirror, grinning, "I see you on television last night!"

Blaring away on his radio was the old Johnny Nash song, "I Can See Clearly Now." The lyrics fit my mood perfectly because dark days, pain, and obstacles were gone, and looking straight ahead, I saw nothing but blue skies.

Having only eight days in Barcelona, we packed as much as we could into every minute. Touring, celebrations, tap jams, eating, sunbathing, swimming, shopping, making new friends, and starting the process all over again. The dance festival culminated in a Friday night performance at the Sant Andrieu Teatre and featured performances by the festival's master teachers and Heartbeat's dancers. Incredible as it was to have dancers from all over the world spend a week in class together, it was profoundly professionally fulfilling to perform in a show with the other master teachers.

Heartbeat's tap dancers' and flamenco dancers' performance piece mixed American jazz music and flamenco guitar in honor of our new dance friends in Barcelona. Kristin performed her infamous dance piece, *Fire*, with Heartbeat's modern dance students. Tap duets and trios added punch to Heartbeat's section of the show, along with Levi's show-stopping hip hop, and Carlos' jaw-dropping break dancing. Heartbeat's group of dancers and teachers watched in heartfelt admiration as Guillem, Basilio, and other dancers from Barcelona thrilled the audience. Yukiko's tap dancing enchanted everyone. Her tap shoes sang so clear and sweet. Backstage, whispers of, "How did I do?" and "You were great!" bounced quietly from one dancer to another.

On stage, we were not people from different areas of the world; we were simply dancers reassuring each other through a strong bond in the arts, a community with no geographic boundaries. The desire to do well, and share with the audience what makes us happy, is the driving force behind all dancers, no matter where they come from. The stage is a dancer's living room, and we are naturally gracious hosts inviting the audience into our homes.

Our week in Barcelona was coming to an end, but for me it was just the beginning of future opportunities for dancers from Yukiko's studio in Tokyo, dancers in Barcelona, and Heartbeat's dancers. Wheels were turning in my mind as I thought about the possibilities for more events to share our common bond.

Out of pure exhaustion from the show, coupled with our Barcelona-high tranquility, Kristin, Tona, Yukiko, and I navigated to an outdoor cafe along Las Ramblas to eat (paella), drink (sangrias), and be merry (laugh until our cheeks hurt). The city seemed exceptionally joyful this evening. We were stunned when we mistook one street performer, disguised in bark and leaves, as a real boulevard tree; that is, until the "tree" stepped off the curb and walked away for a cigarette break. Two other artists fluttered about in eye-catching butterfly regalia, while others resembled copper-plated, derby-capped gentlemen riding turn-of-the-century bicycles. Music carried by the Mediterranean evening breeze permeated every nook and cranny of the city.

Adding a high note to our evening's pleasure were the mimicking antics of a clown. To give the clown due credit, he roused side-splitting laughter from everyone with his ability to deliver perfectly timed imitations of unsuspecting tourists as he casually strutted behind them. His delightful show could have gone on all evening, but was interrupted by approximately two hundred of the two thousand Harley Davidson Motorcycle conventioneers in town, who at that moment sped by with their motors loudly snorting Harley-style. Such was a typical evening in Barcelona. On this splendid and peaceful evening, the thought that at some point we must go home did not enter our minds the remainder of the night.

Looking Back to Tomorrow

The next morning I took a hot, steamy shower to get ready for our first excursion outside of Barcelona. While wiping away condensation that had accumulated on the mirror, I noticed that the damage to my left eyelid, caused by a blow from Richard years ago, had severely worsened. Over time, my upper eyelid had become so weak it was now obstructing half the vision in my eye. Every time I looked into a mirror, it was a sad physical reminder of the past. A few months prior to this trip, I had made an appointment with an ophthalmic surgeon, Dr. Andrew, to schedule corrective surgery upon my return from Barcelona. The startling reflection in the mirror made me realize: the surgery couldn't come fast enough.

Heartbeat's large group of dancers, parents, and teachers, plus Yukiko, climbed into a motor coach and headed to the Montserrat Monastery an hour away. The monastery dates back to the ninth century, and its magnificent buildings jut out from the top of mountains that resemble huge clumps of dripping candle wax.

Our motor coach driver cautiously navigated tight hairpin turns as we climbed through puffs of clouds hovering over an emerald-green valley. The view was breathtaking, and when we stepped off the motor coach, we were just in time to hear the Benedictine monks' chanting voices echoing through the mountaintops. Their voices took our voices away. We proceeded through the monastery in complete reverence and awe, and truly felt removed from the rest of the world. Part of our group lit candles and said prayers, while others gazed at the Black Madonna inside the splendid sanctuary. Throughout the tour, we remained quiet, even as we boarded the motor coach to return to the hotel. Silence was really unusual for our group.

Back at the hotel, we sadly realized that this was our last evening in Barcelona to enjoy as we wished. Sunday evening would be spent packing to go home. The solution to our dismay was to simply party harder, and wander the Las Ramblas and Gothic areas one more time. Yukiko and I decided to attend a show produced by Roxane Butterfly, another distinguished tap professional in Barcelona.

After Roxane's show, Yukiko went to dinner with friends from Tokyo, and I met Basilio for a glass of fine Spanish wine. Basilio and I talked for hours to strategize Heartbeat's next trip to Barcelona and his visit to Heartbeat in the summer of 2009. He, too, had his mind's wheels in motion. We bid adieu, since I would not be seeing him again before Heartbeat's group flew home.

"Deborah, when you kept sending emails to Guillem about a cultural exchange program, that is what inspired me to produce Barcelona's first international tap festival. I want you to know this because the festival happened partly because of you," Basilio said sincerely.

Leaving the cafe in pouring rain, we continued our conversation until a taxi approached us at a rapid clip and sprayed our already wet clothes with more water. Basilio kissed me on each cheek before I got into the taxi, and we continued waving until we could not see each other anymore.

"Take me to the Irish Pub," I said as we sped down the street, splashing everyone who dared to stand on a curb. The pub was already packed with lively Heartbeat folks desperately trying to avoid accepting the truth that we had only one more day in Spain.

Sunday morning meant sun, surf, and sand as our motor coach arrived to carry us away to Spain's popular resort town, Sitges. Two hours later, we immediately claimed our beach chairs and umbrellas, and planned our day along the shore of the Mediterranean. Heartbeat's group split off in all directions, like spurting water in a plaza fountain. Some went on tours of historic cathedrals and museums, while others went shopping in the quaint village of white buildings, terra cotta rooftops, and winding narrow cobblestone streets. Many dove right into the turquoise sea, while others built sandcastles. We literally were kids in a most magnificent playground, and this day was perfect medicine to swallow to unwind and celebrate our Barcelona experience.

Several hours later, many bodies with sunburned faces, wind-tossed hair, and bulging shopping bags boarded the motor coach back to Barcelona. The ride to the hotel was silent, as we knew that in the morning, our next motor coach ride would be to the airport.

With a group as large as Heartbeat's, you are bound to find those who are on time and those who are late, those who are organized and those who do not know what the word means. It was announced: be packed and ready for the ride to the airport by 6:30 a.m.—no later.

Most of Heartbeat's group finished packing, and retired early to have the energy for the grueling process of checking in at the airport, and our long flight home. A few in Heartbeat's group figured they would be smart and stay up all night to get one more chance at this magic city.

"Oh, I'll just pack in the morning because I'll sleep on the plane," they proclaimed.

At 6:30 that morning, the hotel lobby was full of tired dancers, teachers, and parents, and a huge assortment of luggage. The motor coach pulled up to the hotel entrance, and one by one, Heartbeat's members found seats as their luggage was loaded. I did a head count, and realized we were missing two people. They were the all-nighters who decided to pack in the morning, but upon their return to the hotel about 5:00 a.m., fell fast asleep and still were, as the motor coach was ready to drive away.

"Quick, we have to wake them up," one of the parents yelled. A small army of the on-time, organized people ran to the all-nighters' rooms, woke them up, helped them pack, and escorted their near-comatose bodies out of the hotel. Now thirty minutes late for our departure time, I ordered the motor coach driver, "Drive like a taxi driver!" We made it to the airport on time, and quickly nestled into our seats for the long flight home.

Sitting in the window seat next to Kristin as the plane taxied down the runway, I thought of our long journey to get here. I prayed that through it all, I had given her a bigger vision of what she can be.

Closing my eyes, I breathed slowly while peaceful slumber enveloped Kristin, and her head found a comfortable resting place on my shoulder. She is a beautiful woman and a precious child. Our connection is many layers deep, wrapped in an unspoken, indescribable bond like that among soldiers in battle, or explorers sailing into the unknown.

At that moment, I promised myself I would now plan a trip for the two of us to visit Oslo, Norway. There we'd walk on the pier where long ago my great-great-great-grandmother, Ingeborg, longed for her family to see her one last time before she sailed off to her new life in America. When Kristin and I stand on that pier, Ingeborg will be happy to know that, even though generations later, part of her family did show up after all.

Our plane picked up speed, and at the exact moment the plane's tires disengaged from the runway, I embraced our future. Looking out the window, I saw the black tarmac below and imagined it as a shrinking pile of ashes. We were Phoenixes rising.

My heart and head filled with peace. I felt the sun's warmth on my face as the plane flew into the new day. Uncontrollably, tears welled in my eyes, and I had a strong spiritual feeling that God was sending us on our next journey. As the plane continued its powerful climb, the momentum gently swayed it like the lead partner of a waltzing couple. I smiled and thought, "Now it is both of us dancing with the wind."

At that moment, I knew that when I returned home and unlocked my front door, the building blocks of me would be firmly in place. Like my ancestors before me, I was brave and I was hopeful, and would forever be dancing to my heartbeat with a daughter that I love so dearly.

I Can See Clearly Now

JOURNAL ENTRY: (CONTINUED FROM PAGE 1) - JULY 24, 2008

Nearly two hours later, Dr. Andrew's repair work to my damaged eye was complete.

"Deb, your surgery is over. You are in recovery now," the nurse assured me as I slowly escaped from la-la land. Anesthesia makes me nauseated, and I was trying to will myself not to vomit. The feeling in my stomach was not good. For

the next hour, the nurse kept replacing the cold pack on my eyes with a fresh one to keep the swelling down. I was afraid to open my eyes because the doctor did say that my vision may be very cloudy for a period of time, and not being able to see clearly would make me extremely concerned. I was also worried about causing pressure against the stitches under my eyelid. Kristin remained in the hospital waiting room as long as she could before she had to head to the studio to teach, but was able to be there long enough to hear the doctor say that the surgery went well.

I was finally ready to return home, but still could not open my eyes. The nurse gave Paul the go-ahead to get his car from the parking lot, and to meet me at the patient pick-up area. While sitting in the wheelchair with a cold pack on my eye bandages and a prescription for painkillers in my pocket, I felt the soothing warmth of the sun kiss my cheeks. My restful moment was cut short by pain from the surgery becoming fierce, and I was relieved to hear the car pull up. Paul and the nurse guided me into the car and I leaned my head back so the cold pack would stay in place.

"Deb, I will drive carefully, like you are made of glass. Don't worry. I won't take any fast turns." I was so glad at that moment that Paul was not a taxi driver from Barcelona.

Kristin and Paul planned to stay with me for two days to make sure I was not alone if complications from the surgery developed. I arrived intact, and Paul securely held my arm as we walked up the front steps and into the house.

"Do you want another cold pack and a painkiller?" Paul asked.

"Yes, please!" was my reply as I stood in the middle of the kitchen with my eyes closed. "Paul, turn me in the direction of the bathroom. I think I have the courage to take a look in the mirror now."

Several baby steps later I reached out to feel where the sink was located, and stood facing the mirror.

"Paul, please let me be alone a minute."

"Okay, I understand," he obliged, walking into the living room.

In slow motion, like peeling the layers of a cocoon, I nervously and carefully lifted away the cold pack and bandages from my eyes and gazed into the *mirror at a face that no longer told the story of horrible violence. My vision was amazingly clear, better than it had been for years. A staring contest ensued between me and the sparkling Norwegian blue eyes that reflected back. For several quiet minutes I studied the woman who was new to me inside and out, but who had always been there.*

"Nice to meet you," I said.

The End

Domestic Violence Commentary

"To get through the hardest journey we need take only one step at a time, but we must keep on stepping." —*Ancient Chinese proverb*

The best news for a victim of domestic violence, whether a woman, man, child, or elder, is that you do have choices, as there are social, legal, medical, and religious organizations in place to help you. Most importantly, you have it within you to make the choice to leave, and to start over. The sad news for victims of domestic violence is that it still exists. It is too often an "unmentionable" in this country, and sadly, it is culturally acceptable in other countries. The U.S. Department of Justice statistics are startling.

- One-third of all American women have suffered domestic abuse at the hands of an intimate partner.
- Annually, nearly 2,000 people are killed by an intimate partner, and an estimated 3 million incidents of domestic violence are reported.
- Domestic violence is the leading cause of injury to women, and the leading cause of death for women in the workplace.
- Domestic violence is not just a women's issue, although women are the majority of victims.

When I give presentations regarding domestic violence, the following questions are the most often asked of me. I answer them not as a women's issue, but as a humanitarian issue, because it can affect anyone.

Q: "Why didn't you just leave?"
A: I admittedly must take a deep breath and be patient as I answer this question because it automatically assigns blame to the victim—and it throws the victim back into the place from which he/she fought so hard to get out. That question stirs up feelings of guilt, shame and worthlessness that were a daily part of my life. It is my sincere hope that the reader of this book now understands that in addition to being abused, the victim must overcome a multitude of influences and situations in his/her life in order to make the decision to leave. Domestic violence is a systematic whittling down of the makeup of a human being, and it renders them unable to make decisions, let alone the decision to leave. The fear of more severe abuse, if an attempt to leave is made, is overwhelming because that is usually what happens. *The most dangerous, and too often fatal, time for a victim is when she is trying to end a relationship.*

I most often reply to this question by saying, "You are asking the wrong person the wrong question. You should instead ask of the abuser (in my case my ex-husband), 'Why did you do that to your wife and daughter?'"

Q: "What can you do to help someone in this situation?"
A: Don't be afraid to get involved. This is the lesson my family and friends wished they had learned long ago. As the saying goes, "Where there is smoke, there is fire." As an observer, if you suspect something is not right in a particular person's relationship, ask the question, "Is something wrong? You are safe talking to me." This will open the door for your family member or friend, maybe for the first time, to let the words leave his/her lips. As the one asking, if nothing is wrong in the relationship, you may make them angry for asking, but if there is something wrong, you may be instrumental in saving a life. *Remember that things aren't always as they seem.*

More often than not, a victim of abuse will be reluctant to accept help, and will go back to the abuser. This is most puzzling to outsiders. Victims get to a point where they are simply afraid of everything—and do not trust anyone. They are so consumed by fear that fear of the unknown, like leaving the situation, is more than they can handle. Life with the abuser is known and familiar. It should break everyone's heart to know that for this person, living in fear has become a way of life, and seems "normal." If you are trying to help someone who is in this emotional state, immediately call any resource available, including the police department in your area.

Q: "What can society do?"
A: It's simple: realize that domestic violence is a serious crime, and advocate it as a crime against humanity—worldwide. There should be zero tolerance for domestic violence, and children, from early in their lives, should be taught that it is okay to argue, but not to hit.

More efforts need to be made to educate the public, educational institutions, law enforcement agencies, legal and medical associations, and religious organizations. These efforts could include various print and televised media, and scheduled training programs. Parents should discuss this subject with their children, especially when they reach dating age, and it should become part of premarital counseling.

Society also needs to understand that the most devastating insult and disrespect it can give to a victim of abuse is to continue to sweep the problem under the rug, and to continue to believe that it is a family problem, and not a crime. It is not a problem that will go away if it is ignored, and if it is ignored, more people will die spiritual, emotional, and physical deaths. More often than not, the public is unaware of domestic violence until it appears on the news that yet another person, or an entire family, has been murdered by a spouse or domestic partner. A police officer once told me that he sometimes becomes callous to domestic violence complaints because he sees it day in and day out. My reply was that he should try living it day in and day out.

Q: "What did you do to get through all of this?"
A: Early in my marriage, I developed coping mechanisms to get through the incidents of abuse, and over time those mechanisms became fine-tuned. Knowing that it was my job/role to forgive was deeply ingrained, and that was the hardest thing for me to set aside when I made the decision to end my marriage. Kristin and I had (and still have) a lifelong involvement in dance, which gave us periods of safe haven during those years. The healing aspects of dance are not often promoted. It is an art form and a gift that allows people to reclaim who they are.

I was always hopeful that things would get better, and I truly believed that I was doing the right thing by keeping my family together. I prayed for help and guidance every night. I also prayed that one day *someone would ask if something was wrong or would see the pain in our eyes.* I buried each incident of abuse inside me, keeping a journal to ease the pain. Richard made me feel that I deserved this treatment, and that this was my lot in life. The years of abuse had systematically whittled away my ability to ask for help. I also believed that if I asked for help, and no one wanted to get involved, my feelings of worthlessness would be validated.

An absolute fear of dying—as well as divine intervention—catapulted me out of my marriage. Love for my daughter, and a flame deep inside me that one day spontaneously grew to a roaring fire, energized me to make the choices needed to start a new life. Baby steps turned into a full sprint, and, as they say, "The rest is history." Colors are brighter, music is sweeter, and our smiles are genuine. Kristin and I do not need to be "actresses" anymore.

Q: "Do you have any lingering issues related to years of being abused?
A: I still fear the stigma that society places on a person who has been abused. I have lost count of the number of times I have been asked, "What did you do to make him do that to you?" I know in my heart now that that question comes from pure ignorance about domestic violence, and I take it as an opportunity to set the record straight. Victims of abuse are often erroneously viewed as weak. The reality is that incredible stamina and courage are required to gain the strength to leave an abusive situation, no different than that of a prisoner of war.

I have moments of "not feeling good enough" or "not being able to trust," but now those moments disappear quickly. I will always pray that Kristin knows in her heart that I tried to be the best mom for her, and that I did the best that I could. I pray that she knows that she is the angel that spoke the loudest to me.

Q: "What changes have you noticed personally?"
A: Both Kristin and I immediately felt an incredible freedom in our creativity and choreography. It was not stifled anymore. We felt the right to talk freely, and have not stopped. We had a lot of lost years to make up for, and gave birth to a most amazing performing arts center: Heartbeat Studios. We are energized by pushing our creativity to the limit in all aspects of our lives, and are driven to make sure our students develop a healthy sense of self-respect. We have a keen sense of fairness and integrity, and deeply care about everyone who comes into our lives. We understand completely that victims do not have the problem; the abusers do. Both of us have learned that we can fall in love, and be loved.

Q: What changes have you noticed in society?

A: Certainly the medical field has stepped into the forefront to help victims of abuse. I believe it is standard procedure now for female patients in doctors' offices and in emergency rooms to be asked by medical staff if they are in an abusive situation at home. Most police departments have a strict protocol to follow now when an abuse victim calls for help. Domestic violence is a topic that many in elected office publicly speak about, and the media reports on it more frequently.

Q: "What should a person do who is in this situation?"

A: Develop a plan of action to go to a safe location where you can make telephone calls for help or advice. If you remove yourself from the abusive environment, you can think more clearly and make decisions that are best for you. ***Do not be afraid to ask for help***. It will seem overwhelming, so get your mind and heart focused on the fact that you will find the strength to get through it all.

Once you are in a safe location, call your local hotline for domestic violence help, or the national hotline, 1-800-799-7233 (1-800-799-SAFE). Contact your local police department and any other support network such as your extended family members, friends, place of worship, personal doctor, or hospital emergency room. They will help put you in contact with the right organizations. Listen carefully to what they say, follow their advice, and keep moving forward. If you are in immediate danger, call 911. ***Remember that you have it in you to go from victim to victorious and start a new life.***

Purpose and Passion

Now, if you are wondering how my family is doing: we are doing fine. Paul and Kristin have a home in south Minneapolis near the neighborhood where I grew up. She and I are making a living doing what we love most—teaching dance. Our performing arts center, Heartbeat, is more than a business to us—it is a symbol that we are survivors. It is exhilarating to be able to support ourselves doing work about which we are passionate.

Heartbeat has grown into a full-fledged performing arts center with comprehensive programs in dance, acting, singing, piano, and guitar, and a movement program for children with autism. Our productions are admired, and looked forward to, by our community—in fact, in June 2011, we received permission from Lucasfilms Ltd. to produce a stage version of the classic film, *Star Wars,* featuring our young performers. In January 2013, we produced Heartbeat's Fifteenth Anniversary Show featuring Heartbeat's performers along with guest artists, Yukiko Misumi and students from her studio in Tokyo, Guillem Alonso from Barcelona, Dianne Walker from Boston, and Jason Samuels-Smith from New York.

My siblings are married and have beautiful families of their own. Sadly, our mom died suddenly and unexpectedly from a heart attack before this book was completed. While my family stood vigil around her hospital bed, I was holding her hand when her heart stopped beating. I knew at that split second, that was the moment she had been preparing me for—to hold the family together with abundant love, and be their protective shield from all things frightening, as she and Dad had done all of our lives.

"You taught me well, Mom and Dad. I love you."

"I love you, Kristin."

Acknowledgments

I would like to, first of all, thank my lovely daughter, Kristin. This book is inspired by her, and is my gift to her. My love for her is forever. We have been on a journey that bonds us to eternity. I am her, and she is me, and together we survived to build a beautiful life. My Nordic goddess is talented, brilliant, and possesses a loving heart. She also has a pretty cool husband, Paul WonSavage, who has been our rock. He has been instrumental in Heartbeat's business operations, and I love him to pieces.

My thanks goes to my parents, Robert and Jalma, and siblings, Shirlee, Butch, Nancie, Kurt and Mark, who are indeed precious to me, and I will love them always. Laughter, joy, sorrow, courage, and a wealth of memories have built the foundation of "the Lysholm family." This foundation gave me strength, character, gumption, and compassion. Members of the Lysholm family are deserving of their own books, as they, too, have had to travel roads not always smooth. But in true Lysholm fashion, keep smiling and keep moving on. I also want to thank my extended family members, and ancestors, for their love of life and adventurous and entrepreneurial spirits that pulse through our veins.

I want to thank every dance student that I have taught over the past forty years. You kept me going and gave me purpose. Many will never know how much they helped to keep me moving straight ahead, and pursuing my dream of Heartbeat Studios but they need to be thanked regardless. You brought me so much joy, and I am honored to have nurtured your interest and talent in the most beautiful art form dance. I want to thank their parents as well for supporting their children in a most life-enriching endeavor.

I want to thank every dance teacher that I was fortunate to study under. Your dedication to dance, your patience, and your artful teaching, gave me my future. Included in this group are master teachers who shared their artistry and professionalism with passion. Dianne Walker, the late Gregory Hines, Jason Samuels-Smith, Savion Glover, Roxane Butterfly, Guillem Alonso, Yukiko Misumi, the late Henry Le Tang, and the late Jimmy Slyde, are just a few of those who educate, create, and pushed dance to new levels.

My sincere appreciation goes to every legal, medical, and clergy professional who helped Kristin and me put the building blocks of "us" back together. Don, I especially want to thank you and your law firm for your courage and steadfastness as we charted an unknown path. I hold your friendship in my heart. To the staff at Robert Lewis House, you saved my life.

I want to thank my friends who stood by my side and believed in my dream. Patty and Lon Taulbee, Laurie Holien, Gail McCue, Dianne Walker, Barb and Fritz Ferris, MD, Lori Holiday, Tona and Erik Dove, John Lynn,

Bob DeFlores and many more; thank you for the side-splitting laughter, tears, and words of comfort. Thanks for living life with your glass overflowing. Barry Petit, thanks for your vision for Heartbeat Studio's building and your incredible generosity. A shout-out goes my Roosevelt High School buddies; thanks for the memories.

My admiration goes to Heartbeat's teaching staff: Sheila Casey-Best, Levi Martin, Steve Durand, Carlos Garcia, Serena Tritschler, Caitlin Mejia, Angelia Ball, Trudy Gustafson, Andy Ausland, Stephany Himrich, Tona Dove, Patricia Price, Emily Colay, Karen Johnson, and Alexandra West. Without their talent, expertise, and love of teaching, Heartbeat would not be the exceptional school that it is today. Heartbeat's teachers are admired and respected, and I proudly call them my friends. All of us "groove" on the same wavelength.

I want to thank studio owners Yukiko Misumi (Tokyo), Guillem Alonso (Barcelona), and Basilio Gonzalez (Tap on Barcelona) for believing in the friendships and partnerships between our studios. You have become dear friends and our lives are enriched.

And finally, my thanks goes to every proofreader and editor who gave a keen eye and direction to the evolution of my book. Tona Dove, Gail McCue, Diane Anderson, Carol Kallestad, Kristi Smith, Dario Mejia, Caitlin Mejia, Stephany Himrich, Karen Johnson, Patty Taulbee, Laurie Holien, Andrew Miller, Caryn Sullivan, Erik Jensen, Jessica Blank, Karen Johnson, Dennis Hall, Mic Spence, my siblings, and Kristin and Paul thanks for taking the time to read and comment. Anita Coolidge—thanks for your editing, inspiration, and genuine caring. Betty Leidtke and Mary Miller thanks for your wonderful comments and sincere interest in my story. Connie Anderson my heartfelt thanks for your nurturing, editing, caring and vision to help me educate through my book, and for founding Women of Words.

Kristin and I send special thanks our canine kids, Apollo, Saami and Skijee, for their unconditional love, and we remember our dear Aries and Misha.

DEBORAH LYSHOLM

Deborah Lysholm is an accomplished dancer whose professional career spans more than four decades—from performing, choreographing, and teaching thousands of students, to building her own performing arts center, Heartbeat Studios, in Apple Valley, MN. Reaching out to the world dance community, her journey has taken her around the U.S., and to Europe, Asia, and Cuba, where she established travel study and cultural exchange programs and many friendships.

Deborah has been fortunate to study with professionals in ballet and jazz dance, and with luminaries in the tap dance community such as Dianne Walker, the late Gregory Hines, Jason Samuels-Smith, Savion Glover, Guillem Alonso, Roxane Butterfly, and Yukiko Misumi, to name a few. She has been a featured dancer in productions in several Minneapolis/St. Paul venues such as Orchestra Hall Hot Summer Jazz Festival, O'Shaughnessy Auditorium, and several jazz clubs, and internationally in Tokyo, London, and Barcelona. Deborah's choreography is highly original, appearing in a range of productions from dance recitals, musical theater such as *West Side Story, Anything Goes, The Boyfriend, Oklahoma!, Grease,* and *The Wiz,* to public service announcements and major sports events. Several of Deborah's students have pursued the performing arts in their college careers, becoming professional dancers, actors, and teachers.

In addition to a lifetime devotion to dance, Deborah and daughter, Kristin, are survivors of two decades of domestic violence, and the first in the U.S. to file a domestic violence lawsuit in civil court. Their story of survival and starting a new life has been featured in major newspapers and television news shows, and captured the attention of many entertainment celebrities. Deborah is a sought-after speaker, enlightening audiences that violence in the home still affects 25percent of U.S. women (The Centers for Disease Control and Prevention), and that we all have it in us to start over. Deborah is the author of "Surviving in Rhythm" and "East Meets West" articles published in the *International Tap Association* magazine, and now her own memoir, *Dancing to My Heartbeat*. Written with compassion from her heart to the heart of anyone in a difficult situation who desires to start over, Deborah's book educates the public about domestic violence and also the joy of dance and its incredible ability to lift spirits and heal. Deborah dares us to dream big.

KRISTIN FREYA

Kristin's teaching philosophy is to create an educational environment that provides students with experiences to learn skills necessary to build a successful career in dance and theater. Her teaching style develops self-confidence, fosters respect for disciplined work, support through team work, and explores talent through creative opportunities to stretch and to grow. She has deeply enjoyed teaching for over fifteen years.

Kristin is the artistic director of Heartbeat Studios Performing Arts Center in Apple Valley, MN, where she teaches weekly classes in acting, modern, ballet, jazz, and composition. She directs four musical theatrical productions each year and founded the successful Heartbeat Academy Program for students to create and present their original dance composition, scripts, and theater productions. Many of the program's graduates have received full or partial scholarships in theater and dance college programs.

Kristin's professional artistic accomplishments have been diverse. In 1995, she founded, choreographed, and directed the critically acclaimed Vox Medusa Dance Company, where she merges modern and jazz dance, aerial work, fire dancing, video, spoken word, opera, and original music to create epic theatrical productions. She has produced over one hundred dance productions and over sixty multi-medium dance installations that were inspired by female archetypes drawn from ethnically diverse mythological and historical sources. Her works have been performed nationally and internationally, including London, Tokyo, the Falaki Gallery in Cairo, and Barcelona. In the Twin Cities area, her works with Vox Medusa have been commissioned and presented in such venues as Walker Art Center, Weisman Art Center, Theatre De La Jeune Lune, O'Shaughnessy Auditorium, Guthrie Theatre, Fitzgerald Theatre, Loring Playhouse, Pantages Theatre, and many more. Her theatrical dance company has been honored to be the first to stage a production on the altar of the Basilica of St. Mary in Minneapolis.

Kristin also founded Ricochet Kitchen, a multi-art, multi-room cabaret that showcases local and national artists of diverse dance traditions and other art mediums. In its six year history, there have been twenty-five Ricochet Kitchen events where Kristin presented over four hundred artists in unique venues around the Twin Cities.

Kristin has been awarded grants for the creation, direction, and production of dance, theater, and performance art installations from the University of St. Catherine "Women of Substance Series," Metropolitan Regional Arts Council, Falaki Art Gallery (Cairo, Egypt), St. Cloud State University, and Leeds Castle (London, England). In addition, she has received guest artist residency from Menendez Studios (Havana, Cuba), St. Cloud State University, University of Cairo (Egypt), ARTN Dance Studios in Tokyo (Japan), the MN College of Visual Art and Design, and Tap On Barcelona (Spain).

University of Minnesota: Dance and Fine Arts 1995
University of Minnesota Honors: Dance Student of the Year 1995